EXETER MEDIEVAL ENGLISH TEXTS AND STUDIES

General Editors: Marion Glasscoe and M.J. Swanton

A full list of titles in the Exeter Medieval English Texts and Studies series is available from the University of Exeter Press, Reed Hall, Streatham Drive, Exeter, Devon EX4 4QR, UK.

The cover illustration is from a Book of Hours published in Paris by Philippe Pigouchet (late fifteenth century). It depicts (top right to bottom centre) the meeting of Joachim and Anna at the Golden Gate, the birth of Mary, her climbing of the steps into the Temple, and (framed by prophets) her devotions there. It is reproduced with the kind permission of the owner, M. A. Twycross.

D0781819

f.48v.   Passage marked for insertion in Betrothal episode. Dotted paragraph marks show that it is Mary Play material. (See note to ll.685–708 and Introduction p. 3.) Photograph reproduced by permission of the British Library (BLMS Cotton Vespasian D VIII).

The *Mary Play*

From the N. town Manuscript

Edited by

Peter Meredith

UNIVERSITY
of
EXETER
PRESS

Published in 1997 by
University of Exeter Press
Reed Hall, Streatham Drive
Exeter, Devon EX4 4QR
UK

This edition of *The* Mary Play *from the N.town Manuscript* is published by
arrangement with Addison Wesley Longman Ltd, London.

British Library Cataloguing in Publication Data
A catalogue record of this book is available
from the British Library

ISBN 0 85989 547 5

Printed and bound in Great Britain
by Short Run Press Ltd, Exeter

Contents

Preface

It has been apparent since the publication of K. S. Block's edition in 1922 that the N. town manuscript contains not a cycle of pageants but a composite collection of plays, pageants and, in one case, speeches, of distinct origins and varying forms. Despite this, most scholars continue to talk of them as a cycle. This is largely the result of the appearance of the text in the manuscript, the scribe having attempted to give to his heterogeneous material this particular form. The first part of the Passion Play is the only section of the manuscript to have been treated seriously as a separate work, having been edited twice in recent years, once by Peter Happé (in *English Mystery Plays*, Penguin Books 1975) and once by David Bevington (in *Medieval Drama*, Houghton Mifflin 1975). The *Mary Play*, though attracting considerable interest, has never been published separately. Instead, episodes (most commonly the Parliament of Heaven and Annunciation) have been repeatedly anthologised to the detriment of the other episodes and the disruption of the whole play.

There are good reasons why there has been a reluctance to edit the *Mary Play* as a separate whole. The main ones are that parts of it are irrecoverable (though too much can be made of this) and that some doubts remain about those that do survive. I have discussed these problems in the Introduction which follows. My main aim in the present edition is to put forward a text of the play as close as possible to that which existed before its inclusion in the N. town compilation. This has inevitably produced a somewhat different-looking play (especially through the omission of Joseph's Doubts), but it will, I hope, help to ensure that the *Mary Play* despite its uncertainties is treated seriously as an unusual and striking piece of fifteenth-century theatre.

The recent stage history of the play is relatively simple. As Director of Religious Drama in the Diocese of Chichester, E. Martin Browne, so often the pioneer in these matters, made an attractive performing version of the play (though omitting the Visit to Elizabeth and Contemplacio's final speech), which was published as *The Play of the Maid Mary* (Religious Plays 3 Philip Allan, London 1932). There is only one recent production that I know of using the whole original text (including Joseph's Doubts). This was the one designed and produced in Oxford in February 1971 by Meg

Twycross, directed by Christopher McAll, and performed (appropriately) in the University Church of St Mary the Virgin. Most importantly, the performance made careful use of the extensive stage directions contained in the manuscript, and used a place and scaffold lay-out, though with raised stage for the *platea*. Of the individual episodes, there have been regular and successful performances of the Parliament of Heaven and Annunciation in many parts of the world.

Since this was written there have been two further productions of the complete *Mary Play*. The first was directed by John Marshall (Department of Drama, University of Bristol) and performed in the Glynne Wickham Studio Theatre, University of Bristol, in December 1990. The second was directed by John McKinnell (Department of English, University of Durham) for the Durham Medieval Theatre Company and performed on tour in the Great Hall of Brancepeth Castle and in a number of Durham churches in June 1995. The Bristol production effectively used a series of 'island' sets in an open 'place', with a raised temple, and above it heaven, at the rear. The Durham one was centred on the very dominant 15 steps and temple with 'mansions' on either side. At Bristol the humanity of the characters was movingly realised, in Durham the use of partly-sung and partly-spoken Gradual Psalms was successfully demonstrated. Bristol re-introduced the episode of 'Joseph's Doubts', Durham satisfactorily played the play without it. Meg Twycross directed the last section of the play (11.1060 to the end) in a very picturesque and colourful production in the Merchant Adventurers' Hall in York in June 1994.

The N. town plays have been dogged by problems of nomenclature. *Ludus Coventriae*, the earliest, from the description by the seventeenth-century Cotton librarian, Richard James, is the worst of these, but being used by Block it is inevitably still common; 'the Hegge plays', from the first known owner of the manuscript, Robert Hegge, seems to me unhelpful; 'the Lincoln plays', from their supposed home, now seems inappropriate; so that 'N. town' (sometimes written 'N-Town'), the term used in the Proclamation to invite the performers to insert the appropriate town name, seems the best title for plays without a home.

During the many years that I have been caught in the toils of the N. town manuscript, I have discussed it with many people, in particular Richard Beadle, Arthur Cawley, Stanley Kahrl, Stephen Spector and Meg Twycross. I am grateful to them for their wise thoughts, and they should not be held responsible for my rashness. The main shaping and improving of my ideas has been the work of successive MA students from the Workshop Theatre, the Centre for Medieval Studies and the School of English at the University of Leeds. I am most grateful to them for their time and enthusiasm. To my family, for keeping out of my way and allowing me to keep out of theirs, all expressions of gratitude must fall short.

Peter Meredith   *Bramley, September 1985.*

Preface to the 1997 edition:

A small number of additions and corrections have been made to the 1987 edition of the play. Those errors in the text and apparatus of which I am aware have been corrected, the Bibliography has been expanded by the addition of some new editions and recent scholarly work, and the *MED* references in the Glossary have been extended to the point that the *MED* has now reached. The Introduction has not been expanded though I have always been conscious of an absence there of an East Anglian context of Marian devotion. Gail McMurray Gibson's book to some extent supplies this though relying rather too much on non-East-Anglian illustrations and unfortunately rejecting the existence of a separate Mary Play out of hand (p.212). There is no better general introduction to lay devotion in the late Middle Ages than Part I of Eamon Duffy's *Stripping the Altars: Traditional Religion in England 1400–1580* (Yale University Press, New Haven and London 1992), though it is not concentrated on East Anglia

Peter Meredith   *Leeds, August 1996*

For
E.T.M.
and in memory of
E.C.M.

Introduction

The Manuscript

The N. town manuscript of the late fifteenth century (British Library, Cotton Vespasian D VIII), which contains the *Mary Play*, is the most complex of all the major manuscripts of English biblical plays. Whatever the problems of interpreting the manuscripts of York, Chester and Towneley, it is at least clear that they represent cycles of pageants. In the case of York, we also know that the manuscript of the plays is a civic register, the City's official copy of the cycle, and there exists a large body of record material to demonstrate its organisation and performance. Chester is not so clear a case in as much as all the complete cycle manuscripts are late, postdating the last performance of the plays by sixteen years or more; but there is at least no doubt that they represent a series of pageants performed in Chester up to 1575; and once again the text is supported by a considerable amount of evidence for organisation and performance. Towneley, even if its association with Wakefield were an established fact, is not supported in the same way as the other two, nevertheless its form is certainly that of a pageant cycle.[1]

With N. town, on the other hand, very little is certain. First in the manuscript comes a Proclamation, listing and describing forty pageants; a series of 'pageants' then follows, numbered in large red figures in the margin from 1 to 42, with the number 17 missing. The discrepancy of one between the Proclamation and the 'pageants' seems unimportant, but the 'near-fit' is an illusion which conceals far more serious discrepancies in subject-matter. These are most noticeable in the pageants dealing with the conception and early life of Mary:

Proclamation	*'Pageants'*
7 Tree of Jesse	7 Tree of Jesse
8 Betrothal of Mary (i)	8 Conception of Mary
9 Betrothal of Mary (ii)	9 Mary in the Temple
10 The Annunciation	10 Betrothal of Mary
11 Joseph's Doubts about Mary	11 The Annunciation
12 Trial of Mary and Joseph	12 Joseph's Doubts about Mary
	13 Visit to Elizabeth
	14 Trial of Mary and Joseph

It will be immediately apparent that the text has been expanded by the addition of three 'pageants' unmentioned in the Proclamation. Furthermore, the numbering is clearly at variance rather more seriously than at first seems. The scribe has attempted to deal with both these difficulties by altering the numbering in the Proclamation to bring it into line with the text; renumbering both Betrothal pageants, 10, the Annunciation, 11, Joseph's Doubts, 12, and the Trial, 14, perhaps with the intention of adding stanzas to the Proclamation later to deal with the extra 'pageants'. Having renumbered two further pageants, however, he abandoned, even at this mechanical level, the attempt to bring the two into line.

The problem was greater than simple renumbering could ever have solved. The episodes mentioned above which have been added are not individual pageants but parts of a composite play; introduced at the beginning of the Conception, linked in the middle sections, and concluded at the end of the Visit, by an expositor-narrator, Contemplacio. The three episodes not existing at all in the Proclamation are clearly taken over *in toto* from this play, but with the Betrothal, Annunciation and Joseph's Doubts, which already existed as pageants, the case is somewhat different. For the first, the Betrothal, the scribe has used material from both pageants and play and blended it; for the second, the Annunciation, the pageant has apparently been omitted entirely in favour of the episode from the play; and for the last, Joseph's Doubts, since there was only the pageant, it is that which appears in the manuscript.

To integrate this very different material fully into the pageant cycle would have required considerable adjustment and adaptation, and, as with the numbering, the scribe has only just begun the process. This is fortunate, as it turns out, since it means that it is still possible up to a point to distinguish the *Mary Play* from the pageant cycle in which it is now embedded. As the play is unique in English medieval drama in subject matter and form, it is clearly both justifiable and necessary to make the attempt to undo what the scribe was attempting to do, and disentangle the *Mary Play* from its present inappropriate setting.[2]

The *Mary Play*

The first two episodes, the Conception and Mary in the Temple, present few problems. Throughout the two there is a remarkable consistency of stanza form; an indication, if not proof, of a single origin. Apart from the quatrains used for the Gradual Psalms, and the occasional one elsewhere, the stanza is almost entirely an octave rhyming *ababbcbc*, the typical Marian stanza (see 'Metre, Language and Style', p. 7). Any dramatic text at any period is liable to alteration and revision, and there are some minor signs of it here, but they do not seem to be related to the amalgamation of the play with the cycle.

With the third episode, the Betrothal, the situation changes. The scribe clearly had before him the Betrothal episode from the cycle consisting of two pageants, and that from the *Mary Play*. The episode now consists of stanzas which are Marian octaves, and stanzas which are in the main stanza form of the Proclamation, the thirteener, which derive from the two pageants. There are also a number of quatrains, at least some of which are the result of the dividing of one or other of these stanza forms (see notes to ll. 802 and 871). Curiously enough, the scribe has indicated the distinction between the two sources of his copy by placing a red dot in the centre of the paragraph mark which precedes each stanza drawn from the *Mary Play*.[3]

One lesser difficulty in the Betrothal episode is the source of the material added by the interpolation of ff. 51–2 (quire E). It consists of two rather uneven Marian octaves and a quatrain, and is written in a hand different from and later than that of the main text. In as much as it is mainly in Marian octaves, it may have had its origin in parts of the *Mary Play* that the scribe omitted in his initial blending of Marian and cycle material, or it may, as I believe, be an independent composition copying the Marian stanza and later than either *Mary Play* or cycle (see Appendix 1).

The fourth episode, the Parliament of Heaven and the Annunciation, presents a different problem from either of these. It is written almost entirely in Marian octaves but includes four stanzas in a different octave form (rhyming *abababab*; ll. 1324–47 and 1384–91) and also a few quatrains. The evidence from stanza form is therefore very much in favour of a Marian origin. It has nevertheless been suggested that the episode as it has survived is not that of the 'original' *Mary Play*. The evidence for this is first that the Parliament of Heaven is not mentioned in Contemplacio's opening description of the play (ll. 10–13), and therefore, it is suggested, did not form part of the 'original' play; and second, that Contemplacio's speech at the beginning of the Parliament episode was once clearly spoken by two speakers and that its attribution to Contemplacio occurred when the Parliament episode was linked with the Annunciation in the *Mary Play*. As this problem involves other episodes as well as this one, I have delayed discussion of it until the end of this section.

The final episode, the Visit to Elizabeth, shows signs of revision at beginning and end. That at the beginning does seem to be a result of the amalgamation of *Mary Play* and pageant cycle, and is connected with the placing of the pageant of Joseph's Doubts between the Annunciation and the Visit. At the end of the Annunciation there is a stage direction, the end of which, 'and þan Mary sayth', has been deleted (1403sd). If there were no Joseph's Doubts pageant in the manuscript, the next speaker would be Mary (l. 1412) and it is just possible that this represents the earlier form that the play took. Mary's words at the beginning of the Visit are however rather abrupt, especially considering that Joseph has not already entered, and they also imply a continuing conversation. With no Contemplacio to link the two episodes some smoother connection seems likely. Such a possible connection appears at the beginning of Joseph's Doubts. The two quatrains, ll. 13–20, are different in style from the rest of the pageant, and the second of them, ll. 17–20, could provide the first half of a Marian octave if put with the quatrain that begins the Visit (for the effect of this, see the present edition, ll. 1404–15). It may not be the perfect link between the two episodes (the inclusion of Joseph's Doubts, ll. 9–12, would improve it) but it does avoid the abruptness of the present opening and there is some evidence for it in the manuscript (see Appendix 2).

At the end of this episode, the end of the whole play, the manuscript offers alternative endings. One I have included in the main text of the present edition (ll. 1558–96), the other appears in Appendix 3. Strictly speaking, however, there are more than two possible endings. Judging from the way in which the scribe entered this part of the play in the manuscript, he was not sure what should come between ll. 1557 and 1561, since he left a space there which he later filled (crammed would be a better description) with ll. 1–28 of Appendix 3. He seems to have been equally unsure of what followed l. 1568. The explanation may well lie in the variety of possibilities facing him. In the text he was copying, it seems as though the Contemplacio speech was a certainty but the other material, in non-Marian octaves and quatrains, not so. Without knowing the state of the copy from which the scribe was working it is impossible to be sure what the preferred ending was – if there was one. It is quite possible that the choice of ending was left open to the person organising the play.

Early revisions

The alternative endings do not seem to be connected with the amalgamation of *Mary Play* and cycle, but they may be part of some more general revision that seems to have taken place while the play was still separate. There are two possible areas of revision: that involving Contemplacio and that introducing the non-Marian octaves. In Contemplacio's first two speeches, the apparent revisions are the addition of a nine-line stanza at ll. 16–25 and 262–70. These simply expand his expositions by asking for silence and, in one case, by repeating material already mentioned. In both cases the speeches seem to come to a close at the end of the Marian stanzas and then start up again with the nine-liner. Contemplacio's third speech, ll. 577–93, contains no Marian stanzas but consists of two quatrains and a further nine-liner. It is this stanza that introduces the Parliament of Heaven for the first time. Unlike the earlier nine-liners, it does not ask for silence and it does, with the Parliament, introduce new material. The fourth Contemplacio speech is that mentioned earlier which is taken over from two other speakers, and which leads into the Parliament episode. The fifth speech shows no sign of revision, and in the final one it is the introduction of non-Marian octaves that is involved.

It is clearly not easy to know exactly what is revision. The nine-line stanza seems to be, and if so, it suggests that the Parliament episode may also be an addition since it is first introduced in one of them. The absorbing by Contemplacio of the speeches of two other characters also fits with this – as a striking way of replacing an introductory speech which, because of the addition of the Parliament, was no longer appropriate. It must be said, however, that there is no certainty that the Parliament was an addition.

It is only possible to guess at a reason for the inclusion of the two earlier nine-line stanzas with their requests for silence. They could have been the result of a change to a different kind of performance and audience, but equally well they could simply be a response to a practical necessity. Not everyone can be relied upon to keep quiet during the overture.

The non-Marian octaves appear in two series of stanzas and individually, connected with some quatrains, in the Annunciation and Visit to Elizabeth. The first series (ll. 1324–47) consists of three stanzas whose subject matter is all drawn from Nicholas Love's *Mirrour* (see Block, p. lviii). They are detachable from the text, adding to the episode the sense of the whole of creation waiting in suspense for Mary's answer to Gabriel. The single one contained in the Annunciation (ll. 1384–91) creates with its attendant quatrains an extension to Gabriel's leave-taking. The other series occurs in the alternative ending to the play, and depicts Mary and Joseph taking leave of Elizabeth and Zacharias, and the latter's departure for the temple (Appendix 3, ll. 5–28). This section contradicts the description of the episode in the *Meditationes* and Love's *Mirrour*. The final addition, already referred to, of a single octave with quatrains in Contemplacio's final speech (ll. 1577–84) follows the *Meditationes/Mirrour* tradition and therefore contradicts the other addition in the Visit. In as much as the non-Marian octave additions here contradict each other, and therefore could not have been intended to be used together, it seems likely that the very idea of alternative endings derives from this revision.

Neither of these revisions has anything to do with the integration of the *Mary Play* into the cycle, but they are readily explicable as revisions in a self-contained play. Consequently it seems more likely that they were completed before the play was incorporated into the present manuscript, and that they constitute part (even if not original parts) of the *Mary Play*.[4]

Language and Place

All the evidence suggests that the scribe of the N. town manuscript was trained in East Anglia, and there is every reason to believe that the *Mary Play* originated there. There is no obvious clash between the dialect of the scribe as it appears in his spellings and the dialect of the play as it appears in vocabulary and rhymes. There is considerable variety in the forms that words take, but most are explicable in terms of an East Anglian, or more specifically Norfolk, origin.[5]

Most consistent of the scribe's characteristic spellings is the *x-* in *xal(le)*, *xuld(e)*, which is a common East Anglian feature. This East Anglian characteristic is supported by the occasional spellings *-th*, *-t* in words where *-ght* was becoming normal (e.g. *bryth* 'bright', *syth* 'sight', *dowtyr* 'daughter'). In the *Mary Play*, however, the majority form is *-ght* (89:48; the latter boosted by twenty-one examples of *dowtere/-tyr*). Numerically far less significant are two more East Anglian features: the use of *qw-/qwh-* for *wh-*; and the use of *-t*, *-ht*, *-gh(t)* for the third person present indicative singular of verbs (e.g. *discendit* 'descendeth', *growyht* 'groweth', *chargight* 'chargeth', *weldygh* 'wieldeth'). Other East Anglian characteristics are the spellings: *hefne* (20:7 *hevyn*), *sefne* (4:1 *seven*), *mende* (10:0), *kende* (2:2 *kynde*), *werd(e)* 'world' (7:0), *whow* 'how' (3); and the words *swem(e)* (2), *swemful* (1), *swemynge* (1) and *therkeness* (1). *Nyn* (4) is a specifically East Anglian form of *ne* 'nor', and *recure* is used with its East Anglian meaning of 'obtain'.

The area in which the play was copied accounts for a number of unusual spellings. Because of the variation between *-ght* and *-th/-t* on the one hand and the *-ht*, *-gh(t)* spellings for *-th* on the other, which have been mentioned above, and the pronunciation /t/ for *th*, there are a number of confusions in the spelling of final *-t*, *-th*; e.g. *abought* 'about', *dowhte* 'doubt', *pyght* 'pith', *whath* 'what', *ȝough* 'youth'. The variations *wh/w* in words like *why* and *where* produced comparable variations in the spelling of other words containing *w*; e.g. *whande* 'wand', *whith* 'with', *whyght* 'wight' (creature). Other spellings are variations current in East Anglia but also elsewhere; like *e* for *i*, not only in *kende*, *mende* but also, for example, in *dete* 'ditty', *hedyr* 'hither', *hese* 'his', *meracle* 'miracle', *pete* 'pity', *sex* 'six', *trekyl* 'trickle'. *h-* is very occasionally omitted in words of both French and English origin, but more often it is added before an initial vowel; e.g. *a*, *an* (forms of 'have'), *onest* 'honest', *vndryd* 'hundred'; *haddyd* 'added', *haske* 'ask', *helmes* 'alms', *hendyng* 'ending', *hesely* 'easily'. The spellings *were/ware/wore* and *per/pare/pore*, the result of a blending of English and Scandinavian forms, are typical of the East Anglian area, more especially of the more northerly part of it.

The inflections used in the play are among those normal to the area. For the verbs, *-th* is the commonest ending for the third person singular present (for variation in spelling, see above); there are very occasional uses of the Northern *-s* (*lyce/lyse* 'lies', *dwellys* 'dwells'), one form without inflection, *counsell* (l. 1136), and one syncopated form, *sytt* 'sitteth' (ll. 138, 252, 980). The present plural is usually uninflected, very occasionally *-n* (e.g. *faryn* 575, *passyn* 600) and once *-th*, *thynkyth* (l. 1323). The imperative is most commonly without inflection but *-th* exists twice in the singular (*byddyth* 1149, *lystenyth* 1038) and slightly more often in the plural. The infinitive, likewise, is seldom inflected though there are a number of examples with *-n*; the strong past participle varies between no inflection and *-n*. The present participle is almost invariably *-ynge*, though *pleand* appears in Contemplacio's introductory speech (l. 3), and there is an example of *-ende*, *knelende* (as a rhyme, l. 146).

The forms of third person plural pronouns are also those to be expected in this area, but common elsewhere too; *thei/þei*, *hem*, *her(e)*; with occasional variation, e.g. *them* 2 examples; *þer* 2 examples, as against *hem*, 19, and *her(e)*, 22.

Metre, Language and Style

The predominant stanza in the *Mary Play* is the octave or double-quatrain rhyming *ababbcbc*, with the quatrain, rhyming *abab*, used for variation and for special effects like the Gradual Psalms (ll. 355–442) and the Magnificat (ll. 1497–1528). The octave form is common in East Anglian plays of the fifteenth century. It is the main verse form of *Mary Magdalen*, the *Play of the Sacrament*, the *Killing of the Children*, and occurs in *Wisdom* and the N. town *Noah* and elsewhere. There are a scattering of other stanza forms in the play, a number of extra-metrical single lines, and a single couplet (ll. 1432–3). In the Betrothal where the *Mary Play* and pageants are blended, there are a number of 'thirteeners', the stanza characteristic of the Proclamation. The thirteener is the most complicated stanza used in the N. town plays. It consists of thirteen lines, usually rhyming *ababababcdddc*, though variations occur. The number of syllables to a line varies somewhat (5–11), but the *c* lines are normally, though not necessarily, shorter than the others (5–8). The number of stresses also varies; in *c* lines from 1 to 3, and in the others from 3 to 5, with 4 the norm.

Despite variations in numbers of syllables and stresses, the thirteeners commonly have a more distinct metrical rhythm than the surrounding octaves in the Betrothal, mainly because the Marian playwright seems to be more interested in reflecting speech than in metrical regularity, and consequently variation in number of syllables and lack of fit between metrical and sentence stress is far more common. Latin blessings or the marriage service, for example, may not have a regular metrical rhythm, but, it seems, it is more important to have them for their reflection of reality than to retain regularity of metre. This is not to say that the octaves are never metrically regular. For large sections of the play they are, and the writer moves between regularity and freedom of rhythm with considerable skill and dramatic aptness.

A similar freedom is apparent in his division of a stanza between speakers, particularly in the first three episodes. There is no change of stanza form to suit mood, character or situation, except for the rounding-off of a section (e.g. ll. 245–53, 1529–37), but there is a considerable breaking up of stanzas so that thought and expression are not bound by metrical form. After l. 1060, the interchanges between characters are more formal, especially in the Parliament of Heaven and Annunciation episodes, and this is reflected in the relative infrequency with which breaking-up occurs.

The extra-metrical lines, which break up the metre in a different way, are sometimes in Latin, sometimes English. The series at ll. 323–6 combine Latin and English in blessings and Mary's comments and formalise an emotional moment. The two in the Betrothal are in one case an impulsive and somewhat irritated cry ('Comyth thens!', l. 810) and in the other a crowd response ('Mercy, mercy!' 831sd). The other Latin line is the essential 'Ave gracia plena dominus tecum' of the Annunciation (l. 1279). The Latin lines are clearly not the ad-libbing of actors, and there is no reason to believe that the English lines are not also the playwright's own, perhaps second, thoughts.

Rhymes in the *Mary Play* are fairly strict. One or two depend on assonance rather than rhyme, but they are few: e.g. *hond/evesong* (ll. 1539/41), *conclusyon/tecum* (ll. 1561/63). There is also one that equates a vowel followed by an *r*, with one without: *erd* (spelt *erth*)/*fede/blede/nede* (ll. 1069/71/72/74). Some rhymes depend upon a weakly-stressed form of a word: *certeyn* rhyming with *kyn/myn/þin* (ll. 789/91/93, a pageant stanza); and some depend upon the stressing of inflections: e.g. *ay is/weys* (ll. 404/6).

The *Mary Play* is not characterised by a rich literary language. There are places where more 'aureate', or simply more learned, words are used, but they are not many, nor is alliteration used to an extent sufficient to produce a wide range of alliterative words. There are a handful of words that appear here (sometimes in pageant material) for the first time: *celestly* (l. 1021) is recorded in *MED* only here and in the N. town *Assumption* (l. 332); *dissponsacyon* (l. 585) is the first use recorded in *MED* and the only one in this sense – the other is alchemical; *exorte* (l. 1118, see note); *morny* (l. 1052, pageant stanza) is the only example in *MED*; *pleson* (l. 1179) *MED* records as a nonce-word. *Sherherdys* (l. 130) is probably an error for *shepherdys*, but it may be a word in its own right and is unrecorded elsewhere. *Accusatyff* (l. 415), *areste* (l. 624, pag. st.) and *dote* (l. 854, pag. st.), all appear with new meanings here; *parochonerys* (l. 56) is the only literary use of the word recorded in *MED* (earliest recorded use is

Stonor Papers, 1465); and *hestyd* (l. 661 pag. st.) is, apart from a variant reading in the *Castle of Love*, only recorded here and in the N. town *Noah* (l. 165).

Despite the small number of new Latinate words recorded, there are occasionally quite heavily Latinate speeches. Contemplacio's first speech, for example, in common with many fifteenth-century prologues and expositions, is laden with learned terms. It is also more heavily alliterative than most parts of the play; no doubt to create an appropriately weighty solemnity for the opening. Alliteration is scattered through the play but is also concentrated into single stanzas for occasional effects; for example, the angel's acrostic of Mary's name (ll. 545–52), the introduction of the bishop in the Betrothal (ll. 594–9 pag. st.), or Gabriel's parting speech (ll. 1396–1403). Short alliterative phrases also occur throughout, sometimes but not often repeated; e.g. *fayre and fre, tene and tray, se . . . in syght, born of body, leve and leste*.

Rhetorical balance and repetition, sometimes combined with alliteration, also play a part in the style of the *Mary Play*. The salutations and farewells of the angels are obvious examples (ll. 545–52, 1352–5, 1376–9), but there are many briefer ones; e.g. *soferyth – sofron* (l. 129), *grett sorwe – gret grace* (l. 143, and cf.l. 226), *What art þu . . .? What am I . . .?* (l. 152), *lovyd . . . love . . . love* (ll. 459–60), *Endles synne God endles . . .* (l. 1168).

Dramatic and Social Context

East Anglia is now accepted as the home of a large number of the surviving fifteenth-century English play texts; works as diverse as *Mary Magdalen, Mankind, Castle of Perseverance*, the Brome *Abraham and Isaac* and the Norwich pageants, the *Play of the Sacrament*, and the N. town plays. With such a wealth of surviving texts it might be hoped that the records that exist would give some idea of the context in which the plays were written and produced. Apart from Norwich, however, no records so far published can certainly be shown to relate to any of the extant texts.

One of the main difficulties is the sparsity of records from the fifteenth century and earlier. The Middle English Dialect Survey has 'placed' the main scribe of the N. town manuscript in south central Norfolk, and though there is no reason to assume that that marks the home of the N. town plays, it makes a useful starting-point. Almost nothing, unfortunately, in the way of records survives from that area in the fifteenth century. There is the tantalising:

Pd. for the original of an Interlude pleyed at the Cherch gate

from the now lost East Harling church-wardens' accounts, and from the same source a number of references to 'games' from nearby villages. The meaning of the word 'game' is a difficult one to pin down, but if, as it appears to be in the 1566 accounts of the Bungay play, it could be used interchangeably with 'interlude' – at least in the sixteenth century – it is possible that these games of Lopham, Garboldisham and Kenninghall were plays. Thetford priory in its 'necessary expenses' gave rewards to 'jucalars', *mimi*, 'menstrells' and players, but there is nothing here either to suggest the scope and importance of any of the extant plays.[6]

In view of this uncertainty and lack of evidence, it is perhaps more useful to turn to the content of the *Mary Play* to see if a context exists that seems appropriate for it. There is no doubt that later fifteenth-century Norfolk can provide such a context. There were many religious gilds and parish organisations in the area that could have provided exactly the right setting for the kind of devotional tone that the *Mary Play* has. Moreover one particular piece of circumstantial evidence clearly supports a general association of this kind. This is the Commonplace Book of Robert Reynes.[7]

Reynes was a church reeve of Acle, about eleven miles to the east of Norwich, and also an alderman of the St Edmund gild in the late fifteenth century. His commonplace book contains a miscellaneous collection of information of a largely practical kind relating to his personal and professional interests. Among the religious and literary material there are various lists: of the sacraments, of the nine orders of angels, the three kings of Cologne, the twelve apostles; there are rhymes in Latin and English:

> Hac non vade via nisi dicas Aue Maria
> Sis tu procul a ue si michi dicas Aue.   (p. 300)
> (Do not go this way without saying *Ave Maria*;
> You may be far 'from woe' if you say to me *Ave*.)

Our Lady's Psalter is mentioned in a rhyme obviously intended to stand above a set of beads for common use:

> Man, in chirche not idyll thow stande,
> But take thy bedys in thyn hande.
> And yf thow haue here none of thyne,
> I pray the, take these for the tyme,
> And seye a sauter with glad chere
> In worcheppe of Oure Lady dere.   (pp. 287–8)

For which he is offered pardon:

> And whanne thow wylt no lenger stonde,
> Leve the bedys ther thow hem fonde.   (p. 288)

Even these devotional interests are reminiscent of the play. Among this extensive assembly of items there are, however, some of more particular relevance: a poem in honour of St Anne covering much the same story as the play (a text of the *Life of St Anne (3)*), a note on Anne's parentage, and two genealogies (one rhymed) of Mary. There is here an obvious overlap with the content of the play; moreover, the St Anne poem is clearly connected with a gild:

> And Mary and her moder maynteth this gylde,
> To þe worchep of God, and of his plesaunce,
> And alle þat it mayntene, be it man or chylde,
> God of his hey grace ʒeue hem good chaunse.   (ll. 453–6,
>   p. 228)

It seems quite possible that it was intended for performance at the gild meeting. The two genealogies and the note also show an interest in Anne, and it has been suggested that the section of the book that contains these, once a separate booklet, previously belonged to or was compiled for a gild of St Anne. The genealogies suggest the same kind of interest that prompted the inclusion of the genealogy in the N. town manuscript (see note to l. 25). The concern with Mary's ancestry was a common one in the fifteenth century (it was part of the *Legenda Aurea* treatment of the Nativity of Mary) but the names in the Reynes genealogies (especially the unrhymed one on f. 20v) and those in the N. town manuscript are remarkably alike; what is more they both contain the same error, *Beatus Geruasius episcopus* for *Legenda*'s *Servatius* (p. 586). The single-line note in the commonplace book:

> Est tuus Anna pater Izakar, Nazaphat tua mater

also appears, though in rather a different form, in the N.town manuscript. This is not enough to show that the *Mary Play* was the property of a St Anne's gild or that it was performed at Acle, but it does anchor it firmly in this kind of fifteenth-century Norfolk context.

Besides these pieces which show an interest in Mary and Anne, there are also in the book a number of dramatic pieces. The first is a series of single stanza speeches for three of the 'Worthies'; the second is a complete pageant of the Nine Worthies, with couplets for each character; the third is part of a dialogue between an unnamed female character and Delight, mainly consisting of an attractive speech for Delight; and the last is the epilogue of a play clearly for performance in aid of the church:

> Vnto Holy Chirche to ben incressement,
> All that excedith þe costis of oure play.   (p. 273)

Reynes may have come across these pieces through hearing them or through reading them; he may have copied them or he may even have composed them himself; what is clear is that they show an interest in drama. In the case of the epilogue, bearing in mind that he was a church-reeve (and also perhaps the relative unattractiveness of the piece), the likely reason for including it is the practical one of making use of it for the benefit of his own church – perhaps it had already proved its worth. All in all, Reynes, in his commonplace book, reveals exactly the range of interest that would have relished the *Mary Play*.

One other dramatic piece may be relevant to the setting of the performance of the *Mary Play*, the *Killing of the Children*. In its prologue Poeta explains that it is being performed in honour of St Anne, and later to 'worshippe Oure Ladye and Seynt Anne' (l. 18). Finally (l. 51) it is 'to the honour of God, Oure Lady, and Seynt Anne'; fitting descriptions too of the *Mary Play*. The play was one of a series performed to celebrate a feast; the previous year it had been *The Shepherds*, the following it was to be *The Doctors in the Temple*. There is no way of knowing where the play was performed, but it seems at least a possibility that it was for a St Anne's gild or for a parish church dedicated to St Anne. The presence of minstrels in the play fits in a general way with normal gild celebrations, and curiously enough even the dancing of the 'virgyns', which is part of the presentation of the play, is paralleled in a gild of St John the Baptist at Baston in Lincolnshire, where the sisters came together on St John's day to dance with each other.[8] It is, I suppose, not impossible that the *Killing of the Children* provides us with an example of gild entertainment.

It has to be admitted, however, that there is no evidence, apart from the St Anne poem, to connect literary or dramatic work with the celebrations of a Norfolk religious gild. There is nothing to parallel the Pater Noster guild at York, specifically founded to keep the play going; nor is there any sign of a William Revetour to leave his play-books to a likely guild.[9] Nevertheless the existence of both these shows that gild interest in drama could exist. Alternatively, there is later in Norfolk a good deal of evidence of dramatic activity in towns and villages, sometimes specifically in aid of church funds; such performance at an earlier date could also have provided a setting for the *Mary Play*.

This is of course speculation, but the *Mary Play* fits well with a devotional audience of the kind that a gild or parish would provide; one that has come together for the particular celebration of a saint's day or a gild feast. The coincidence of interest and information that exists between the Reynes Commonplace Book and the *Mary Play* is unlikely to be chance. I do not think it fixes the place of the N.town *Mary Play* but it does clarify the kind of person and the kind of lay society for which the play could have been written and performed.

Teaching

The didactic aim of the English vernacular plays has often been stressed, no doubt partly in response to an earlier emphasis on entertainment, but also in an attempt to show that teaching does not equal boredom. To what extent is the *Mary Play* didactic? In a direct, expository way, it is so only very briefly and sporadically. For example, the audience is told by Joachim to observe:

> So xulde euery curat . . .   (l. 54)
> So xulde childyr . . .   (l. 342)

Even here, however, the remarks spring very naturally from the situation. The same is true of the 'teaching' about the conception. Mary explains how Christ has been conceived, quoting and adapting the words of *Legenda Aurea* and Nicholas Love (ll. 1356–67). It is teaching but it is expressed through the over-flowing joy of Mary. It is exposition conveyed in emotion. Moreover the expressions of joy are sufficient to show the ecstatic nature of Mary's experience and hence explain her understanding of the event. More apparent teaching appears in Mary's words about the psalter. The content of her speech is undoubtedly teaching, but, in a rather more subdued way than at the moment of the conception, she is rejoicing in God's grace to man.

Where one might expect to find direct teaching, in the speeches of Contemplacio, there is none until the end. There he explains the structure of the *Ave Maria* and its value for Christians, and comments on Our Lady's Psalter and on the other liturgical pieces which have arisen from the episodes of the play. But by this time he is very much a character within the play. This is the Contemplacio who prayed for men before the Annunciation, as well as the by now familiar expositor who has been our guide through the scenes of Mary's life; and what he says carries a greater significance and emotional appeal. It is astonishing how information given by a character within a play is transformed into something other than pure fact. He is not like a preacher conveying information, more like Christ in the pageants after the Resurrection explaining the Eucharist.

More all-pervasive in the play, however, is exemplary teaching. Joachim and Anne are idealised human beings. Their righteousness is stated, but more importantly their affection and concern for each other, their eagerness to do God's will and their fear of his displeasure, their loving treatment of Mary, are all demonstrated in their actions. Mary is even more so the ideal. Joachim draws attention to this, but it is apparent throughout. It is exactly the same kind of attention to Mary's character and behaviour that is apparent in such works as the *Meditationes*; attention to the detail of human actions, explaining what the gospels did not, in order to show what

human behaviour at its best can be. Nor is it only the central
characters, Mary, Joachim and Anne, that are exemplary, but the
others combine to create an 'exemplary' world. Ysachar's rejection
of Joachim is harsh but there is no suggestion that it is unjust. His
re-admission of Joachim is correspondingly just and humane. The
bishop's treatment of Joseph is abrupt and reproving, but Joseph
needs to be brought to a proper sense of his duty. Even the
shepherds, with their homely concern for their master and mistress,
contribute to this world. The 'exemplary' world is very much that of
the fourteenth Gradual Psalm:

> Se how good and how glad it is
> Bretheryn for to dwelle in on.

The stated aim of the play is teaching for another purpose,
namely to tell the story, 'þe processe'. This is not a play with a set
teaching programme, though in the teaching of Mary in the temple
elements of that do appear, but to put in the audience's minds the
human and superhuman agents of the coming of salvation. It is in
honour of Mary ('This matere here mad is of þe modyr of mercy')
and it is therefore primarily her part, the human part, that is re-
enacted. The purpose of the re-enactment is again similar in many
ways to the purpose of the *Meditationes*; to make the audience
visualise and feel emotionally how the events occurred. It is similar
also to the purpose (or at least the effect) of pilgrimage to the Holy
Land. Christ's and Mary's lives become again living events of which
the fifteenth-century Christian can become a part, whether it is
primarily an emotional involvement, as with Margery Kempe from
Lynn, or a deeper understanding of the scriptures, as with Felix Fabri
from Ulm.[10]

The Treatment of Sources

Almost the whole of the story in the *Mary Play* is apocryphal. The
only biblical episodes are the Annunciation (Luke i, 26–38) and the
Visit to Elizabeth (ibid. 39–58). For the apocryphal story a number
of accounts existed in Latin and translated and adapted into English.
The story up to the Annunciation is contained in the Greek
Protevangelium, the Latin gospels of *Pseudo-Matthew* and the *Nativity
of Mary*, and a later re-telling of parts of the story in the *Legenda Aurea*
and the *Meditationes Vitae Christi*. For the Annunciation there was
not only Luke's gospel, but also versions of the episode in
Protevangelium, *Pseudo-Matthew*, *Nativity of Mary*, *Legenda Aurea* and
Meditationes. The Visit to Elizabeth only appears in expanded form in
Meditationes. Most vernacular re-tellings of the episode made use of
one or other of these, sometimes combined, often probably at

second hand. The playwright of the *Mary Play* certainly made use of *Legenda Aurea* and *Meditationes*, but there is no convincing sign of a first-hand use of *Protevangelium* or *Pseudo-Matthew*. *Legenda Aurea* and the *Nativity of Mary* differ little since the former drew on the latter, but where the play makes close use of a source it is the *Legenda*. Parts of the Annunciation episode stay very close to Luke's gospel.

The texts of the incipits of the Gradual Psalms and of the whole Magnificat could come from either the Bible or a liturgical service book, though both were commonplace elements in lay worship and frequently appear in Primers. For the hymns, sequences and quotations from the service of the mass, the source must have been liturgical. How much use the playwright made of the liturgy apart from these it is difficult to say, since so many of the ideas found there had a general currency.

The same is true of a large number of expansions of the basic story. They can usually be parallelled in other vernacular versions or Latin works, but it is seldom possible to show any closer connection. The two exceptions to this amongst vernacular works are *The Charter of the Abbey of the Holy Ghost* and Nicholas Love's translation and adaptation of the *Meditationes*, *The Mirrour of the Blessed Lyf of Jesu Christ*.

I shall look more closely at the playwright's use of these and other sources in the individual sections which follow.[11]

The Conception

In the episode of the Conception of Mary the playwright is drawing on the *Legenda Aurea* for the overall outline of the narrative, some speeches and some isolated ideas and expressions, and on the liturgy for the service in the temple and the angelic singing. Though the plot is by and large that of the *Legenda*, the playwright adds and expands in such a way as to make a very much more complex re-telling of the story. The *Legenda* version in Graesse's edition is after all only fifty-five lines long, twenty-three of which are taken up by the angel's speech to Joachim – the only part of the *Legenda* to be translated almost literally by the playwright.

The episode has at its centre the rejection of Joachim from the temple. It is therefore important that the temple should dominate the early part, and the gravity of the rejection be apparent from the beginning. Ysakar's opening speech, an addition to the source, emphasises the importance of his own high office of priesthood and his duty to exclude from the temple all who are unworthy. It also draws attention to the name of the feast by the gloss "þe newe fest", and therefore to an implied sense of renewal. The playwright's use of the phrase *regal sacerdocium* is interesting. In the *Legenda* it appears a few lines earlier in a discussion of the joining of the kingship and the priesthood of Israel in Christ. The phrase in itself is appropriate – a

kingly priesthood – though in its original context, 1 Peter ii, 9, and in
the *Legenda* it refers to all Christians. The playwright is clearly
making use of the phrase not to conjure up associations from the
Legenda or from the epistle, but for itself, as a further emphasis on the
grandeur of the temple and its officers.

Another way of building up the authority of the temple and of
emphasising the seriousness of Joachim's rejection is through the
temple service. No other surviving English play goes to such lengths
to re-create a solemn church ritual, nor uses the Christian liturgy so
imaginatively. The singing of the sequence in honour of the Trinity,
the solemn censing of the altar, the presence not only of the bishop
but also of his ministers, the echoes of the preparation of the mass, all
serve to establish the grandeur of 'Goddys hous'.

Mary in the Temple

This episode is contained in all the early accounts of Mary's early life,
but only in *Pseudo-Matthew* and the *Meditationes* is it at all developed.
None of the Middle English versions of this episode is a source of the
play, each running at times parallel to the play and at others
diverging from it. *Meditationes* is clearly the ultimate source of the
episode but the play goes far beyond what is contained there.
Meditationes has no clear narrative line, since it is a report supposedly
given by Mary to St Elizabeth and an account by Jerome, and the
development in the play is consequently freer.

I have not found a single source for the treatment of the Gradual
Psalms, though the relation between the steps and the psalms was a
commonplace. They are a common element in popular devotions
and it seems likely that Mary's sometimes rather awkward
commentaries and translations stem from popular teaching. They fit
her own situation, however, and were presumably made specially
for the play. From her desire to be with God (1), she moves through:
eagerness to know God's will (2), hope of salvation (3), the virtues of
obedience and humility (4–5, 8), trust and hope in God (6–7), fear
and love of God (9), bearing temptation and confessing (10–11),
meekness (12), faith and works (13); and finally through longing for
love among humans (14) to the unity in God's love. Many of the
ideas mentioned here appear later in her instruction in the temple,
others stress elements in her own character, and all are appropriate to
her and her situation, and through her to the audience.

This is the learning period of Mary's life and it is not surprising
that the playwright makes use of the episode for the exposition of
Christian doctrine as well as to demonstrate through the allegorical
priests and maidens the extent of Mary's instruction and the growth
of her understanding.

The Betrothal

One problem with this episode lies in the blending of three texts, two pageants and one play. There seems no reason to believe, however, that the basic story was very different. The source of the Mary version was clearly the *Legenda*, and that of the pageants could have been the same, though treated more freely and using material from elsewhere.

There are many differences between the version of the story in the *Legenda* (and the *Nativity of Mary*, which is its source) and the other early versions. *Protevangelium* is different enough from the play version to make it clear that it had no direct influence. *Pseudo-Matthew* comes nearer but even here there are details that transform the story. Abiathar the priest, for example, wishes to marry his son to Mary, but she refuses, having vowed chastity. When Mary is twelve (or fourteen – both ages appear) the priests can by custom no longer keep her in the temple. They send for all the tribes and Abiathar, now high priest, tells them that there have always been virgins in the temple but that at the proper age they were married. Now, he says, 'a new order of life has been found out by Mary alone', who wished to remain a virgin. They decide to cast lots to see which tribe shall look after her, and it falls on Judah. The story then follows the lines of the others. The Middle English *Life of St Anne* (1) clearly derives from this. In *Pseudo-Matthew* both Mary and Abiathar have speeches that could have furnished material for the play, but neither is made use of. In *St Anne* (1) both are used (ll. 446–56 and 466–81). In all these details, the story which is followed in pageant and play texts is that contained in the *Legenda*.

Considerable expansions and additions have been made but many of these are merely the result of turning a prose account into a play. The seeds of the whole of the incident of Joseph's hesitation (ll. 748–811), for example, are contained in: 'Erant inter caeteros Joseph de domo David, cui cum incongruum videretur, si vir tam provectae aetatis tam teneram virginem duceret in uxorem, caeteris virgas suas afferentibus solus ipse virgam suam subtraxit'. Joseph's reluctance because of his age, the offering of the rods by the others, the holding back of Joseph, all are there simply turned into speech and dialogue. It is worth noting here that in the *Nativity of Mary* 'cui cum incongruum . . . in uxorem' is lacking. If the playwright needed hints for the development of the attitude of Joseph, the *Legenda* rather than the *Nativity* would have provided them. Reliance on *Legenda* is also clear in the bishop's speech (ll. 685–92) where *Vovete et reddite* is quoted (*Leg.* p. 589), but even here there is not the close reliance upon the source which is clear in the angel's speech in the Conception.

Continuing the sense of 'reality' that he created by the use of the liturgy in the temple scene in the Conception, is the use of the marriage service here (ll. 883–6). The use of this kind of precise image of reality seems to be a characteristic of the Marian playwright.

The Parliament of Heaven and the Annunciation

This episode is somewhat different from the others in as much as it derives not from the *Legenda* or the apocryphal gospels, but from a variety of sources including two vernacular works and the gospel of Luke.

The Charter of the Abbey of the Holy Ghost is used in the first part of the Parliament. As Hemingway pointed out, the speech of Contemplacio and the speeches of the daughters of God are translations of the Latin texts quoted and translated in the *Charter*, with very considerable additions and expansions. Sometimes a stanza is made up almost entirely of translated quotations, sometimes they are merely used to validate what a character is saying. Contemplacio's last stanza, for example, is almost wholly translation and adaptation of three quotations from Jeremiah and Lamentations, used in the same order as the *Charter*, but there in a fuller form. There is no connection, however, in this instance between the English of the *Charter* and the play. Truth's two stanzas ll. 1119–34) make use of two quotations only, at the beginning and end of the second stanza; but here the English of the *Charter* does exert an influence. Compare, for example:

> þou seydest þat what-tyme þat man ete of þat appul þat he
> schulde dieye & gon to helle   (*Charter* p. 349)

with:

> Whan Adam synnyd, þu seydest þore
> þat he xulde deye and go to helle . . .   (ll. 1123–4)

There is no doubt about the influence, but the use that is made of the *Charter* is a highly selective one. In the *Charter*, for example, there are four suppliants to God for man, David, Solomon, Isaiah, and Jeremiah; the playwright has made no use of the first two whatsoever, and with the second two has chosen to use only some of the possible quotations and those only in part. There is in the *Charter* no intervention by the angels on man's behalf, and the order of events is quite different.

The continuous use of the *Charter* ceases with Christ's first words (ll. 1199). The Council of the Trinity occasionally reflects it but the playwright appears to be creating his own version of the story, making use of a number of sources, including, it seems, Bernard's sermon and the *Meditationes*.

For the Annunciation, the use of Luke's gospel, allowing for the necessities of rhyme and metre, amounts in one place to close translation:

Missus est angelus Gabriel a Deo	1251	
in civitatem Galilaeae	1252	
cui nomen Nazareth	1253	
ad virginem desponsatam viro	1254	
cui nomen erat Joseph	1255	
de domo David,	1256	
et nomen virginis Maria	1257–8	(Luke i, 26–7)

In general, however, the playwright has used Luke's text as the basis for a series of imaginative and lyrical flights.

The Visit to Elizabeth

The main sources of this episode are the *Legenda Aurea* and the *Meditationes* (making use of Love's *Mirrour* for what is probably an addition at ll. 1569–88). The *Legenda* is used for Contemplacio's description of the announcement to Zacharias of Elizabeth's conception (ll. 1434–49), and the play is at times very close to its source. The interpretations of Luke's account of the episode and the additions to it seem to come largely from the *Meditationes*, either in the Latin or Love's translation. The Magnificat, which takes up a large part of the episode, was an even more frequently used devotional item than the Gradual Psalms. Its antiphonal speaking here creates a formal atmosphere of meditation, as to some extent the Psalms do in the earlier episode. Its text appears to be drawn from the liturgy, though there is only one difference from the Vulgate (l. 1522).

Contemplacio's comments on the Ave Maria are popular teaching material, used here not only to round off the play but also to draw together the transcendental story which the audience has just been watching, and their own everyday devotions.

Staging

Stage directions, though one of the most valuable pieces of evidence for the staging of a play, are difficult to interpret. Though in many cases it is likely that their origin is a practical one, it is seldom clear whether they are the ideas of the original playwright or the result of subsequent performance (or a mingling of the two) and it is therefore uncertain at what stage in the development of the text they were included. I have for this reason not increased the complication by adding stage directions of my own. It is often clear what is happening from the text, and where it is not I have tried to indicate the action in the notes. The stage directions that do exist by no means cover all the action of the play, but in a number of cases they supply information totally absent from the text. The striking pause in the action of the Annunciation at l.1323 would go unnoticed without the stage direction that describes it, and there is nothing in the text to indicate the musically accompanied coming and going of angels bringing presents to the child Mary (560sd).

There are twenty-four stage directions in the *Mary Play*. They seem to be of varying origins since some are Latin and some English; some are centred on the page and were therefore prepared for in the laying-out of the text, while others are squeezed into the margin. All those in the margin are in Latin. The majority of stage directions are concerned with actions of some kind (e.g. kneeling, kissing) or with movement (e.g. retiring, descending). A smaller number refer to music and properties, and one to costume. Only one of them suggests that the play was staged around a 'platea' or place (1433sd). This is far too small a body of evidence, even when taken with that from the text, to show how the overall staging of the play was managed. What we have, besides the single reference to the 'platea', are references to five 'locations': the Temple, Heaven, and the houses of Joachim and Anne, Mary and Joseph, and Elizabeth and Zacharias. If one thinks in terms of place and scaffold staging, then there are five (or with doubling-up three) scaffolds bordering an open space; which is a possible arrangement, especially for outdoor performance. In what follows, I have used place and scaffold not to exclude other methods of staging but as a way of talking about the organisation of performance. Given the absence of evidence, the play is as likely to have been performed indoors as out, and the main central scaffold could easily be the rood screen and loft of a church, or the screens and gallery of a medieval hall.

The most elaborate of the scaffolds, to judge by stage directions and text, are the Temple, which holds at least fourteen people at one time and where the service takes place (including the censing of the altar), and the Heaven, which holds the choir, the Trinity, the four daughters of God, and Gabriel, and from which angels descend. The Temple is reached by fifteen steps and the Heaven is also clearly raised. The action takes place, as far as it is possible to tell, on or at the scaffolds rather than in the place. The major action in the place is that involving Joachim and his shepherds in the Conception, and the gathering of the kindred of David in the Betrothal. There is movement in the place but almost all is for the purpose of getting from one scaffold to another rather than for its own sake. Given the lack of attention to movement of this kind, it is perhaps reasonable to consider that a small number of scaffolds, fairly close together, was preferred. It is possible to reduce the five to three by doubling that of

Joachim and Anne with that of Elizabeth and Zacharias, and by placing the Heaven above the Temple. This latter allows for a large structure for the scaffold where the most action, and the most complex action, takes place, and also puts Heaven in a raised position. The choir, needed for Heaven and the Temple, could easily move from one to the other (if necessary), and so could the angels on their visits to Mary. It is worth noting that apart from singing, no action takes place in Heaven until after the end of the Betrothal, and that with the Betrothal the action in the Temple comes to an end. Whether or not the scaffolds could be closed off, there is time for the main area of the Temple to become Heaven for the latter part of the play, the Parliament and the Annunciation, before the action moves to the houses of Mary and Joseph and Elizabeth and Zacharias. Appropriately the action begins with the temple of the Old Law as its dominant feature, moves to Heaven, and finally to the human dwellings from which the salvation of man and the New Law is to come.[12]

There is considerable stress on music in the play. There are seven stage directions referring to music, all indicating the singing of liturgical pieces. Besides these there are four references to music in the text. The liturgical pieces are performed either in Heaven or in the Temple; the only 'earthly' music is the singing of the shepherds (l. 212). The stress on music goes side by side with a concentration on set-pieces, which in turn emphasise the formal aspects of the play. In each section, except the Betrothal, the stage directions or the text describe or create a set-piece. In the Conception it is the elaborate service in the Temple (ll. 96–120); in Mary in the Temple it is the formal recital of the Gradual Psalms as Mary ascends the fifteen steps, and later the bringing of presents by the angels (560sd). In the Parliament and Annunciation there are a series of set-pieces; the kissing of the four daughters (1250sd) and the farewells of Gabriel (ll. 1376–1403) flanking the elaborate visual presentation of the incarnation (1355sd). In the last episode it is the antiphonal reciting of the Magnificat. The absence of a set-piece in the Betrothal could simply be the result of the blending of play and pageant material and the consequent removal of a stage direction. A stage direction is after all the main evidence for the Temple service and the only evidence for the visual display at the incarnation. Either the flowering of the Joseph's rod or the marriage service could have provided an appropriate moment.

A number of stage directions describing actions of one kind and another underline formality. The repeated Latin blessings on Mary (ll. 323–6) echo the earlier kneeling of Mary and Joachim when they make their vows to God (294sd, 310sd). Mary's kissing the ground (560sd) and the kissing of the daughters of God (1250sd) are also formal actions. What little evidence there is for properties hints at richness of appearance – the cup of gold which holds the manna 'lyke to confeccions' (560sd), the presents brought by the angels, and the dishes of food brought by the priest from Ysakar (560sd). The flowering rod implies a use of the old and effective conjuror's trick, though whether the dove appeared in the same way is not clear. The single costume reference, to Mary's white dress (270sd), indicates a symbolic use of costume, though a fairly commonplace one.

Stress must be laid on the formal aspects of the presentation of the play, but not to the exclusion of everything else. Truth, Justice, Mercy and Peace may be the daughters of God, but their words to each other are often politely sisterly. Joachim and Anne are exemplary characters, types of the good married couple and the good parents, but their language can also be affectingly natural. It is difficult to know how the playwright treated Joseph because of the intrusion of pageant and other material into the Marian Betrothal, but his appearance in the final section emphasises the naturally good-humoured as well as the typically old. The presentation of the Gradual Psalms is pictorially and verbally formal, but it should not be forgotten that it is performed by a very young child. Nor should the effect of the prologue be misunderstood. Despite his occasionally learned and cumbersome language, Contemplacio, like all links between actors and audience, has the effect of drawing the audience into the play, not of distancing the action into greater formality.

Notes to the Introduction

1. The dramatic records of York and Chester have been published by Records of Early English Drama, edited by Alexandra F. Johnston and Margaret Rogerson (Toronto 1979), and Lawrence M. Clopper (Toronto 1979) respectively. For Chester, see also R. M. Lumiansky and David Mills, *The Chester Mystery Cycle: Essays and Documents* (Chapel Hill and London 1983). What there is for Wakefield appears in *The Wakefield Pageants in the Towneley Cycle*, ed. A. C. Cawley (Manchester 1958), pp. 124–6.★

2. I have called the *Mary Play* unique amongst English medieval plays. I think this is justified but it does need modifying slightly since one other East Anglian play, the *Conversion of St Paul*, has a somewhat similar form. Its similarity lies in the prologue-figure, Poeta, who links together the three parts of the play. The play is far briefer however (662 lines as opposed to 1596) and far more limited in scope than the *Mary Play*, and the staging also seems to have been different. The playwright envisages a series of separate locations ('stacions' or 'pagents', as they are called) to which the audience is led by Poeta and where each scene is played. There is certainly similarity between the two plays, but sufficient difference to justify emphasising the unusualness of the *Mary Play*.

3. The red dots are briefly described and discussed in Meredith and Kahrl (1977), p. xvii, and Spector (1977), p. 71.

4. Some discussion of the amalgamation and earlier revisions appears in Greg (1914), Spector (1977), Fletcher (1982) and Meredith (1983).

5. The most useful collection of material on the language of the area and of the plays appears in Richard Beadle's D.Phil thesis (University of York 1978) *The Medieval Drama of East Anglia: studies in dialect, documentary records and stagecraft*, and the works cited there; but see also the introductions to the editions of *The Macro Plays* (see Bibliography under *Castle of Perseverance*), the Digby plays (see Bibliography under *Conversion of St. Paul*), and the *Play of the Sacrament* and the Norwich pageants (see Bibliography).

6. For references to dramatic activity in the area, see *Records of Plays and Players in Norfolk and Suffolk, 1330–1642*, ed. David Galloway and John Wasson, Malone Society Collections Volume XI (Oxford 1980). Gail McMurray Gibson argues strongly for Bury St Edmunds as the home of all the N. town plays (Gibson 1981).

7. All references are to the edition by Cameron Louis (see *Reynes* in Bibliography). There the manuscript is divided up into 'articles'. The St Anne material composes articles 46–9; the dramatic pieces are articles 51 (3 Worthies), 53 (9 Worthies), 85 (Delight) and 86 (Epilogue).

8. H. F. Westlake, *The Parish Gilds of Mediæval England* (London 1919), p. 155.

9. For the Pater Noster guild, see REED *York* pp. 645–8, and for Revetour, see Twycross (1983), p. 65.

10. The best work on the interaction between teaching and theatre is Meg Twycross 'Books for the Unlearned' (1983).

11. Alan Fletcher deals usefully with the sources of the Conception episode in his MA thesis (University of Leeds 1974), *An Edition of the N-Town Conception of Mary, with an introduction and notes*. For more general discussion of sources see M. P. Forrest, 'Apocryphal Sources of the St Anne's Day Plays in the Hegge Cycle', *Medievalia et Humanistica* 17 (1966), pp. 38–50.

12. John Marshall in his MA thesis (University of Leeds 1974), *The Staging of the Marian Group from the N-Town Cycle*, deals with scaffold lay-out and use in some detail. He suggests a structure for the Golden Gate on one side of the Temple, with possibly a matching gateway (for Nazareth?) on the other side (p. 35). Certainly the Golden Gate seems a likely addition.

* The Wakefield evidence referred to in Note 1 should now be corrected from the *Leeds Studies in English* articles (ns 7 (1974) 108–16 + appendices and ns 19 (1988) 85–104) in which A.C. Cawley, Jean Forrester and, in the latter article, John Goodchild demonstrate the errors in the Walker transcriptions of the Wakefield Burgess Court Rolls which refer to the Corpus Christi play.

Bibliography

This Bibliography consists of works referred to in the introduction and notes, and more recent works relating to the *Mary Play*. For work on the N. town plays, see the general bibliographies, *Annual Bibliography of English Language and Literature* and *The Year's Work in English Studies*, and the specialised *Bibliography of Medieval Drama* (Carl J. Stratman, 2 vols, New York 1972) and *A Manual of the Writings in Middle English 1050–1500* (J. Burke Severs *et al.*, New Haven 1967–). The works referred to in the notes are listed under the short titles used there.

References to the Bible are to the Douai-Rheims (English) and Vulgate (Latin).

Analecta Hymnica Medii Aevi, ed. G. M. Dreves and C. Blume (Leipzig 1886–1922) and index (1978)

Ancient Liturgy, see William Maskell, *The Ancient Liturgy of the Church of England* (Oxford 1882)

Ancrene Riwle, see *The Ancrene Riwle*, trans. M. B. Salu (London 1955)

Augustine (on the Psalms), *Expositions on the Book of Psalms by St Augustine*, trans. J. Tweed *et al.*, 6 vols, A Library of Fathers of the Holy Catholic Church (Oxford 1847–57) [*Enarrationes in Psalmos*, PL 36–7 (1861 and 1865)]

Beadle, H. R. L., *The Medieval Drama of East Anglia: studies in dialect, documentary records and stagecraft* (unpublished D. Phil thesis, York 1978)

Bernard, see PL 183 (Paris 1854)

Block, see *Ludus Coventriae or the Plaie called Corpus Christi*, ed. K. S. Block, EETS ES 120 (London 1922)

Breviary, see *Breviarium ad Usum . . . Sarum*, ed. Francis Proctor and Christopher Wordsworth, 3 vols (Cambridge 1882–86)

Brome *Abraham and Isaac*, see *Non-Cycle Plays and Fragments*, ed. Norman David, EETS SS 1 (London 1970)

Brown *Lyrics XV*, see *Religious Lyrics of the Fifteenth Century*, ed. Carleton Brown (Oxford 1939)

Cassiodorus, see PL 70 (Paris 1865)

Castle of Love, see under *Vernon*, I pp. 355–406

Castle of Perseverance, see *The Macro Plays*, ed. Mark Eccles, EETS 262 (London 1969)

Cawley, A. C., Marion Jones, Peter F. McDonald and David Mills, *Medieval Drama*, The Revels History of Drama in English 1 (London and New York 1983)

Charter, see 'The Charter of the Abbey of the Holy Ghost', in *Yorkshire Writers: Richard Rolle of Hampole*, ed. C. Horstman, 2 vols (London 1895) 1

Chester, see *The Chester Mystery Cycle*, ed. R. M. Lumiansky and David Mills, EETS SS 3 (London 1974)

Comestor, see *PL* 198 (Paris 1855)

Conversion of St Paul, see *The Late Medieval Religious Plays of Bodleian MSS. Digby 133 and E. Museo 160*, ed. Donald C. Baker, John L. Murphy and Louis B. Hall Jr., EETS 283 (London 1982)

Cursor Mundi, see *Cursor Mundi*, ed. Richard Morris, 7 vols, EETS OS 57, 59, 62, etc. (London 1874–93)

Enchiridion, see 'The Enchiridion', trans. J. F. Shaw, in *Works of Aurelius Augustine*, ed. Marcus Dods, vol. 9 (Edinburgh 1873) [Aurelii Augustini Opera Pars XIII, 2, Corpus Christianorum Series Latina 46 (Turnholt 1969) pp. 21–114]

Fabri, see *The Wanderings of Felix Fabri*, trans. Aubrey Stewart, 2 vols, Palestine Pilgrims Text Society (London 1887–97) [Fratris Felicis Fabri, *Evagatorium in Terrae Sanctae, Arabiae et Aegypti*, ed. Conrad Dietrich Hassler, 3 vols, Bibliothek des literarischen Vereins in Stuttgart (Stuttgart 1843–9)]

Fletcher, Alan J., 'The "Contemplacio" Prologue to the N-Town Play of the Parliament of Heaven', *Notes and Queries* 27 (1980), pp. 111–12

Fletcher, Alan J., 'Marginal Glosses in the N-Town Manuscript, British Library MS Cotton Vespasian D VIII', *Manuscripta* 25 (1981), pp. 113–17

Fletcher, Alan J., 'The Design of the N-Town Play of Mary's Conception', *Modern Philology* 79 (1981) pp. 166–73

Fletcher, Alan J., 'Layers of Revision in the N-Town Marian Cycle', *Neophilologus* 66 (1982) pp. 469–78

Forrest, Sister M. P., 'Apocryphal Sources of the St Anne's Day Plays in the Hegge Cycle', *Medievalia et Humanistica* 17 (1966) pp. 38–50

Forrest, Sister M. P., 'The Role of the Expositor Contemplacio in the St Anne's Day Plays of the Hegge Cycle', *Medieval Studies* 28 (1966), pp. 60–76

Gibson, Gail McMurray, 'Bury St Edmunds, Lydgate, and the *N-Town Cycle*', *Speculum* 56 (1981), pp. 56–90.

Gospel of Nicodemus, see *Apocryphal Gospels, Acts and Revelations*, trans. Alexander Walker, Ante-Nicene Library 16 (Edinburgh 1890) [*Evangelia Apocrypha*, ed. Constantinus Tischendorff (Leipzig 1853)]

Gray *Lyrics*, see *A Selection of Religious Lyrics*, ed. Douglas Gray (Oxford 1975)

Greene, see *The Early English Carols*, ed. Richard Leighton Greene (2nd. edn, Oxford 1977)

Greg, Walter W., *Bibliographical and Textual Problems in the English Miracle Cycles* (London 1914)

Happé, see *English Mystery Plays*, ed. Peter Happé (Penguin Books, 1975)

Hemingway, see *English Nativity Plays*, ed. Samuel B. Hemingway, Yale Studies in English 38 (New York 1909)

History of Joseph, see under *Gospel of Nicodemus*

Horae, see *Horae Eboracenses, the Prymer or Hours of the Blessed Virgin Mary*, ed. Christopher Wordsworth, Surtees Society 132 (Durham 1920)

Isidore, see Isidori Hispalensis Episcopi, *Etymologiarum sive Originum*, ed. W. M. Lindsay, 2 vols (Oxford 1911)

Jacob's Well, see *Jacob's Well*, ed. Arthur Brandeis, EETS OS 115 (London 1900)

Jacques de Vitry, *The History of Jerusalem*, trans. Aubrey Stewart in Palestine Pilgrims Text Society (London 1896)

Killing of the Children, see under *Conversion of St Paul*

Lanterne of Light, see *The Lanterne of Light*, ed. Lilian M. Swinburn, EETS OS 151 (London 1917)

Lay Folks' Catechism, see *The Lay Folks' Catechism*, ed. Thomas Frederick Simmons and Henry Edward Nolloth, EETS OS 118 (London 1901)

Lay Folks Mass Book, see *The Lay Folks Mass Book*, ed. Thomas Frederick Simmons, EETS OS 71 (London 1879)

Legenda, see Jacobus de Voragine, *Legenda Aurea*, ed. Theodor Graesse (3rd. edn, Breslau 1890)

Life of St Anne, see *The Middle English Stanzaic Versions of the Life of St Anne*, ed. Roscoe E. Parker, EETS OS 174 (London 1928). The three texts edited are referred to as (1), (2) and (3) respectively

Love's *Mirrour*, see *The Mirrour of the Blessed Lyf of Jesu Christ . . . by Nicholas Love*, ed. Lawrence F. Powell (Oxford 1908)

Lydgate, see *The Minor Poems of John Lydgate*, ed. Henry Noble MacCracken, 2 vols, EETS ES 107, 192 (London 1911, 1934) 1

Lydgate's *Life of Our Lady*, see *A Critical Edition of John Lydgate's Life of Our Lady*, ed. Joseph A. Lauritis, Ralph A. Klinefelter and Vernon D. Gallagher, DuQuesne Studies: Philological Series 2 (Pittsburgh, Pa., 1961) [Upper case roman numerals in references refer to Books]

Mankind, see under *Castle of Perseverance*

Margery Kempe, see *The Book of Margery Kempe*, ed. Sanford Brown Meech and Hope Emily Allen, EETS OS 212 (London 1940)

Mary Magdalen, see under *Conversion of St Paul*

Maskell, see *Monumenta Ritualia Ecclesiae Anglicanae*, ed. William Maskell, 3 vols (Oxford 1882)

Meditationes, see 'Meditationes Vitae Christi', in *S. Bonaventurae . . . Opera Omnia*, ed. A. C. Peltier, vol. 12 (Paris 1868) [*Meditations on the Life of Christ*, trans. Isa Ragusa, ed. Isa Ragusa and Rosalie B. Green, Princeton Monographs in Art and Archaeology 35 (Princeton, NJ, 1961)]

Meredith, Peter, 'A Reconsideration of Some Textual Problems in the N-Town Manuscript (BL MS Cotton Vespasian D VIII)', *Leeds Studies in English* NS 9 (1977), pp. 35–50

Meredith, Peter, and Stanley J. Kahrl, *The N-Town Plays, a facsimile of BL MS Cotton Vespasian D VIII*, Leeds Texts and Monographs, Medieval Drama Facsimiles 4 (Leeds 1977)

Meredith, Peter, 'Scribes, Texts and Performance', in *Aspects of Early English Drama*, ed. Paula Neuss (Cambridge 1983)

Mézières, see *Philippe de Mézières' Campaign for the Feast of Mary's Presentation*, ed. William E. Coleman (Toronto 1981)

Middle English Sermons, see *Middle English Sermons*, ed. Woodburn O. Ross, EETS OS 209 (London 1940)

Mirk, see *Mirk's Festial*, ed. Theodor Erbe, EETS ES 96 (London 1905)

Mirrour, see under Love's *Mirrour*

Missal, see *Missale ad Usum . . . Sarum*, ed. Francis Henry Dickinson (Burntisland 1861–83)

Nativity of Mary, see under *Gospel of Nicodemus*

Norwich pageants, see 'The Norwich Grocers' Play' in *Non-Cycle Plays and Fragments*, ed. Norman Davis, EETS SS 1 (London 1970)

On the Properties, see *On the Properties of Things*, John Trevisa's translation of Bartholomaeus Anglicus' *De Proprietatibus Rerum*. ed. M. C. Seymour *et al.*, 2 vols (Oxford 1975)

Ormulum, see *The Ormulum*, ed. Robert Meadows White, 2 vols (Oxford 1852)

Passion Play, see *The Passion Play from the N. town Manuscript*, ed. Peter Meredith (London 1990)

Pepysian Gospel Harmony, see *The Pepysian Gospel Harmony*, ed. Margery Goates, EETS OS 157 (London 1922)

Piers Plowman, see William Langland, *The Vision of Piers Plowman*, ed. A. V. C. Schmidt (London 1978)

Play of the Sacrament, see under Brome *Abraham and Isaac*

Protevangelium, see under *Gospel of Nicodemus*

Prymer, see *The Prymer or Lay Folks' Prayer Book*, ed. Henry Littlehales, 2 vols, EETS OS 105, 109 (London 1895, 1897)

Pseudo-Matthew, see under *Gospel of Nicodemus*

REED *York*, see *York*, ed. Alexandra F. Johnston and Margaret Rogerson, Records of Early English Drama (Toronto 1979)

Religious Pieces, see *Religious Pieces in Prose and Verse*, ed. George G. Perry, EETS OS 26 (London 1867, 1914)

Reynes, see *The Commonplace Book of Robert Reynes of Acle*, an edition of Tanner MS 407, ed. Cameron Louis (New York and London 1980)

Rolle, see *Yorkshire Writers: Richard Rolle of Hampole*, ed. C. Horstman, 2 vols (London 1895)

Rosarium, see *The Middle English Translation of the Rosarium Theologiae*, ed. Christina von Nolcken, Middle English Texts 10 (Heidelberg 1979)

Rushforth, see G. McN. Rushforth, *Medieval Christian Imagery* (Oxford 1936)

Schiller, see Gertrud Schiller, *Iconography of Christian Art*, trans. Janet Seligman, 2 vols (London 1971)

Specimens, see *Specimens of the Pre-Shakesperean Drama*, ed. John Matthews Manly, 2 vols (New York 1897, repr. 1967)

Spector, Stephen, 'The Composition and Development of an Eclectic Manuscript: Cotton Vespasian D VIII', *Leeds Studies in English* NS 9 (1977), pp. 62–83

Spector, Stephen, 'Symmetry in Watermark Sequences', *Studies in Bibliography* 31 (1978), pp. 162–78

Speculum Sacerdotale, see *Speculum Sacerdotale*, ed. Edward H. Weatherly, EETS OS 200 (London 1936)

Staging of Religious Drama, see Peter Meredith and John E. Tailby, *The Staging of Religious Drama in Europe in the Later Middle Ages: texts and documents in English translation* (Kalamazoo 1983)

Stanzaic Life, see *A Stanzaic Life of Christ*, ed. Frances A. Foster, EETS OS 166 (London 1926)

St-Jacques, Raymond, 'The Hegge "Mary in the Temple" and the Liturgy of the Consecration of Virgins', *Notes and Queries* 27 (1980), pp. 295–7

The Myroure, see *The Myroure of Oure Ladye*, ed. John Henry Blount, EETS ES 19 (London 1873)

Towneley, see *The Towneley Plays*, ed. George England and Alfred W. Pollard, EETS ES 71

28   Bibliography

Twycross, Meg. 'Books for the Unlearned', in Themes in Drama 5: *Drama and Religion* (Cambridge 1983)

Vernon, see *The Minor Poems of the Vernon MS*, ed. Carl Horstman (vol 1) and Frederick J. Furnivall (vol 2), 2 vols, EETS OS 98, 117 (London 1892, 1901)

Vita Christi, see *Vita Jesu Christi . . . Ludolphum de Saxonia*, ed. A-C. Bolard, L-M. Rigollot and J. Carnandet (Paris and Rome 1865)

Vriend, see J. Vriend S.J., *The Blessed Virgin Mary in the Medieval Drama of England* (Purmerend 1928)

Whiting, see Bartlett Jere Whiting, *Proverbs, Sentences, and Proverbial Phrases from English Writings mainly before 1500* (Cambridge, Mass. 1968)

Wisdom, see under *Castle of Perseverance*

Woolf *Lyric*, see Rosemary Woolf, *The English Religious Lyric in the Middle Ages* (Oxford 1968)

Woolf *Mystery Plays*, see Rosemary Woolf, *The English Mystery Plays* (London 1972)

York, see *The York Plays*, ed. Richard Beadle (London 1982)

York Manual, see *Manuale et Processionale ad Usum . . . Eboracensis*, ed. W. G. Henderson, Surtees Society 63 (Durham 1875)

Additions to Bibliography:

New editions have now appeared of *N.town* (appearing in the Bibliography under 'Block'), *Towneley* and Love's *Mirrour* as follows:

The N-town Play, ed. Stephen Spector, EETS SS 11 and 12 (Oxford 1991)

The Towneley Plays, ed. Martin Stevens and A.C. Cawley, EETS SS 13 and 14 (Oxford 1994)

Nicholas Love's 'Mirror of the Blessed Life of Jesus Christ': a critical edition based on Cambridge University Library MSS 6578 and 6686, ed. Michael G. Sargent (New York and London 1992)

There is a handy new annotated bibliography which supplements Stratman:

Berger, Sidney E., *Medieval English Drama, an annotated bibliography of recent criticism* (New York and London 1990)

The following should also be added:

Fletcher, Alan J., 'The N-Town plays', in *The Cambridge Companion to Medieval English Theatre*, ed. Richard Beadle (Cambridge 1994)

Gibson, Gail McMurray, *The Theater of Devotion: East Anglian drama and society in the late Middle Ages* (Chicago and London 1989)

Meredith, Peter, 'Manuscript, scribe and performance: further looks at the N.town manuscript', in *Regionalism in Late Medieval Manuscripts and Texts*, ed. Felicity Riddy (Cambridge 1991)

Meredith, Peter, 'Performance, Verse and Occasion in the N.town *Mary Play*', in *Individuality and Achievement in Middle English Poetry*, ed. O. S. Pickering (Cambridge 1997)

Spector, Stephen, *The Genesis of the N-town Cycle* (New York and London 1988)

Twycross, Meg, '"As the sun with his beams when he is most bright"', *Medieval English Theatre* 12:1 (1990) 34–79

Editorial Procedures

1. Capitalisation, word division and punctuation are editorial.
2. The manuscript distinction between *u* and *v*, has been retained. Manuscript *ff* and *ss* have been simplified to *f/F* and *s* when initial. In the manuscript *þ* and *y* are written as *y*. For the sake of clarity I have distinguished between them.
3. For the convenience of the reader, stressed final *-e* has been marked with an acute accent.
4. All abbreviations have been expanded silently. Among suspensions, only that of final *-r* has been regularly expanded since the others appear in most cases to be merely final flourishes.
5. The form *þu* is used throughout for the expansion of the abbreviation in the manuscript. Though forms with *-ou/-ow* occur when the word is written in full, they are less common than those with *-u*.
6. The scribe uses a wide variety of spellings, especially for final *-th/-t*. These have been retained except where indicated in the textual notes.
7. Speakers' names in the manuscript are all in the right margin. Stage directions in the manuscript are usually underlined in red and centred on the page. Attention is drawn in the textual notes to any not underlined or which are placed in the margin.
8. All roman numerals in text and stage directions have been replaced by the forms appearing most commonly elsewhere. In the case of *twelve*, which appears only as *xij*, the modern form has been used. All roman numerals in speakers' names when followed by a Latin sign of abbreviation have been silently expanded using the appropriate Latin form.
9. Editorial emendations or additions are enclosed within square brackets in the text only when the emendation or addition results in a new word. All emendations or additions are noted in the textual notes.
10. Stanza division in the manuscript is normally indicated by a paragraph mark preceding the first line of a new stanza, and sometimes also by a space. The scribe has occasionally failed to indicate a new stanza and in a very few cases has indicated one wrongly. I have followed his stanza division except where it seems to be wrong or inadequate.

The *Mary Play*

f. 37v *Contemplacio*

Cryst conserve þis congregacyon
Fro perellys past, present and future,
And þe personys here pleand, þat þe pronunciacyon
Of here sentens to be seyd mote be sad and sure,
And þat non oblocucyon make þis matere obscure,   5
But it may profite and plese eche persone present,
From þe gynnynge to þe endynge so to endure
Þat Cryst and every creature with þe conceyte be
                                        content.

This matere here mad is of þe modyr of mercy;
How be Joachym and Anne was here concepcyon,   10
Sythe offred into þe temple, compiled breffly,
Than maryed to Joseph, and so, folwyng þe
                                        salutacyon,
Metyng with Elyzabeth, and þerwith a conclusyon
In fewe wurdys talkyd þat it xulde nat be tedyous
To lernyd nyn to lewd, nyn to no man of reson.   15
Þis is þe processe; now preserve ȝow, Jhesus!

Perffore of pes I ȝow pray all þat ben here present,
And tak hed to oure talkyn, what we xal say.
I beteche ȝow þat Lorde þat is evyr omnypotent
To governe ȝow in goodnes as he best may—   20
    In hevyn we may hym se.
Now God þat is hevyn kynge
Sende us all hese dere blyssynge,
And to his towre he mote vs brynge,
    Amen, for charyté!   25

2–5] *large red numeral 8 in right margin*   16 now preserve] of oure *deleted
before* now   *below* 25] *for the five Annes and conclusion of genealogy, see notes
to l. 25*

f. 38   *Ysakar*

The prestys of God offre sote ensens
Vnto here God and þerfore they be holy.
We þat mynistere here in Goddys presens,
In vs xuld be fownd no maner of foly.
Ysakar, prynce of prestys, am I   30
Þat þis holyest day here haue mynystracyon,
Certyfyenge all tribus in my cure specyaly,
Þat this is þe hyest fest of oure solennyzacyon.

This we clepe *Festum Encenniorum*,
Þe newe fest, of which thre in þe ȝere we exercyse.   35
Now all þe kynredys to Jerusalem must cum
Into þe temple of God, here to do sacryfyse.
Tho þat be cursyd my dygnyté is to dysspyse,
And þo þat be blyssyd, here holy sacrefyse to take.
We be *regal sacerdocium*; it perteyneth vs to be wysse, 40
Be fastyng, be prayng, be almes and at du tyme to
                                                    wake.

Joachym

Now all þis countré of Galylé,
With þis cetye of Nazareth specyal,
Þis fest to Jerusalem must go we
To make sacrefyce to God eternal.   45
My name is Joachym, a man in godys substancyall.
Joachym is to say, "he þat to God is redy";
So haue I be and evyrmore xal,
For þe dredful domys of God sore drede I.

I am clepyd ryghtful; why, wole ȝe se?   50
For my godys into thre partys I devyde:
On to þe temple and to hem þat þer servyng be,
Anodyr to þe pylgrimys and pore men, þe thrydde
                                    for hem with me abyde.
f. 38v   So xulde euery curat in þis werde wyde
ȝeve a part to his chauncel, iwys,   55
A part to his parochonerys þat to povert slyde,
The thryd part to kepe for hym and his.

But blyssyd wyff, Anne, sore I drede
In þe temple þis tyme to make sacryfice.
Becawse þat no frute of vs doth procede,   60
I fere me grettly þe prest wole me dysspice;
Than grett slawndyr in þe tribus of vs xulde aryse.
But þis I avow to God with all þe mekenes I can:
Ȝyff of his mercy he wole a childe us devyse,
We xal offre it up into þe temple to be Goddys man.   65

Anna

Ȝour swemful wurdys make terys trekyl down be my
                                                                            face;
Iwys, swete husbond, þe fawte is in me.
My name is Anne, þat is to sey "grace" –
We wete not how gracyous God wyl to us be.
A woman xulde bere Cryst, þese profecyes haue we –   70
If God send frute and it be a mayd-childe,
With all reuerens I vow to his magesté,
Sche xal be here foot-mayd to mynyster here most
                                                                        mylde.

Joachym

Now lete be it as God wole, þer is no more!
Tweyn turtelys for my sacryfice with me I take,   75
And I beseche, wyff, and evyr we mete more,
Þat hese grett mercy vs meryer mut make.

Anna

For dred and for swem of ȝour wourdys I qwake.
Thryes I kysse ȝow with syghys ful sad,
And to þe mercy of God mekely I ȝow betake;   80
And þo þat departe in sorwe, God make þer metyng
                                                                            glad!

Senior Tribus

Worchepful sere Joachym, be ȝe redy now?
All ȝour kynrede is come ȝow to exorte,
f. 39   Þat þei may do sacrifice at þe temple with ȝow,
For ȝe be of grett wurchep as men ȝow report.   85

---

71 God send] If *deleted before* God *and written again in left margin*
80 mekely] ? *deleted before* mekely; -ly *of* mekely *above line*   84 may]
written above line + caret

Joachym

    All synfull, seke and sory, God mote comforte;
    I wolde I were as men me name!
    Thedyr in Goddys name now late us all resorte.
    A, Anne, Anne, Anne, God scheeld us fro shame!

Anne

    Now am I left alone, sore may I wepe.   90
    A, husbond, ageyn God wel mote ȝow brynge,
    And fro shame and sorwe he mote ȝow kepe!
    Tyl I se ȝow ageyn, I kannot sees of wepynge.
Senior
    Prynce of oure prestys, if it be ȝour plesynge,
    We be com mekely to make our sacrefice.   95
Ysakar
    God do ȝow mede, bothe elde and ȝynge,
    Than devowtly we wyl begynne servyse.

There they xal synge þis sequens: Benedicta sit beata
Trinitas. *And in þat tyme Ysakar with his ministerys
ensensyth þe autere, and þan þei make her offryng and Isaker
seyth*:

    Comyth up, serys, and offeryth all now,
    Ȝe þat to do sacryfice worthy are.
    Abyde a qwyle, sere! Whedyr wytte þu?   100
    Þu and þi wyff arn barrany and bare,
    Neyther of ȝow fruteful nevyr ȝett ware.
    Whow durste þu amonge fruteful presume and
                               abuse?
    It is a tokyn þu art cursyd þare;
    Whereffore with grett indygnacyon þin offeryng I
                               refuse.   105
               Et refudit sacrificium Joachim.

    Amonge all þis pepyl barreyn be no mo,
    Therefore comyth up and offeryth here alle! –
    Þu, Joachym, I charge þe fast out þe temple þu go! –
                     Et redit flendo.
    Than with Goddys holy wourde blysse ȝow I shalle.

Ministro cantando
f. 39v   *Adiutorium nostrum in nomine domini,*   110

97 *sd*] *Stage direction preceded by red* Memorandum *abbreviation*   105 *sd* and
108 *sd*] *in right margin*   109 holy] *written above line + caret*

Chorus
> *Qui fecit celum et terram.*

Minister
> *Sit nomen domini benedictum:*

Chorus
> *Ex hoc nunc et usque in seculum.*

Episcopus
> *Benedicat vos diuina maiestas et vna deitas*
> ✠ *Pater* ✠ *et Filius* ✠ *et Spiritus Sanctus.*   115

Chorus
> *Amen.*

Signando manu cum cruce solenniter et recedant tribus extra templum.

[*Ysakar*]
> Now of God and man blyssyd be ȝe alle.
> Homward aȝen now returne ȝe,
> And in þis temple abyde we xalle
> To servyn God in Trinyté.   120

Joachym
> A, mercyfful Lord, what is þis lyff?
> What haue I do, Lorde, to haue þis blame?
> For hevynes I dare not go hom to my wyff,
> And amonge my neyborys I dare not abyde for
>   shame.
> A, Anne, Anne, Anne, al our joye is turnyd to
>   grame!   125
> From ȝour blyssyd felacheppe I am now exilyd;
> And ȝe here onys of þis fowle fame,
> Sorwe wyl sle ȝow to se me thus revylyd.
>
> But sen God soferyth thys, vs must sofron nede.
> Now wyl I go to my sherherdys and with hem
>   abyde,   130
> And þer evyrmore levyn in sorwe and in drede.
> Shame makyth many man his hed for to hyde.
> Ha, how do ȝe, felas? In ȝow is lytel pryde.
> How fare ȝe and my bestys? Þis wete wolde I veryly.

---

114 maiestas] & una *deleted before* maiestas   117 *sn* Ysakar] *omitted in*
MS.   123 hevynes] dare *deleted before* hevynes

Primus Pastor
    A, welcom hedyr, blyssyd mayster! We pasture hem
                      ful wyde.   135
    They be lusty and fayr and grettly multyply.

    How do ȝe, mayster? Ȝe loke al hevyly.
    How doth oure dame at hom? Sytt she and sowyht?
Joachym
    To here þe speke of here it sleyth myn hert veryly.
    How I and sche doth, God hymself knowyth;   140
    The meke God lyftyth up, þe proude overthrowyht.
    Go, do what ȝe lyst! Se ȝour bestys not stray!
Secundus Pastor
    Aftere grett sorwe, mayster, evyr gret grace
                      growyht.
    Sympyl as we kan, we xal for ȝow pray.

Tertius Pastor
    Ȝa, to pray for careful, it is grett nede.   145
    We all wul prey for ȝow knelende.
    God of his goodnes send ȝow good spede,
    And of ȝour sorwe ȝow sone amende!

Joachym
    I am nott wurthy, Lord, to loke up to hefne;
    My synful steppys an venymyd þe grounde.   150
    I, lothfolest þat levyth: þu, Lord, hyest in þi setys
                      sefne.
    What art þu, Lord? What am I, wrecche, werse þan
                      an hownde?
    Þu hast sent me shame, which myn hert doth
                      wounde –
    I thank þe more herefore þan for all my prosperité.
    Þis is a tokyn þu lovyst me, now to the I am bounde;   155
    Þu seyst þu art with hem þat in tribulacyon be.

    And hoso haue þe, he nedyth not care thanne;
    My sorwe is feryng I haue do sum offens.
    Punchyth me, Lorde, and spare my blyssyd wyff
                      Anne

f. 40

135ff] *For the lettering of the following speeches and the dividing off of this section,* *see note to ll. 133–212*   139 sn Joachym] ij pastor *deleted*   150 venymyd] *MS.* vemynyd

Þat syttyth and sorwyth ful sore of myn absens.   160
Ther is not may profyte but prayour to ʒour presens.
With prayorys prostrat byfore þi person I wepe;
Haue mende on oure avow for ʒour mech
                                    magnyficens,
And my lovyngest wyff Anne, Lord, for þi mercy
                                    kepe.

Anna
A, mercy, Lord, mercy, mercy, mercy!   165
We are synfolest, it shewyth þat ʒe send us all þis
                                    sorwe.
Why do ʒe thus to myn husbond, Lord? Why, why,
                                    why?
For my barynes, [ʒe] may amend þis þiself, and þu
                                    lyst, tomorwe,
And it plese so þi mercy; þe, my Lord, I take to
                                    borwe.
I xal kepe myn avow qwhyl I leve and leste.   170
I fere me I haue offendyd þe, myn hert is ful of
                                    sorwe.

f. 40v   Most mekely I pray þi pety, þat þis bale þu wyl breste.

Here þe aungel descendith; þe hefne syngyng: Exultet celum
laudibus resultet terra gaudijs archangelorum gloria
sacra canunt solennia.

Joachym
Qwhat art þu, in Goddys name, þat makyst me
                                    adrad?
It is as lyth abowt me as al þe werd were fere.
Angelus
I am an aungel of God, com to make þe glad.   175
God is plesyd with þin helmes and hath herd þi
                                    prayere;
He seyth þi shame, þi repreff and þi terys cler.
God is a vengere of synne, and not nature doth lothe;
Whos wombe þat he sparyth and makyth barreyn
                                    her,
He doth to shewe his myth and his mercy bothe.   180

Thu seest þat Sara was nynty ʒere bareyn;
Sche had a son, Ysaac, to whom God ʒaff his
                                    blyssynge.
Rachel also had þe same peyn;

168 ʒe] *MS.* he   173 *sn Joachym] placed before sd.*

She had a son, Joseph, þat of Egypt was kynge.
A strongere þan Sampson nevyr was, be wrytynge,   185
Nor an holyere þan Samuel, it is seyd thus;
3ett here moderys were bareyn bothe in þe
                                gynnynge.
Þe concepcyon of all swych, it is ful mervelyous.

And in þe lyke wyse, Anne, þi blyssyd wyff,
Sche xal bere a childe xal hygth Mary,   190
Which xal be blyssyd in here body and haue joys fyff;
And ful of þe Holy Goost, inspyred syngulyrly,
Sche xal be offryd into þe temple, solemply,
Þat of here non evyl fame xuld sprynge thus;
And as sche xal be bore of a barrany body,   195
So of here xal be bore, without nature, Jhesus,

f. 41   That xal be savyour vnto al mankende.
In tokyn, whan þu come to Jherusalem, to þe Gyldyn
                                Gate,
Þu xalt mete Anne, þi wyff – haue þis in þi mende.
I xal sey here þe same, here sorwys to rebate.   200

Joachym

Of þis incomparabyl comfort I xal nevyr forgete þe
                                date.
My sorwe was nevyr so grett, but now my joy is
                                more.
I xal hom in hast, be it nevyr so late.
A, Anne, blyssyd be þat body of þe xal be bore!

Now, farewel, myn shepherdys! Governe 3ow now
                                wysly!   205

Primus Pastor

Haue 3e good tydyngys, mayster, þan be we glad.

Joachym

Prayse God for me, for I am not wourthy.

Secundus Pastor

In feyth, sere, so we xal, with all oure sowlys sad.

Tertius Pastor

I holde it helpfful þat on of vs with 3ow be had.

Joachym

Nay, abyde with 3our bestys, sone, in Goddys
                                blyssynge!   210

194 of here] *written above line + caret*   196] *at foot of page are catchwords* Þat
xal be s*avyour*   201 incomparabyl] *MS.* imcomparabyl

Primus Pastor
> We xal make us so mery now þis is bestad,
> Þat a myle on ӡour wey ӡe xal here us synge.

Anne
> Alas, for myn husbond me is ful wo!
> I xal go seke hym, whatsoevyr befalle.
> I wote not in erth which wey is he go.   215
> Fadyr of hefne, for mercy to ӡour fete I falle!

Angelus
> Anne, þin husbond ryght now I was withall,
> Þe aungel of God þat bar hym good tydynge.
> And as I seyd to hym, so to þe sey I xal:
> God hath herd þi preyour and þi wepynge.   220

> At þe Goldyn Gate þu xalte mete hym ful mylde,
> And in grett gladnes returne to ӡour hous.
> So be proces þu xalt conseyve and bere a childe
> Whiche xal hyght Mary; and Mary xal bere Jhesus
> Which xal be savyour of all þe werd and us.   225
> Aftere grett sorwe, evyr grett gladnes is had.
> Now myn inbassett I haue seyd to ӡow thus;
> Gooth in oure Lordys name, and in God beth glad!

f. 41v

Anne
> Now blyssyd be oure Lorde and all his werkys ay!
> All heffne and erthe mut blysse ӡow for this.   230
> I am so joyful, I not what I may say.
> Þer can no tounge telle what joye in me is.
> I to bere a childe þat xal bere all mannys blys,
> And haue myn hosbonde ageyn – ho myth haue joys
> more?
> No creature in erth is grauntyd more mercy, iwys.   235
> I xal hyӡe me to þe ӡate to be þer before.

Here goth þe aungel aӡen to hefne.

> A, blyssyd be our Lord, myn husbond I se!
> I xalle on myn knes and to-hym-ward crepe.

Joachym
> A, gracyous wyff Anne, now fruteful xal ӡe be!

211 þis is] is *deleted before* þis

For joy of þis metyng in my sowle I wepe.   240
Haue þis kusse of clennesse and with ȝow it kepe.
In Goddys name now go we, wyff, hom to our hous!

Anne

Þer was nevyr joy sank in me so depe.
Now may we sey, husbond, God is to us gracyous,
    Veryly.   245

Joachym

Ȝa, and if we haue levyd wel herebefore,
I pray þe, Lord, þin ore,
So mote we levyn evyrmore
    And be þi grace more holyly.

Anne

f. 42   Now homward, husbond, I rede we gon,   250
Ryth hom al to our place,
To thank God þat sytt in tron,
Þat þus hath sent us his grace.

Contemplacio

Sovereynes, ȝe han sen shewyd ȝow before,
Of Joachym and Anne, here botherys holy metynge.   255
How Our Lady was conseyvid and how she was
                                                bore,
We passe ovyr þat, breffnes of tyme consyderynge;
And how Our Lady in here tendyr age and ȝyng
Into þe temple was offryd, and so forth, proced.
Þis sentens sayd xal be hire begynnyng.   260
Now þe modyr of mercy in þis be our sped!

And as a childe of thre ȝere age here she xal appere
To alle pepyl þat ben here present;
And of here grett grace now xal ȝe here,
How she levyd evyr to Goddys entent   265
    With grace;
That holy matere we wole declare,
Tyl fortene ȝere, how sche dyd fare.
Now of ȝour speche I pray ȝow spare
    All þat ben in þis place.   270

---

240 metyng] wepy *deleted before* metyng   243 nevyr] *written above line* +
caret   259–63] *large red numeral* 9 *in right margin*   262 thre] MS.
iij   264 now xal] here she xal *deleted before* now

Here Joachym and Anne, with Oure Lady betwen hem beyng
al in whyte as a childe of thre ȝere age, presente here into þe
temple; thus seyng Joachym:

f. 42v   Joachim

Blyssyd be oure Lord, fayr frute haue we now.
Anne, wyff, remembyr wole ȝe
Þat we made to God an holy avow
Þat oure fyrst childe þe servaunt of God xulde be.
The age of Mary, oure dowtere, is ȝerys thre,   275
Þerfore to thre personys and on God lete us here
                                        present;
Þe ȝonger she be drawyn þe bettyr semyth me,
And for teryeng of our avow of God we myth be
                                        shent.

Anne

It is as ȝe sey, husbond, indede.
Late us take Mary, our dowtere, us betwen   280
And to þe temple with here procede.
Dowtere, þe aungel tolde us ȝe xulde be a qwen;
Wole ȝe go se þat Lord ȝour husbond xal ben,
And lerne for to love hym, and lede with hym ȝour
                                        lyff?
Telle ȝour fadyr and me her, ȝour answere let sen;   285
Wole ȝe be pure maydyn, and also Goddys wyff?

Maria

Fadyr and modyr, if it plesynge to ȝow be,
Ȝe han mad ȝour avow, so sothly wole I,
To be Goddys chast seruaunt whil lyff is in me –
But to be Goddys wyff, I was nevyr wurthy.   290
I am þe sympelest þat evyr was born of body.
I haue herd ȝow sey, God xulde haue a modyr swete;
Þat I may leve to se hire, God graunt me for his
                                        mercy,
And abyl me to ley my handys vndyr hire fayr fete!

Et genuflectet ad Deum.

---

270 *sd* thre] *MS.* iij;   *thus seyng*] s *deleted before* thus   292 sey] *MS.*
seyd   293 his] *written above line*;   mercy] ȝour *deleted before* mercy

Joachym
    Iwys, dowtere, it is wel seyd.   295
    ȝe answere and ȝe were twenty ȝere olde!
Anne
f. 43   Whith ȝour speche, Mary, I am wel payd.
    Can ȝe gon alone? Lett se – beth bolde!
Maria
    To go to Goddys hous wole ȝe now beholde;
    I am joyful thedyrward as I may be.   300
Joachym
    Wyff, I ryght joyful oure dowtere to beholde.
Anne
    So am I, wys, husbond, now in Goddys name go
                                         we.

Joachym
    Sere prince of prestes, and it plese ȝow,
    We þat were barreyn, God hath sent a childe;
    To offre here to Goddys service we mad our avow;   305
    Here is þe same mayde, Mary, most mylde.
Isakar
    Joachym, I haue good mende how I ȝow revyled;
    I am ryght joyful þat God hath ȝove ȝow þis grace
    To be amonge fruteful; now be ȝe reconsylid.
    Com, swete Mary, com! ȝe haue a gracyous face.   310

Joachym flectendo ad Deum sic dicens:

Joachym
    Now, Fadyr and Sone and Holy Gost,
    On God and personys thre,
    We offre to þe, Lorde of myghtys most,
    Oure dowtere, þi servaunt evyrmore to be.
Anna
    Therto most bounde evyrmore be we.   315
    Mary, in þis holy place leve ȝow we xall;
    In Goddys name now up go ȝe;
    Oure fadyr, oure prest, lo, doth ȝow call.

Maria
Modyr, and it plese ʒow, fyrst wole I take my leve
Of my fadyr and ʒow my modyr, iwys.   320
I haue a Fadyr in hefne, þis I beleve;
Now, good fadyr, with þat Fadyr ʒe me blysse.

Joachym
f. 43v   *In nomine Patris et Filij et Spiritus Sancti.*
Maria
Amen. Now ʒe, good modyr.
Anne
In nomine Patris et Filij et Spiritus Sancti.   325
Maria
Amen.

Now oure Lord thank ʒow for this.
Here is my fadyr and my modyr bothe,
Most mekely I beseche I may ʒow kys.
Now forʒeve me yf evyr I made ʒow wrothe.   330

Et explexendo osculabit patrem et matrem.

Joachym
Nay, dowtere, ʒe offendyd nevyr God nor man.
Lovyd be þat Lord, ʒow so doth kepe!
Anne
Swete dowtyr, thynk on ʒour modyr, An,
ʒour swemynge smytyht to myn hert depe.
Maria
Fadyr and modyr, I xal pray for ʒow and wepe   335
To God with al myn hert specyaly.
Blysse me day and nyght, evyr her ʒe slepe,
Good fadyr and modyr, and beth mery.

Joachym
A, ho had evyr suche a chylde!
Nevyr creature ʒit þat evyr was bore.   340
Sche is so gracyous, she is so mylde;
So xulde childyr to fadyr and modyr evyrmore.

326 *Maria* Amen.] *MS. Speaker's name and Amen follows end of previous line. Speaker's name repreated in margin.*   335 *sn Maria] omitted in MS. and added by a later hand*   338 beth] -th *deleted, perhaps by later hand*

Anne
>   Than xulde thei be blyssyd and plese God sore.
>   Husbond, and it plese ʒow, not hens go we xal
>   Tyl Mary be in þe temple above thore.   345
>   I wold not for al erthe se here fal.

Episcopus
>   Come, gode Mary! Come, babe, I þe call!
>   Þi pas pratyly to þis plas pretende.
>   Þu xalt be þe dowtere of God eternall

f. 44
>   If þe fyftene grees þu may ascende.   350
>   It is meracle if þu do. Now God þe dyffende!
>   From Babylony to hevynly Jherusalem þis is þe way.
>   Every man þat thynk his lyff to amende,
>   Þe fyftene psalmys in memorye of þis mayde say.

Maria (et sic deinceps usque ad finem quindecim psalmorum)
>   The fyrst degré gostly applyed   355
>   It is holy desyre with God to be:
>   In trobyl to God I haue cryed,
>   And in sped þat Lord hath herde me.

>   *Ad dominum cum tribularer clamaui;*
>   *et exaudiuit me.*   360

>   The secunde is stody with meke inquysissyon,
>   veryly,
>   How I xal haue knowynge of Godys wylle:
>   To þe mownteynes of hefne I haue lyfte myn ey,
>   From qwens xal comyn helpe me tylle.

>   *Leuaui oculos meos in montes;*   365
>   *vnde ueniat auxilium mihi.*

>   The thrydde is gladnes in mende in hope to be,
>   That we xall be savyd all thus:
>   I am glad of these tydyngys ben seyd to me,
>   Now xal we go into Goddys hous.   370

>   *Letatus sum in hijs que dicta sunt mihi;*
>   *in domum domini ibimus.*

---

354 *sd ad finem*] MS. ad fine;   *quindecim*] MS. xv^cim

The fourte is meke obedyence as is dette
To hym þat is above þe planetys sefne:
To þe I haue myn eyn sette   375
Þat dwellys above þe skyes in hefne.

Ad te leuaui oculos meos;
qui habitas in celis.

The fyfte is propyr confessyon,
Þat we be nought withowth God thus: 380
But God in vs haue habytacyon,
Peraventure oure enemyes shulde swelle vs.

f. 44v   *Nisi quia dominus erat in nobis dicat nunc Israel;*
         nisi quia dominus erat in nobis.

The sexte is confidens in Goddys strenght alon;   385
For of all grace from hym comyth þe strem:
They þat trust in God as þe Mownt Syon,
He xal not be steryd endles þat dwellyth in
                                          Jherusalem.

Qui confidunt in domino sicut mons Syon:
non commouebitur in eternum qui habitat in Hierusalem.   390

The sefte is vndowteful hope of immortalyté
In oure Lorde-is grace and mercy:
Whan oure Lord conuertyth oure captiuité,
Than are we mad as joyful mery.

In conuertendo dominus captiuitatem Syon;   395
facti sumus sicut consolati.

The eyted is contempt of veynglory in vs,
For hym þat al mankende hath multyplyed:
But yf oure Lord make here oure hous,
They an laboryd in veyn þat it han edyfied: 400

Nisi dominus edificauerit domum; in uanum
laborauerunt qui edificant eam.

---

392 Lorde–is grace] *MS.* lorde is as gracy   394 mery] s *deleted before* mery
400 han edyfied] ? *deleted before* han   402 laborauerunt] *MS.* laborauerut

The nynte is a childely fer indede,
With a longyng love in oure Lorde þat ay is:
Blyssyd arn all they þat God drede,   405
Whiche þat gon in his holy weys.

Beati omnes qui timent dominum: qui
ambulant in vijs eius.

The tende is myghty soferauns of carnal temptacyon;
For þe fleschly syghtys ben fers and fel: 410
Ofte ȝough is fowth with, with suech vexacyon;
Þu seynge God say so, clepyd Israel.

Sepe expugnauerunt me a iuuentute mea; dicat
nunc Israel.

The elefnte is accusatyff confessyon of iniquité,   415
Of which ful noyous is þe noyis:
Fro depnes, Lord, I haue cryed to the,
Lord, here in sped my sympyl voys.

f. 45   *De profundis clamaui ad te domine: domine*
         exaudi uocem meam.   420

The twelfte is mekenes þat is fayr and softe
In mannys sowle withinne and withowte:
Lord, myn herte is not heyued on lofte,
Nyn myn eyn be not lokynge abowte.

Domine non est exaltatum cor meum; neque   425
elati sunt oculi mei.

The threttene is feyth þerwith,
With holy dedys don expresse:
Haue mende, Lorde, of Davyth
And of all his swettnes.   430

Memento domine Dauid; et omnis
mansuetudinis eius.

The fourtene is brothyrly concorde, iwys,
Þat norchyth love of creaturys echon:
Se how good and how glad it is,   435
Bretheryn for to dwelle in on.

Ecce quam bonum et quam jocundum;
habitare fratres in vnum.

The fyftene is gracyous with on acorde,
Whiche is syne of godly love, semyth me: 440
Se now, blysse oure Lord,
All þat oure Lordys servauntys be.

Ecce nunc benedicite dominum:
omnes serui dominj.

Episcopus
A, gracyous Lord, þis is a mervelyous thynge   445
Þat we se here all in syght;
A babe of thre ȝer age so ȝynge
To come vp þese grecys so vpryght.
It is an hey meracle and by Goddys myght,
No dowth of, she xal be gracyous.   450
Maria
Holy fadyr, I beseche ȝow forthryght,
Sey how I xal be rewlyd in Goddys hous.

Episcopus
f. 45v   Dowtere, God hath ȝovyn vs comaundementys ten,
Which shortely to say be comprehendyd in tweyn,
And þo must be kept of all crysten men   455
Or ellys here jugement is perpetual peyn.
Ȝe muste love God sovereynly and ȝour evyn crystyn
                                                 pleyn;
God fyrst for his hyȝ and sovereyn dygnyté;
He lovyd ȝow fyrst, love hym ageyn,
For of love to his owyn lyknes he made the.   460

Love Fadyr, Sone and Holy Gost:
Love God þe Fadyr, for he gevyth myght;
Love God þe Son, for he gevyth wysdam, þu wost;
Love God þe Holy Gost, for he gevyth love and
                                                 lyght.
Thre personys and on God þus love of ryght,   465
With all þin hert, with all þi sowle, with all þi mende
And with all þe strenghthis in þe bedyght;
Þan love þin evyn crystyn as þiself withowtyn ende.

457 sovereynly] MS. severeynly   466 Þi mende] myght *deleted after*
mende

Thu xalt hate nothynge but þe devyl and synne –
God byddyth the lovyn þi bodyly enmy.   470
And as for ȝourself here, þus xal ȝe begynne:
Ȝe must serve and wurchep God here dayly,
For with prayȝer [come] grace and mercy;
Sethe haue a resonable tyme to fede;
Thanne to haue a labour bodyly,   475
Þat þerin be gostly and bodely mede.

Ȝour abydynge xal be with ȝour maydenys fyve,
Swyche tyme as ȝe wole haue consolacyon.
Maria
This lyff me lyketh as my lyve –
Of here namys I beseche ȝow to haue informacyon.   480
Episcopus
f. 46   There is þe fyrst, Meditacyon;
Contryssyon, Compassyon, and Clennes,
And þat holy mayde, Fruyssyon;
With these blyssyd maydenes xal be ȝour besynes.

Maria
Here is an holy felacheppe; I fele   485
I am not wurthy amonge hem to be.
Swete systerys, to ȝow all I knele,
To receyve me I beseche ȝour charyté.
Episcopus
They xal, dowtere. And on þe tothere syde se
Ther ben sefne prestys indede,   490
To schryve, to teche, and to mynystryn to the,
To lerne þe Goddys lawys and scrypture to rede.

Maria
Fadyr, knew I here namys, wele were I.
Episcopus
Ther is Dyscressyon, Devocyon, Dylexcyon, and
                               Deliberacyon,
They xal tende upon ȝow besyly,   495
With Declaracyon, Determynacyon, Dyvynacyon.
Now go, ȝe maydenys, to ȝour occupacyon,
And loke ȝe tende þis childe tendyrly;

---

473 come grace and] *MS.* with grace and   488 beseche] -seke *deleted after*
be-

And ȝe, serys, knelyth and I xal gyve ȝow Goddys
benyson:
In nomine Patris et Filij et Spiritus Sancti.   500

Et recedet cum ministris suis. Omnes virgines dicent: Amen.

[*Maria*]
    To ȝow, fadyr and modyr, I me comende,
    Blyssyd be þe tyme ȝe me hedyr brought.
Joachym
    Dowtere, þe Fadere of oure feyth þe mot defende,
    As he of his myght made all thynge of nowth!
Anne
    Mary, to þi sowle solas he sende   505
    In whos wysdam all þis werd was wrought!
    Go we now hens, husbonde so hende,
    For owth of care now are we brought.

Hic Joachim et Anna recedent domum.

Maria
f. 46v   Be þe Holy Gost at hom be ȝe brought!
          (*Ad virgines*) Systerys, ȝe may go do what ȝe xall,   510
          To serve God fyrst here is al my thought.
          Beforn þis holy awtere on my knes I fall.

          Lord, sefne petycyons I beseche ȝow of here:
          Fyrst, þat I may kepe þi love and þi lawe;
          Þe secunde, to lovyn myn evyn crystyn as myself
                                                              dere;   515
          Þe thrydde, from all þat þu hatyst me to withdrawe;
          The fourte, all vertuys to þi plesauns knawe;
          Þe fyfte, to obey þe ordenaryes of þe temple echon;
          Þe sexte, and þat all pepyl may serve þe with awe,
          Þat in þis holy tempyl fawte be non.   520

          The sefnte, Lord, I haske with grett fere:
          Þat I may se onys in my lyve
          Þat lady þat xal Goddys sone bere,
          Þat I may serve here with my wyttys fyve,
          If it plese ȝow, and ellys it is not þerwith to stryve.   525

500 *sd recedet*] *MS.* recedent   **501** *sn Maria*] *omitted in MS.*   **508** *sd*] in
right margin

With prayers prostrat for þese gracys I wepe;
O, my God, devocyon depe in me dryve
Þat myn hert may wake in þe, thow my body slepe.

Here þe aungel bryngyth manna in a cowpe of gold, lyke to
confeccyons; þe hefne syngynge. Þe aungel seyth:

[*Angelus*]
Merveyle not, mekest maydon, of my
                mynystracyon;
I am a good aungel sent of God allmyght   530
With aungelys mete for ȝour sustentacyon,
Ȝe to receyve it for natural myght.

f. 47   We aungellys xul serve ȝow day and nyght.
Now fede ȝow þerwith in Goddys name.
We xal lerne ȝow þe lyberary of oure Lordys lawe
                lyght,   535
For my sawys in ȝow shewyth sygnes of shame.

Maria
To thank oure soveryen Lord not sufficyth my
                mende,
I xal fede me of þis fode my Lord hath me sent.
All maner of savowrys in þis mete I fynde,
I felt nevyr non so swete ner so redolent.   540
Angelus
Eche day þerwith ȝe xal be content,
Aungelys alle howrys xal to ȝow apere.
Maria
Mercy, my makere, how may þis be ment?
I am þe sympelest creature þat is levynge here.

Angelus
In ȝour name, Maria, fyve letterys we han: 545
M – mayde most mercyfull, and mekest in mende;
A – auerte of þe anguysch þat Adam began;
R – regina of regyon, reyneng withowtyn ende;
I – innocent be influens of Jessés kende;
A – aduocat most autentyk, ȝour antecer, Anna.   550
Hefne and helle here kneys down bende
Whan þis holy name of ȝow is seyd: Maria.

529 *sn* Angelus] *omitted in* MS.   542 Aungelys] *MS.* Aunge

Maria

    I qwake grettly for dred to here þis comendacyon;

    Good swete aungel, why wole ȝe sey thus?

Aungell

    For ȝe xal hereaftere haue a salutacyon   555

    Þat xal þis excede, it is seyd amonge vs;

    The deyté þat dede xal determyn and dyscus.

    Ȝe xal nevyr, lady, be lefte here alone.

Maria

f. 47v   I crye þe mercy, Lorde, and þin erthe cus,

    Recomendynge me to þat Godhȳd þat is tryne in

                        trone.   560

Hic osculet terram. Here xal comyn alwey an aungel with dyvers presentys goynge and comyng, and in þe tyme þei xal synge in hefne þis hympne: Jhesu corona virginum. And after þer comyth a minister fro þe busschop with a present and seyth:

Minister

    Prynce of oure prestes, Ysakare be name,

    He hath sent ȝow hymself his servyce indede;

    And bad ȝe xulde fede ȝow – spare for no shame;

    In þis tyme of mete, no lenger ȝe rede.

Maria

    Recomende me to my fadyr, sere, and God do hym

                        mede.   565

    These vesselys aȝen sone I xal hym sende.

    I xal bere it my systerys, I trowe þei haue more nede –

    Goddys foyson is evyr to his servauntys hendyr þan

                        we wende.

    Systerys, oure holy fadyr, Isakare,

    Hath sent vs hese servyce here ryght now.   570

    Fede ȝow þerof hertyly, I pray ȝow nat spare.

    And if owght be leve, specyaly I pray ȝow

    That þe pore men þe relevys þerof haue now.

    Fayn and I myth I wolde do þe dedys of mercy.

    Pore folk faryn God knowyth how,   575

    On hem evyr I haue grett pety.

Contemplacio

    Lo, sofreynes, here ȝe haue seyn

    In þe temple of Oure Ladyes presentacyon;

555 haue a] a *deleted before* haue

f. 48

She was nevyr occapyed in thyngys veyn,
But evyr besy in holy ocupacyon.   580

And we beseche ȝow of ȝoure pacyens
Þat we pace þese materys so lythly away;
If þei xulde be do with good prevydens,
Eche on wolde suffyce for an hool day.

Now xal we procede to here dissponsacyon, 585
Which aftere þis was fourtene ȝere.
Tyme sufficyth not to make pawsacyon;
Hath pacyens with vs we besech ȝow her,
 And in short spas
The Parlement of Hefne sone xal ȝe se, 590
And how Goddys sone com man xal he;
And how þe salutacyon aftere xal be,
 Be Goddys holy gras.

f. 49 *Tunc venit Abysakar episcopus.*

[*Episcopus*]
Listenyth, lordyngys, bothe hye and lowe,
And tendyrly takyth heyd onto my sawe. 595
Beth buxom and benyngne ȝour busshopp to knowe,
For I am þat lord þat made þis lawe.
With hertys so hende, herkyn nowe!
Ȝoure damyselys to weddyng, ȝa, loke þat ȝe drawe,
Þat passyn fourtene ȝere, for what þat ȝe owe. 600
Þe lawe of God byddyth þis sawe:
 Þat at fourtene ȝere of age,
Euery damesel, whatso sche be,
To þe encrese of more plenté,
Xulde be browght in good degré 605
 Onto here spowsage.

Joachym
Herke now, Anne, my jentyl spowse,

584–87] *large red numeral* 10 *in right margin*   586 fourtene] *MS.* xiiij   594 sn Episcopus] *omitted in MS.*   594 lowe] ll *or* w *deleted before* lowe   594–97] *large red numeral* 10 *repeated in right margin*   594, 624, 633, 672, 685, 709, 726] *each line preceded by a letter*, a–g *respectively*   600, 602, 610, 623 fourtene] *MS.* xiiij

How þat þe buschop his lawe hath tolde;
Þat what man hath a dowtyr in his house
Þat passyth fourtene ӡerys olde,   610
He muste here brynge, I herde hym rowse,
Into þe tempyl a spowse to wedde.
Wherfor oure dowtyr ryth good and dowse
Into þe tempyl sche must be ledde,
　　And þat anoon ryght sone.   615

Anne
Sere, I grawnt þat it be so,
Aӡen þe lawe may we not do.
With here togedyr lete us now go;
　　I hold it ryght weyl done.

Joachym
Sere busshopp, here aftyr þin owyn hest,   620
We haue here brought oure dowtyr dere,
Mary, my swete childe; she is ful prest,
Of age she is ful fourtene ӡere.

Episcopus
f. 49v　Welcome, Joachym, onto myn areste,
Bothe Anne, þi wyff, and Mary clere!   625
Now Mary, chylde, to þe lawe þu leste
And chese þe a spowse to be þi fere –
　　Þat lawe þu must fulffylle.

Maria
Aӡens þe lawe wyl I nevyr be,
But mannys felachep xal nevyr folwe me;   630
I wyl levyn evyr in chastyté
　　Be þe grace of Goddys wylle.

Episcopus
A, fayre mayde, why seyst þu so?
What menyth the for to levyn chast?
Why wylt þu not to weddyng go?   635
Þe cawse þu telle me and þat in hast.

Maria
My fadyr, and my modyr sertys also,
Er I was born, ӡe may me trast,
Thei were bothe bareyn, here frute was do;
They come to þe tempyl at þe last   640
　　To do here sacryfice.
Bycause they hadde nothyr frute nere chylde

Reprevyd þei wore, of wykkyd and wyllde,
With grett shame þei were revylyd,
    Al men dede them dyspyce.   645

My fadyr and my modyr, thei wepte full sore,
Full hevy here hertys wern of þis dede,
With wepynge eyn þei preyd þerfore
Þat God wolde socowre hem and sende hem sede.
Iff God wold graunt hem a childe be bore,   650
They behest þe chylde here lyff xulde lede
In Goddys temple to serve evyrmore,
And wurchep God in loue and drede.
    Than God ful of grace
He herd here longe prayour   655
And þan sent hem both seed and flowre.
Whan I was born in here bowre
    To þe temple offryd I was.

Whan þat I was to þe temple brought
And offerde up to God above,   660
Ther hestyd I as myn hert thought
To serve my God with hertyly love.
Clennesse and chastyté myn hert owth,
Erthely creature nevyr may shoue.
Such clene lyff xuld ȝe nouht   665
In no maner wyse reprove.
    To þis clennesse I me take.
This is þe cawse, as I ȝow tell,
Þat I with man wyll nevyr mell.
In þe servyse of God wyl I evyr dwell;   670
    I wyl nevyr haue other make.

Episcopus
    A, mercy, God! þese wordys wyse
Of þis fayr mayde clene,
Thei trobyl myn hert in many wyse.
Her wytt is grett and þat is sene.   675
In clennes to levyn in Godys servise,
No man here blame, non here tene;
And ȝit in lawe þus it lyce
Þat such weddyd xulde bene.
    Who xal expownd þis oute?   680
Þe lawe doth after lyff of clennes;
Þe lawe doth bydde such maydenes expres

f. 50 *(margin, at line 655)*

Þat to spowsyng they xulde hem dres –
God help us in þis dowhte!

f. 48v   This ansuere grettly trobelyth me: 685
To mak avow to creaturys it is lefful,
Vovete et reddite in scripture haue we;
And to observe oure lawe also it is nedful;
In þis to dyscerne to me it is dredful.
Þerfore to cowncell me in þis cas, I calle   690
Þe holde and þe wyse and swiche as ben spedful –
In þis sey ȝour avyse, I besech ȝow alle.

Minister
To breke oure lawe and custom it wore hard indede,
And on þat other syde to do aȝen scrypture;
To ȝeve sentens in þis degré ȝe must take good hede,   695
For dowteles þis matere is dyffuse and obscure.
Myn avyse here in þis I ȝow ensure,
Þat we prey all God to haue relacyon,
For be prayour grett knowlech men recure;
And to þis I counsell ȝow to ȝeve assygnacyon.   700

Episcopus
Trewly ȝour counsell is ryght good and eylsum,
And as ȝe han seyd, so xal it be.
I charge ȝow, bretheryn and systerys, hedyr ȝe com,
And togedyr to God now pray we
That it may plese his [infynyte] deyté   705
Knowleche in þis to sendyn vs.
Mekely eche man falle down on kne
And we xal begynne: *Veni creator spiritus*.

Et hic cantent: Veni creator. *And whan* Veni creator *is don,
þe buschop xal seyn*:

f. 50v   Now, lord God, of lordys wysest of alle,
I pray þe, Lorde, knelynge on kne,   710

684] *line followed by reference sign and incipit for inserted passage; see
notes*   685–708sd] *passage inserted from f.* **48v**   690 cowncell] *MS.*
cowcell   694 aȝen] a- *written above line*   695 good] *MS.* goo   705
infynyte] *MS.* fynyte   708 sd] *The first sentence of the sd. is in the right margin
against l.* 706;   seyn] *MS.* seyng   709] *the spelling of this line is identical with
that of the catchwords on f.* 48v *with the exception of* whysest *and* all. *The line is
preceded by a reference sign for the end of the insertion.*

With carefull herte I crye and calle,
Þis dowteful dowte enforme þu me.

Angelus

Thy prayour is herd to hyȝ hevyn halle,
God hath me sent here down to the,
To telle þe what þat þu do xalle   715
And how þu xalt be rewlyd in iche degré;
   Take tent and vndyrstond!
This is Goddys owyn byddyng:
Þat all kynsmen of Dauyd þe kyng
To þe temple xul brynge here du offryng,   720
   With whyte ȝardys in þer honde.

Loke wele what tyme þei offere there,
All here ȝardys in þin hand þu take;
Take heed whose ȝerde doth blome and bere
And he xal be þe maydenys make.   725

Episcopus

I thank þe, Lord, with mylde chere,
Thi wurde xal I werkyn withowtyn wrake;
I xal send for hem bothyn fer and nere,
To werke þi wyl I vndyrtake,
   Anon it xal be do.   730
Herk, masangere, þu wend þi way,
Dauyd kynsmen, as I þe say,
Byd hem come offyr þis same day
   And brynge white ȝardys also.

Nuncius

Oy! Al maner men takyth to me tent   735
That be owgth of kynrede to Dauid þe kyng.
My lord þe busshop hath for ȝow sent
To þe temple þat ȝe come with ȝour offryng.
f. 53   He chargight þat ȝe hast ȝow, for he is redy bent
   Ȝow to receyve at ȝour comyng.   740
He byddyth ȝow ferthermore in handys þat ȝe hent
A fayre white ȝerde, everych of ȝow ȝe bryng
   In hyght.
Tary not, I pray ȝow
My lord, as I say ȝow,   745
Now to receyve ȝow
   Is full redy dyght.

734 also] *written twice, the first deleted*

Joseph

    Benedicite, I cannot vndyrstande
    What oure prince of prestys doth men,
    Þat every man xuld come and brynge with hym a
                          whande.   750
    Abyl to be maryed þat is not I, so mote I then;
    I haue be maydon evyr, and evyrmore wele ben.
    I chaungyd not ȝet of all my long lyff,
    And now to be maryed – sum man wold wen
    It is a straunge thynge, an old man to take a ȝonge
                          wyff.   755

    But nevyrþelesse, no doute of, we must forth to
                          towne.
    Now, neyborys and kynnysmen, lete us forth go;
    I xal take a wand in my hand and cast of my gowne.
    Yf I falle, þan I xalle gronyn for wo,
    Hoso take away my staff, I say, he were my fo.   760
    Ȝe be men þat may wele ren, go ȝe before!
    I am old and also colde, walkyng doth me wo,
    Þerfore now[wolde] I, so my staff holde I, þis jurny
                          to wore.

Episcopus

    Serys, ȝe xal vndyrstande
    Þat þis is þe cawse of our comynge,   765
    And why þat ech of ȝow bryngyth a wande.
    For of God we haue knowynge,
    Here is to be maryde a mayde ȝynge.
    All ȝour roddys ȝe xal brynge vp to me
    And on hese rodde þat þe Holy Gost is syttynge,   770
    He xal þe husbond of þis may be.

Hic portent virgas

Joseph

f. 53v   It xal not be [I], I ley a grote!
    I xal abyde behynde preuyly.
    Now wolde God I wore at hom in my cote,
    I am aschamyd to be seyn, veryly.   775

748] *line preceded by a reference sign indicating the position of the interpolation on f. 51. For text, see Appendix 1.*   748 *sn* Joseph] Primus generacionis david *deleted*   763 wolde] *MS.* wole   771 *sd*] *in right margin against l. 770*   772 be I, I ley] *MS.* be I ley

Primus generacionis Dauid

    To wurchep my lord God, hedyr am I come,
    Here for to offyr my dewe offrynge.
    A fayr white ȝarde in hand haue I nome,
    My lord sere busshop, at ȝour byddynge.

Secundus generacionis Dauid

    Off Dauythis kynred, sertys, am I com,   780
    A fayr white ȝarde in hand now I bryng;
    My lord þe busshop, after ȝour owyn dom,
    Þis ȝarde do I offre at ȝour chargyng
        Ryht here.

Tercius generacionis Dauid

    And I a ȝarde haue, both fayr and whyght,   785
    Here in myn hond it is redy dyght;
    And here I offre it forth within syght,
        Ryght in good manere.

Quartus generacionis Dauid

    I am þe fourte of Dauidis kyn,
    And with myn offrynge my God I honoure.   790
    Þis fayr whyte ȝarde is offryng myn,
    I trost in God of sum socoure.
    Com on, Joseph, with offrynge þin,
    And brynge up þin as we han oure.
    Þu taryst ryth longe behynde, certeyn,   795
    Why comyst not forth to Goddys toure?
        Com on, man, for shame!

Joseph

    Com? Ȝa, ȝa – God help, full fayn I wolde.
    But I am so agyd and so olde
    Þat both myn leggys gyn to folde,   800
        I am ny almost lame.

Episcopus

f. 54   A, mercy, Lord, I kan no sygne aspy!
    It is best we go ageyn to prayr.

Vox

    He brought not up his rodde ȝet trewly
    To whom þe mayd howyth to be maryed her.   805

---

776 wurchep] my *deleted before* wurchep   777 dewe] dw *deleted before*
dewe   782 owyn] *MS.* owym   785 whyght] -gh- *deleted by a later hand*

Episcopus
　　Whath, Joseph, why stande ȝe there byhynde?
　　Iwys, sere, ȝe be to blame.

Joseph
　　Sere, I kannot my rodde fynde,
　　To come þer in trowth methynkyht shame.

Episcopus
　　Comyth thens!　　　　　　　　　　　　　　　　810

Joseph
　　Sere, he may euyl go þat is ner lame!
　　In soth I com as fast as I may.
Episcopus
　　Offyr up ȝour rodde, sere, in Goddys name!
　　Why do ȝe not as men ȝow pray?

Joseph
　　Now in þe wurchep of God of hevyn　　　　　815
　　I offyr þis ȝerde as lely whyte,
　　Prayng þat Lord of gracyous stewyn,
　　With hert, with wytt, with mayn, with myght,
　　And as he made þe sterrys seven,
　　Þis sympyl offrynge þat is so lyght,　　　　　820
　　To his wurchep he weldygh evyn;
　　For to his wurchep þis ȝerd is dyght.
　　　　Lord God, I þe pray,
　　To my herte þu take good hede
　　And nothynge to my synful dede;　　　　　　825
　　Aftyr my wyl þu qwyte my mede,
　　　　As plesyth to þi pay.

　　I may not lyfte myn handys heye --
　　Lo, lo, lo! What se ȝe now?
Episcopus
　　A, mercy, mercy, mercy, Lord, we crye!　　　830
　　Þe blyssyd of God we se art thou.

Et clamant omnes: Mercy, mercy!

f. 54v　　A, gracyous God in hevyn trone,
　　　　Ryht wundyrful þi werkys be!

810] *sn. and speech in right margin*　　813 Offyr] holde *deleted and* Offyr
written above　　831 sd] *in right margin*

Here may we se a merveyl one,
A ded stok beryth flourys fre.   835
Joseph, in hert withoutyn mone,
Þu mayst be blyth with game and gle,
A mayd to wedde þu must gone,
Be þis meracle I do wel se;
   Mary is here name.   840

Joseph
What, xuld I wedde? God forbede!
I am an old man, so God me spede,
And with a wyff now, to levyn in drede,
   It wore neyther sport nere game.

Episcopus
Aȝens God, Joseph, þu mayst not stryve,   845
God wyl þat þu a wyff haue.
Þis fayr mayde xal be þi wyve,
She is buxum and whyte as laue.

Joseph
A, shuld I haue here, ȝe lese my lyff.
Alas, dere God, xuld I now rave?   850
An old man may nevyr thryff
With a ȝonge wyff, so God me saue.
   Nay, nay, sere, lett bene!
Xuld I now in age begynne to dote?
If I here chyde she wolde clowte my cote,   855
Blere myn ey and pyke out a mote,
   And þus oftyntymes it is sene.

Episcopus
Joseph, now as I þe saye,
God hath assygnyd here to þe;
f. 55 Þat God wol haue do, sey þu not nay,   860
Oure lord God wyl þat it so be.

Joseph
Aȝens my God not do I may,
Here wardeyn and kepere wyl I evyr be.
But, fayr maydon, I þe pray,
Kepe þe clene as I xal me.   865
   I am a man of age,
Therfore, sere busshop, I wyl þat ȝe wete

861 so be] *MS.* be so

Þat in bedde we xul nevyr mete;
For, iwys, mayden suete,
   An old man may not rage.   870

Episcopus
   This holyest virgyn xalt þu maryn now,
   ʒour rodde floreschyth fayrest þat man may se;
   Þe Holy Gost we se syttyht on a bow.
   Now ʒelde we all preysyng to þe Trenyté.

Et hic cantent: Benedicta sit beata Trinitas.

   Joseph, wole ʒe haue þis maydon to ʒour wyff   875
   And here honour and kepe as ʒe howe to do?
Joseph
   Nay, sere, so mote I thryff!
   I haue ryght no nede þerto.
Episcopus
   Joseph, it is Goddys wyl it xuld be so;
   Sey aftyr me as it is skyl.   880
Joseph
   Sere, and to performe his wyl I bow þerto,
   For all thynge owyght to ben at his wyl.

Episcopus (et idem Joseph)
   Sey þan after me: Here I take þe, Mary, to wyff...
   To hauyn, to holdyn ... as God his wyll with us wyl
                                                   make ...
   And as longe as bethwen us ... lestyght oure lyff...   885
   To loue ʒow as myselff ... my trewth I ʒow take.

(nunc ad Mariam, sic dicens)

f. 55v   Mary, wole ʒe haue þis man
          And hym to kepyn as ʒour lyff?
Maria
          In þe tenderest wyse, fadyr, as I kan,
          And with all my wyttys fyff.   890

Episcopus
   Joseph, with þis ryng now wedde þi wyff,
   And be here hand now þu here take.

874 sd] *in right margin against l.* 873   887 sn] Episcopus *repeated in MS. after* s

Joseph
    Sere, with þis rynge I wedde here ryff,
    And take here now here for my make.
Episcopus
    Mary, mayd withoutyn more stryff   895
    Onto þi spowse þu hast hym take.
Maria
    In chastyté to ledyn my lyff
    I xal hym nevyr forsake
        But evyr with hym abyde.
    And, jentyll spowse, as ʒe an seyd,   900
    Lete me levyn as a clene mayd –
    I xal be trewe, be not dysmayd,
        Both terme-tyme and tyde.

Episcopus
    Here is þe holyest matremony þat evyr was in þis
                                werd!
    Þe hyʒ names of oure Lord we wole now syng hy.   905
    We all wole þis solempn dede record
    Devowtly: *Alma chorus domini nunc pangat nomina*
                                  summi.

    Now goth hom all in Godys name
    Where-as ʒour wonyng was before.
    Maydenys, to lete here go alone it wore shame,   910
    It wold hevy ʒour hertys sore;
    ʒe xal blysse þe tyme þat sche was bore,
    Now loke ʒe at hom here brynge.
Maria
    To haue ʒour blyssyng, fadyr, I falle ʒow before.
Episcopus
    He blysse ʒow þat hath non hendyng: 915

    In nomine Patris et Filij et Spiritus Sancti.

f. 56   Joseph, þiselph art old of age
    And þi wyff of age is ʒonge,
    And as we redyn in old sage
    Many man is sclepyr of tonge;   920
    Þerfore euyl langage for to swage,
    Þat ʒour good fame may leste longe,
    Thre damysellys xul dwelle with ʒow in stage,

917 *sn*] Episcopus *repeated in MS. at foot of f. 55v*

With þi wyff to be evyrmore amonge.
   I xal these thre here take: 925
Susanne, þe fyrst xal be,
Rebecca, þe secunde xal go with the,
Sephore, þe thrydde. Loke þat ʒe thre
   Þis maydon nevyr ʒe forsake!

Susanne
   Sere, I am redy att ʒour wyll   930
   With þis maydon for to wende.
Rebecca
   ʒour byddyng, sere, [I] xall fulffyl
   And folwe þis maydon fayr and hende.
Sephor
   To folwe hyre it is good skyl,
   And to ʒour byddynge wole I bende.   935
Joseph
   Now, sere buschop, hens go I wyl,
   For now comyth onto my mende
      A matere þat nedful is.
Episcopus
   Farewel, Joseph and Mary clere,
   I pray God kepe ʒow all in fere   940
   And sende ʒow grace in good manere
      To serve þe kynge of blysse.

Maria
   Fadyr and modyr, ʒe knowe þis cas,
   How þat it doth now stonde with me;
   With myn spowse I must forth passe   945
   And wott nevyr whan I xal ʒow se.
f. 56v   Therfore I pray ʒow here in þis plas
   Of ʒour blyssynge, for charyté,
   And I xal spede þe betyr and haue more gras
   In what place þat evyr I be.   950
      On knes to ʒow I falle;
   I pray ʒow, fadyr and modyr dere,
   To blysse ʒour owyn dere dowtere
   And pray for me in all manere;
      And I for ʒow all.   955

925 thre] *MS.* iij   932 I xall fulfyll] *MS.* xall fulfyll
944 How þat] ll *deleted before* How

Joachym

    Almyghty God, he mote þe blysse

    And my blyssynge þu haue also;

    In all godnesse God þe wysse

    On londe or on watyr wherevyr þu go!

Anna

    Now God þe kepe from every mysse   960

    And saue þe sownd in welth from wo!

    I pray þe, dowtyr, þu onys me kys

    Or þat þi modyr parte þe fro.

        I pray to God þe saue!

    I pray þe, Mary, my swete chylde,   965

    Be lowe and buxhum, meke and mylde,

    Sad and sobyr and nothyng wylde,

        And Goddys blyssyng þu haue.

Joachym

    Farwel, Joseph, and God ȝow spede

    Wherso ȝe be in halle or boure!   970

Joseph

    Almyghty God ȝour weys lede

    And saue ȝow sownd from all doloure!

Anna

    Goddys grace on ȝow sprede!

    Farewel, Mary, my swete flowre,

    Fareweyl, Joseph, and God ȝow rede,   975

    Fareweyl, my chylde and my tresowre,

f. 57   Farewel, my dowtere ȝyng!

Maria

    Farewel, fadyr and modyr dere,

    At ȝow I take my leve ryght here;

    God þat sytt in hevyn so clere   980

    Haue ȝow in his kepyng!

Joseph

    Wyff, it is ful necessary þis ȝe knowe,

    Þat I and my kynrede go hom before,

    For in soth we haue non hous of oure owe.

    Þerfore I xal gon ordeyn and thanne come ȝow fore.   985

    We ar not ryche of werdly thynge

    And ȝet of oure sustenauns we xal not mys;

969 Farwel] *MS.* Forwel

Therfore abydyth here stylle to ȝour plesynge;
To worchep ȝour God is all ȝour blysse.

He þat is and evyr xal be   990
Of hefne and helle ryche kynge,
In erth hath chosyn poverté
And all ryches and welthis refusynge.
Maria
Goth, husbond, in oure Lordys blyssynge!
He mote ȝow spede in all ȝour nede.   995
And I xal here abyde ȝour aȝen-comynge,
And on my sawtere-book I xal rede.

Now blyssyd be oure Lord for this,
Of hefne and erthe and all þat beryth lyff!
I am most bound to ȝow, Lord, iwys,   1000
For now I am bothe mayde and wyff.

Now lord God dysspose me to prayour
Þat I may sey þe holy psalmes of Dauyth,
Wheche book is clepyd þe sawtere,
Þat I may preyse the, my God, þerwith.   1005
f. 57v   Of þe vertuys þerof þis is þe pygth:
It makyht sowles fayr þat doth it say,
Angelys be steryd to help us þerwith,
It lytenyth therkeness and puttyth develys away.

Þe song of psalmus is Goddys deté,   1010
Synne is put awey þerby;
It lernyth a man vertuysful to be,
It feryth mannys herte gostly;
Who þat it vsyth custommably,
It claryfieth þe herte and charyté makyth cowthe.   1015
He may not faylen of Goddys mercy
Þat hath þe preysenge of God evyr in his mowthe.

O holy psalmys! O holy book!
Swetter to say than any ony;
Þu lernyst hem love, Lord, þat on þe look,   1020
And makyst hem desyre thyngys celestly.
With these halwyd psalmys, Lord, I pray the
                              specyaly,

For all þe creatures qwyke and dede,
Þat þu wylt shewe to hem þi mercy,
And to me specyaly þat do it rede.   1025

I haue seyd sum of my sawtere and here I am
At þis holy psalme indede:
Benedixisti domine terram tuam;
In this holy labore, Lord me spede!

Joseph

Mary, wyff and mayd most gracyous,   1030
Displese ʒow not, I pray ʒow, so long I haue be.
I haue hyryd for us a lytyl praty hous
And þerin ryght hesely levyn wole we.

Come forth, Mary, and folwe me,
To Nazareth now wele we go.   1035
f. 58   And all þe maydonys bothe fayr and fre
With my wyff comyth forth also!
Now lystenyth well, wyff, what I tell þe:
I must gon owth hens fer þe fro.
I wyll go laboryn in fer countré   1040
With trewth to maynteyn oure housholde so;
    Þis nyn monthis þu seyst me nowth.
Kepe þe clene, my jentyl spowse,
And all þin maydenys in þin howse,
Þat evyl langage I here not rowse,   1045
    For hese love þat all hath wrought.

Maria

I pray to God he spede ʒour way,
And in sowle helth he mote ʒow kepe
And sende ʒow helth bothe nyth and day.
He shylde and saue ʒow from al shenschepe!   1050
Now, Lord of grace, to þe I pray,
With morny mood on kne I krepe,
Me saue from synne, from tene and tray;
With hert I murne, with eye I wepe,
    Lord God of peté!   1055
Whan I sytt in my conclaue
All myn hert on þe I haue,

1023 creatures] *the second* e *has perhaps been altered to* y   1042 nyn] *MS.*
ix   1054 murne] *MS. perhaps intended for* mourne

> Gracyous God, my maydenhed saue,
> Euyr clene in chastyté!

f. 58v   *Contemplacio*

> Fowre thowsand sex vndryd foure ȝere, I telle,   1060
> Man for his offens and fowle foly
> Hath loyn ȝerys in þe peynes of helle,
> And were wurthy to ly þerin endlesly;
> But thanne xulde perysche ȝour grete mercye.
> Good Lord, haue on man pyté;   1065
> Haue mende of þe prayour seyd by Ysaie;
> Lete mercy meke þin hyest magesté.
>
> Wolde God þu woldyst breke þin hefne myghtye
> And com down here into erth,
> And levyn ȝerys thre and threttye,   1070
> Thyn famyt folke with þi fode to fede;
> To staunche þi thrysté lete þi syde blede,
> For erste wole not be mad redempcyon.
> Cum vesyte vs in þis tyme of nede;
> Of þi careful creaturys, Lord, haue compassyon!   1075
>
> A, woo to vs wrecchis of wrecchis be,
> For God hath haddyd sorwe to sorwe!
> I prey þe, Lorde, þi sowlys com se,
> How þei ly and sobbe for syknes and sorwe.
> With þi blyssyd blood from balys hem borwe,   1080
> Thy careful creaturys cryenge in captyvyté.
> A, tary not, gracyous Lord, tyl it be tomorwe!
> The devyl hath dysceyved hem be his iniquité.
>
> A, quod Jeremye, who xal gyff wellys to myn eynes
> Þat I may wepe bothe day and nyght   1085
> To se our bretheryn in so longe peynes?
> Here myschevys amende may þi mech myght.

f. 59
> As grett as þe se, Lord, was Adamys contryssyon
>   ryght;
> From oure hed is falle þe crowne;

1060] 1us *in red in centre above line*   1060–63] *large red numeral* 11 *in right margin*   1069 into] to *deleted after* in-   1076] *line preceded by* 2 *in red in left margin*; of] *altered above line to* that *by a later hand*   1077 haddyd] h- *later deleted*   1079 for syknes and sorwe] *later altered above the line to* bothe eve and morewe   1084 eynes] e *added above second* e

Man is comeryd in synne. I crye to þi syght: 1090
Gracyous Lord, gracyous Lord, gracyous Lord,
                                    come downe!

Virtutes
Lord, plesyth it þin hyȝ domynacyon,
On man þat þu made to haue pyté.
Patryarchys and prophetys han made supplycacyon,
Oure offyse is to presente here prayerys to the.   1095
Aungelys, archaungelys, we thre,
Þat ben in þe fyrst ierarchie,
For man to þin hy magesté,
Mercy, mercy, mercy, we crye!

The aungel, Lord, þu made so gloryous,   1100
Whos synne hath mad hym a devyl in helle,
He mevyd man to be so contraryous;
Man repentyd, and he in his obstynacye doth dwelle.
Hese grete males, good Lord, repelle,
And take man onto þi grace;   1105
Lete þi mercy make hym with aungelys dwelle,
Of Locyfere to restore þe place.

Pater
Propter miseriam inopum
Et gemitum pauperum
Nunc exurgam.   1110

For þe wretchydnes of þe nedy
And þe porys lamentacyon,
Now xal I ryse þat am almyghty.
Tyme is come of reconsyliacyon.
f. 59v   My prophetys with prayers haue made supplicacyon, 1115
My contryte creaturys crye all for comforte,
All myn aungellys in hefne withowte cessacyon
They crye þat grace to man myght exorte.

Veritas
Lord, I am þi dowtere, Trewth,
Þu wylt se I be not lore;   1120

1095 prayerys] sory *deleted before* prayerys   1101 hath] hath *written
twice. The first apparently written* had, *corrected to* hath, *and deleted*

Thyn vnkynde creaturys to save were rewthe,
The offens of man hath grevyd þe sore.
Whan Adam had synnyd, þu seydest þore
Þat he xulde deye and go to helle,
And now to blysse hym to resstore –   1125
Twey contraryes mow not togedyr dwelle.

Thy trewthe, Lord, xal leste withowtyn ende,
I may in no wyse fro þe go.
Þat wretche þat was to þe so vnkende,
He may not haue to meche wo.   1130
He dyspysyd þe, and plesyd þi fo;
Þu art his creatour, and he is þi creature;
Þu hast lovyd trewthe, it is seyd, evyrmo,
Þerfore in peynes lete hym evyrmore endure.

Misericordia
O, Fadyr of mercy and God of comforte,   1135
Þat counsell us in eche trybulacyon,
Lete 30ur dowtere, Mercy, to 30w resorte,
And on man þat is myschevyd haue compassyon.
Hym grevyth ful gretly his transgressyon,
All hefne and erthe crye for mercy;   1140
f. 60   Mesemyth þer xuld be non excepcyon
Ther prayers ben offeryd so specyally.

Trewth seyth she hath evyr be than –
I graunt it wel she hath be so –
And þu seyst endlesly þat mercy þu hast kept for
                                               man;   1145
Than, mercyabyl Lorde, kepe us bothe to.
Thu seyst: *Veritas mea et misericordia mea cum ipso.*
Suffyr not þi sowlys, than, in sorwe to slepe;
Þat helle-hownde þat hatyth þe, byddyth hym ho!
Þi love, man, no lengere lete hym kepe.   1150

Justicia
Mercy, me merveylyth what 30w movyth!
3e know wel I am 30ur systere, Ryghtwysnes;
God is ryghtful and ryghtffulnes lovyth.
Man offendyd hym þat is endles,

1143 Trewth] *MS.* Threwth.

Therfore his endles punchement may nevyr sees.   1155
Also he forsoke his makere þat made hym of clay,
And þe devyl to his mayster he ches –
Xulde he be savyd? Nay, nay, nay!

As wyse as is God, he wolde a be;
This was þe abhomynabyl presumpcyon!   1160
It is seyd, ȝe know wel þis, of me
Þat þe ryghtwysnes of God hath no diffynicyon –
Therffore late þis be oure conclusyon:
He þat sore synnyd ly stylle in sorwe.
He may nevyr make aseyth be resoun;   1165
Whoo myght thanne thens hym borwe?

Misericordia

f. 60v   Systyr Ryghtwysnes, ȝe are to vengeabyl;
Endles synne God endles may restore.
Above all hese werkys God is mercyabyl.
Þow he forsook God be synne, be feyth he forsook
                            hym neverþemore;   1170
And þow he presumyd nevyr so sore,
ȝe must consyder þe frelnes of mankende.
Lerne, and ȝe lyst, þis is Goddys lore:
Þe mercy of God is withowtyn ende.

Pax

To spare ȝour speches, systerys, it syt;   1175
It is not onest in vertuys to ben dyscencyon.
The pes of God ovyrcomyth all wytt.
Þow Trewth and Ryght sey grett reson,
ȝett Mercy seyth best, to my pleson.
For yf mannys sowle xulde abyde in helle,   1180
Betwen God and man evyr xulde be dyvysyon,
And than myght not I, Pes, dwelle.

Therefore mesemyth best ȝe thus acorde,
Than hefne and erthe ȝe xul qweme;
Putt bothe ȝour sentens in oure Lorde   1185
And in his hyȝ wysdam lete hym deme –
This is most syttynge me xulde seme –

1155 sees] -e- *added above final* -s *by main scribe; a later hand has altered the last two letters to* -es   1173 *Lerne*] ? *deleted before* Lerne

And lete se how we fowre may all abyde.
Þat mannys sowle it xulde perysche, it wore sweme,
Or þat ony of vs fro othere xulde dyvyde.   1190

Veritas
In trowthe hereto I consente;
I wole prey oure Lorde it may so be.
Justicia
I, Ryghtwysnes, am wele contente,
For in hym is very equyté.
Misericordia

f. 61   And I, Mercy, fro þis counsel wole not fle;   1195
Tyl Wysdam hath seyd, I xal ses.
Pax
Here is God now, here is vnyté;
Hefne and erth is plesyd with Pes.

Filius
I thynke þe thoughtys of pes and nowth of
                              wykkydnes.
This I deme to ses ʒour contraversy: 1200
If Adam had not deyd, peryschyd had Ryghtwysnes,
And also Trewth had be lost þerby;
Trewth and Ryght wolde chastyse foly.
ʒiff another deth come not, Mercy xulde perysch,
Þan Pes were exyled fynyaly;   1205
So tweyn dethis must be, ʒow fowre to cherysch.

But he þat xal deye, ʒe must knawe
Þat in hym may ben non iniquyté,
Þat helle may holde hym be no lawe,
But þat he may pas at hese lyberté.   1210
Qwere swyche on his, prevyde and se,
And hese deth, for mannys deth, xal be redempcyon.
All hefne and erth seke now ʒe;
Plesyth it ʒow þis conclusyon?

Veritas
I, Trowthe, haue sowte þe erthe, withowt and
                              withinne,   1215

1203 Trewth] *MS. has a loop on* T, *apparently the headstroke of an abandoned* h,
cf. l. 1143, rather than an -er *abbreviation mark*   1215 withowt] -inne *and*
with- *deleted after* with-

And in sothe þer kan non be fownde,
Þat is of o day byrth, withowte synne,
Nor to þat deth wole be bownde.

Misericordia

I, Mercy, haue ronne þe hevynly regyon rownde
And þer is non of þat charyté   1220
Þat for man wole suffre a deddly wounde –
I cannott wete how þis xal be.

Justicia

f. 61v   Sure I can fynde non sufficyent,
For servauntys vnprofytable we be echon.
Hes love nedyth to be ful ardent   1225
That for man to helle wolde gon.

Pax

That god may do, is non but on;
Þerfore þis is Pesys avyse:
He þat ȝaff þis counsell, lete hym ȝeve þe comforte
                                                          alon,
For þe conclusyon in hym of all þese lyse.   1230

Filius

It peyneth me þat man I mad,
Þat is to seyn, peyne I must suffre fore.
A counsel of þe Trinité must be had,
Whiche of vs xal man restore.

Pater

In ȝour wysdam, Son, man was mad thore,   1235
And in wysdam was his temptacyon;
Þerfor, Sone, Sapyens, ȝe must ordeyn herefore
And se how of man may be salvacyon.

Filius

Fadyr, he þat xal do þis must be both God and man;
Lete me se how I may were þat wede.   1240
And syth in my wysdam he began,
I am redy to do þis dede.

Spiritus Sanctus

I, the Holy Gost, of ȝow tweyn do procede;

1222 I cannott] I *written twice, the first an odd 's'-like form*   1225 Hes] *MS.*
He, *the* -s *added later*   1228 Pesys] *later altered to* be hys   1236 wysdam
was] ? *deleted before* was

This charge I wole take on me:
I, Love, to ȝour lover xal ȝow lede –   1245
Þis is þe assent of oure vnyté.

Misericordia

f. 62   Now is þe loveday mad of us fowre fynialy,
Now may we leve in pes as we were wonte:
Misericordia et Veritas obviauerunt sibi,
Justicia et Pax osculate sunt.   1250

Et hic osculabunt pariter omnes.

Pater

From vs, God, aungel Gabryel þu xalt be sende
Into þe countré of Galylé –
The name of þe cyté, Nazareth is kende –
To a mayd, weddyd to a man is she
Of whom þe name is Joseph, se,   1255
Of þe hous of Davyd bore;
The name of þe mayd fre
Is Mary, þat xal al restore.

Filius

Say þat she is withowte wo and ful of grace,
And þat I, þe Son of þe Godhed, of here xal be bore.   1260
Hyȝe þe, þu were there apace,
Ellys we xal be there the beffore.
I haue so grett hast to be man thore
In þat mekest and purest virgyne.
Sey here she xal restore   1265
Of ȝow aungellys þe grett ruyne.

Spiritus Sanctus

f. 62v   And if she aske þe how it myth be,
Telle here I, þe Holy Gost, xal werke al this.
Sche xal be savyd thorwe oure vnyté.
In tokyn here bareyn cosyn, Elyzabeth, is   1270
Qwyk with childe in here grett age, iwys.
Sey here to vs is nothynge impossyble;
Here body xal be so fulfylt with blys
Þat she xal sone thynke þis sownde credyble.

1245 ȝow lede] procede *deleted before* ȝow

Gabriel

In thyn hey inbassett, Lord, I xal go,   1275
It xal be do with a thought.
Beholde now, Lord, I go here to,
I take my flyth and byde nowth.

Ave gracia plena dominus tecum!

Heyl, ful of grace, God is with the!   1280
Amonge all women blyssyd art thu.
Here þis name, *Eva*, is turnyd *Aue*;
Þat is to say: withowte sorwe ar ȝe now.

Thow sorwe in ȝow hath no place,
ȝett of joy, lady, ȝe nede more,   1285
f. 63   Therfore I adde and sey: ful of grace,
For so ful of grace was nevyr non bore;
ȝett who hath grace, he nedyth kepyng sore,
Therfore I sey: God is with the,
Whiche xal kepe ȝow endlesly thore;   1290
So amonge all women blyssyd are ȝe.

Maria

A, mercy, God! Þis is a mervelyous herynge!
In þe aungelys wordys I am trobelyd her;
I thynk how may be þis gretynge.
Aungelys dayly to me doth aper,   1295
But not in þe lyknes of man þat is my fer;
And also thus hyȝly to comendyd be
And am most vnwurthy – I cannot answere;
Grett shamfastnes and grett dred is in me.

Gabryel

Mary, in þis take ȝe no drede,   1300
For at God grace fownde haue ȝe.
ȝe xal conceyve in ȝour wombe, indede,
A childe, þe sone of þe Trynyté,
f. 63v   His name of ȝow, Jhesu clepyd xal be.
He xal be grett, þe son of þe hyest clepyd of kende,   1305

1279 Ave gracia] Maria *deleted after* Ave, *perhaps by main scribe*   1280 of
grace] of *written twice and the second deleted*   1292 herynge] he- *written above
line; the* -r- *altered from an* h

And of his fadyr, Davyd, þe Lord xal ȝeve hym þe se,
Reynyng in þe hous of Jacob, of which regne xal be
                                        non ende.

Maria

Aungel, I sey to ȝow,
In what manere of wyse xal þis be?
For knowyng of man I haue non now;   1310
I haue evyrmore kept, and xal, my virginyté.
I dowte not þe wordys ȝe han seyd to me,
But I aske how it xal be do.

Gabryel

The Holy Gost xal come fro above to the,
And þe vertu of hym hyest xal schadu þe so.   1315

Therfore þat Holy Gost of þe xal be bore,
He xal be clepyd þe Son of God, sage.
And se, Elyzabeth, ȝour cosyn, thore,
She hath conseyvid a son in hyre age –
This is þe sexte monyth of here passage,   1320
Of here þat clepyd was bareyn –
Nothynge is impossyble to Goddys vsage.
They thynkyth longe to here what ȝe wyl seyn.

f. 64

*Here þe aungel makyth a lytyl restynge and Mary beholdyth
hym, and þe aungel seyth:*

Mary, come of and haste the,
And take hede in thyn entent   1325
Whow þe Holy Gost, blyssyd he be,
Abydyth þin answere and þin assent.
Thorwe wyse werke of dyvinyté,
The secunde persone, verament,
Is mad man by fraternyté   1330
Withinne þiself in place present.

Ferthermore take hede þis space
Whow all þe blyssyd spyrytys of vertu
Þat are in hefne byffore Goddys face,
And all þe gode levers and trew   1335
That are here in þis erthely place –
Thyn owyn kynrede þe sothe ho knew –
And þe chosyn sowlys þis tyme of grace
Þat are in helle and byde rescu,

f. 64v   As Adam, Abraham, and Davyd, in fere,   1340
　　　　 And many othere of good reputacyon,
　　　　 Þat þin answere desyre to here
　　　　 And þin assent to þe incarnacyon,
　　　　 In which þu standyst as persevere
　　　　 Of all mankende savacyon.   1345
　　　　 Gyff me myn answere now, lady dere,
　　　　 To all these creaturys comfortacyon.

Maria
　　　　 With all mekenes I clyne to þis acorde,
　　　　 Bowynge down my face with all benyngnyté;
　　　　 Se here þe hand-mayden of oure Lorde,   1350
　　　　 Aftyr þi worde be it don to me.
Gabryel
　　　　 Gramercy, my lady fre!
　　　　 Gramercy, of ȝour answere, on hyght!
　　　　 Gramercy, of ȝour grett humylyté!
　　　　 Gramercy, ȝe lanterne off lyght!   1355

Here þe Holy Gost discendit with thre bemys to Our Lady,
the Sone of þe Godhed nest with thre bemys to þe Holy Gost,
the Fadyr godly with thre bemys to þe Sone, and so entre all
thre to here bosom, and Mary seyth:

Maria
f. 65   A, now I fele in my body be
　　　　 Parfyte God and parfyte man,
　　　　 Havyng al schappe of chyldly carnalyté;
　　　　 Evyn al at onys, þus God began.

　　　　 Nott takynge fyrst o membyr and sythe another,   1360
　　　　 But parfyte childhod ȝe haue anon.
　　　　 Of ȝour hand-mayden, now ȝe haue mad ȝour
　　　　　　　　　　　　　　　　　　　　　 modyr.
　　　　 Withowte peyne in flesche and bon,
　　　　 Thus conceyved nevyr woman non
　　　　 Þat evyr was beynge in þis lyff.   1365
　　　　 O myn hyest Fadyr in ȝour tron,

1344 persevere] *second* e *altered from* y   1352 my lady] my *written above line*
+ *caret*   1354 of ȝour] of *written twice and the second deleted*   1355 sd thre]
MS. *the first three instances* iij

It is worthy ȝour son, now my son, haue a
                              prerogatyff.

I cannot telle what joy, what blysse,
Now I fele in my body!
Aungel Gabryel, I thank ȝow for thys!   1370
Most mekely recomende me to my Faderys mercy.
To haue be þe modyr of God, ful lytyl wend I!
Now myn cosyn, Elyzabeth, fayn wold I se,
How sche hath conseyvid as ȝe dede specyfy.
Now blyssyd be þe hyȝ Trynyté!   1375

Gabryel

f. 65v   Fareweyl, turtyl, Goddys dowtere dere!
Farewel, Goddys modyr, I þe honowre!
Farewel, Goddys sustyr and his pleynge-fere!
Farewel, Goddys chawmere and his bowre!

Maria

Farewel, Gabryel, specyalye!   1380
Farewel, Goddys masangere expresse!
I thank ȝow for ȝour traveyl hye.
Gramercy of ȝour grett goodnes,

And namely of ȝour comfortabyl massage;
For I vndyrstande by inspyracyon,   1385
Þat ȝe knowe by syngulere preuylage,
Most of my sonys incarnacyon.
I pray ȝow take it into vsage,
Be a custom ocupacyon,
To vesyte me ofte be mene passage –   1390
Ȝour presence is my comfortacyon.

Gabriel

At ȝour wyl, lady, so xal it be,
Ȝe gentyllest of blood, and hyest of kynrede
Þat reynyth in erth in ony degré
Be pryncypal incheson of þe Godhede.   1395

I comende me onto ȝow, þu trone of þe Trinyté!
O, mekest mayde, now þe modyr of Jhesu!
f. 66   Qwen of hefne, lady of erth, and empres of helle be
                                        ȝe;

Socour to all synful þat wole to ȝow sew,
Thour ȝour body beryth þe babe oure blysse xal
                                    renew.   1400
To ȝow, modyr of mercy, most mekely I
                            recomende,
And as I began, I ende, with an *Ave* new,
Enjonyd hefne and erth – with þat I ascende.

Angeli cantando istam sequenciam: Aue Maria gratia plena
dominus tecum uirgo serena. *And þan Mary seyth:*

[f. 67 *Maria*

Husbond, ryght gracyously now come be ȝe.
It solacyth me sore, sothly, to se ȝow in syth.   1405

Joseph

Me merveylyth, wyff, surely, ȝour face I cannot se,
But as þe sonne with his bemys qwan he is most
                                        bryth.

Maria

Husbond, it is as it plesyth oure Lord, þat grace of
                                    hym grew.
Who þat evyr beholdyth me, veryly,
They xal be grettly steryed to vertu;   1410
For þis ȝyfte and many moo, good Lord, gramercy!]

f. 71   Bvtt, husbond, of oo thynge I pray ȝow most
                                    mekely:
I haue knowyng þat oure cosyn Elyzabeth with
                                    childe is,
Þat it plese ȝow to go to here hastyly;
If owught we myth comforte here, it wore to me
                                    blys.   1415

Joseph

A Godys sake, is she with childe, sche?
Than wole here husbond, Zakarye, be mery.
In Montana they dwelle, fer hens, so moty the,
In þe cety of Juda, I knowe it veryly.

1403 *sd serena*] MS. *sesena*;   And þan Mary seyth] *deleted in MS. by the*
scribe   1404–11] *For the passage inserted here from f. 67, see note to l.*
1404ff.   1405 *se ȝow*] *ȝw deleted before ȝow*   1412] *sn* Maria *in right*
margin, beginning pageant 13 in MS   1419–22] *large red numeral* 13 *in right*
margin   1419 I knowe] *m deleted before* I

It is hens, I trowe, myles two and fyfty –   1420
We are lyke to be wery or we come at þat same.
I wole with a good wyl, blyssyd wyff Mary;
Now go we forthe than in Goddys name!

Maria
Goth, husbond, þow it be to зow peyne.
This jurny I pray зow lete us go fast,   1425
For I am schamfast of þe pepyl to be seyne,
And namely of men, þerof I am agast.
Pylgrymagys and helpyngys wolde be go in hast;
Þe more þe body is peynyd, þe more is þe mede.
Say зe зour devocyonys and I xal myn i-cast.   1430
Now in þis jurny, God mote us spede!

Joseph
Amen, amen and evyrmore!
Lo, wyff, lo, how starkly I go before!

Et sic transient circa placeam

Contemplacio
f. 71v   Sovereynes, vndyrstondyth þat kynge Davyd here
Ordeyned foure and twenty prestys of grett
                                   devocyon   1435
In þe temple of God, aftere here [lot] apere.
Þei weryn clepyd *summi sacerdotes* for here
                                   mynistracyon,
And on was prynce of prestys, havynge
                                   dominacyon.
Amonge whiche was an old prest clepyd Zakarye,
And he had an old woman to his wyff of holy
                                   conversacyon   1440
Whiche hyth Elizabeth, þat nevyr had childe,
                                   verylye.

In hese mynistracyon, the howre of incense,
The aungel Gabryel apperyd hym to;
Þat hese wyff xulde conseyve, he зaff hym
                                   intelligence.

1422 I wole] wyl *deleted before* wole   1450 i–cast] MS. ?jicast   1433 sd]
in right margin   1434 sn Contemplacio] MS. Comtemplacio   1436 lot]
MS. let   1437 weryn] MS. weryd   1440 woman] wyff *deleted before*
woman

He, seinge hese vnwurthynes and age, not belevyd,
                                            so   1445
The plage of dompnesse hise lippis lappyd, lo.
Thei wenten hom and his wyff was conseyvenge.
This concepcyon Gabryel tolde Oure Lady to,
And in soth sone aftere þat sage sche was sekynge:
And of here tweyners metyng,   1450
Here gynnyth þe proces.
Now God be oure begynnynge
And of my tonge I wole ses.

Joseph

A, a, wyff, in feyth I am wery!
Therfore I wole sytt downe and rest me ryght here.   1455
Lo, wyff, here is þe hous of Zakary –
Wole ӡe I clepe Elyzabeth to ӡow to apere?

Maria

f. 72   Nay, husbond, and it plese ӡow, I xal go ner.
Now þe blyssyd Trynité be in þis hous!
A, cosyn Elizabeth, swete modyr, what cher?   1460
Ӡe grow grett; a, my God, how ӡe be gracyous!

Elizabeth

Anon as I herd of ӡow þis holy gretynge,
Mekest mayden and þe modyr of God, Mary,
Be ӡour breth þe Holy Gost vs was inspyrynge
Þat þe childe in my body enjoyd gretly   1465
And turnyd down on his knes to oure God
                                    reverently;
Whom ӡe bere in ӡour body, þis veryly I ken.
Fulfyllyd with þe Holy Gost, þus lowde I cry:
Blyssyd be þu amonge all women!

And blyssyd be þe frute off þi wombe also,   1470
Þu wurthyest virgyne and wyff þat evyr was
                                    wrought!
How is it þat þe modyr of God me xulde come to,
Þat wrecche of all wrecchis, a whyght wers þan
                                    nought?

1445 He, seinge] *MS.* Hese juge *or* jnge   1446 lippis] *written above line* +
caret   lo] to *deleted before* lo   1448 Gabryel tolde] gab *deleted before* tolde

And þu art blyssyd þat belevyd veryly in þi thought
Þat þe wurde of God xulde profyte in the;   1475
But how þis blyssydnes abought was brought,
I cannot thynk nyn say how it myght be.

Maria

To þe preysynge of God, cosyn, this seyd mut be.
Whan I sat in my lytyl hous onto God praynge,
Gabryel come and seyd to me "*Ave*";   1480
Ther I conceyvyd God at my consentynge,

f. 72v   Parfyte God and parfyte man at onys beynge.
Than þe aungel seyd onto me
Þat it was sex monethys syn ȝour conseyvynge;
Þis cawsyth my comynge, cosyn, ȝow to comfort
                and se.   1485

Elizabeth

Blyssyd be ȝe, cosyn, for ȝour hedyr comynge!
How I conseyvyd I xal to ȝow say:
Þe aungel apperyd þe howre of incensynge
Seynge I xulde conseyve, and hym thought nay.
Sethe for his mystrost he hath be dowm alway –   1490
And þus of my concepcyon I haue tolde ȝow sum.
Maria
For þis holy psalme I begynne here þis day:
Magnificat: anima mea dominum
Et exultauit spiritus meus: in deo salutari meo
Elizabeth
Be þe Holy Gost with joye Goddys son is in þe cum,   1495
Þat þi spyryte so injouyid þe helth of þi God so.

Maria

Quia respexit humilitatem ancille sue
Ecce enim ex hoc beatam me dicent omnes generaciones
Elizabeth
For he beheld þe lownes of hese hand-maydeȝe,
So ferforthe for þat all generacyonys blysse ȝow in
                pes.   1500

Maria

Quia fecit mihi magna qui potens est
Et sanctum nomen eius

1485 cosyn] *? deleted before* cosyn   1488 of] *written above line + caret*

Elizabeth
    For grett thyngys he made and also myghtyest,
    And ryght holy is þe name of hym in vs.

Maria
f. 73   *Et misericordia eius a progenie in progenies*   1505
    Timentibus eum
Elizabeth
    3a, þe mercy of hym fro þat kynde into þe kynde of
                                       pes,
    For all þat hym drede, now is he cum.

Maria
    Fecit potenciam in brachio suo
    Disspersit superbos mente cordis sui   1510
Elizabeth
    The pore in his ryght arme he hath mad so;
    Þe prowde to dyspeyre and þe thought of here hertys
                                          only.

Maria
    Deposuit potentes de sede
    Et exaltauit humiles
Elizabeth
    The prowde men fro hey setys put he,   1515
    And þe lowly vpon heyth in þe sete of pes.

Maria
    Esurientes impleuit bonis
    Et diuites dimisit inanes
Elizabeth
    Alle þe pore and þe nedy he fulfyllyth with his
                                     goodys,
    And þe ryche he fellyth to voydnes.   1520

Maria
    Suscepit Israel puerum suum
    Recordatus est misericordie sue
Elizabeth
    Israel for his childe vptoke he to cum,
    On his mercy to thynk for hese þat be.

Maria
    Sicut locutus est ad patres nostros   1525
    Abraham et semini eius in secula

Elizabeth
> As he spak here to oure forfaderys in clos,
> Abraham and to all hese sed of hym in þis werd sa.

Maria
> Gloria Patri et Filio
> *Et Spiritui Sancto*   1530

Elizabeth
> Preysyng be to þe Fadyr in hevyn, lo,
> Þe same to þe Son here be so,
> > Þe Holy Gost also to ken;

Maria
f. 73v   *Sicut erat in principio et nunc et semper*
> *Et in secula seculorum Amen*   1535

Elizabeth
> As it was in þe begynnynge, and now is, and xal be
> > for evyr,
> And in þis werd in all good werkys to abydyn then.

Maria
> This psalme of prophesye seyd betwen vs tweyn,
> In hefne it is wretyn with aungellys hond;
> Evyr to be songe and also to be seyn,   1540
> Euery day amonge us at oure evesong.

> But, cosyn Elyzabeth, I xal ȝow here kepe,
> And þis thre monethis abyde here now
> Tyl ȝe han childe, to wasche, skore and swepe,
> And in all þat I may to comforte ȝow.   1545

Elizabeth
> A, ȝe modyr of God, ȝe shewe us here how
> We xulde be meke þat wrecchis here be;
> All hefne and herthe wurcheppe ȝow mow,
> Þat are trone and tabernakyl of þe hyȝ Trinité.

Joseph
> A, how do ȝe, how do ȝe, fadyr Zacharye?   1550
> We falle fast in age, withowte oth.
> Why shake ȝe so ȝour hed? Haue ȝe þe palsye?
> Why speke ȝe not, sere? I trowe ȝe are not wroth.

1553 Why] h *deleted before* Why

Elizabeth

Nay, wys, fadyr Joseph, þerto he were ful loth.
It is þe vesytacyon of God; he may not speke, veryly. 1555
Lete us thank God þerffor, both;
He xal remedy it whan it plesyth his mercy.

Come, I pray ʒow specialy!
Iwys, ʒe are welcome, Mary!
For þis comfortabelest comynge, good God,
gramercy! 1560

f. 74   *Contemplacio*

Lystenyth, sovereynys, here is a conclusyon;
How þe *Aue* was mad, here is lernyd vs:
Þe aungel seyd: *Ave gracia plena dominus tecum*
Benedicta tu in mulieribus;
Elyzabeth seyd: *et benedictus* 1565
Fructus uentris tui; thus þe Chirch addyd *Maria* and
Jhesus her.
Who seyth Oure Ladyes sawtere dayly for a ʒer þus,
He hath pardon ten thowsand and eyte hundryd ʒer.

Than ferther to oure matere for to procede:
Mary with Elizabeth abod þer stylle, 1570
Thre monthys fully, as we rede,
Thankynge God with hertly wylle.

A, lord God, what hous was þis on!
Þat þese childeryn and here moderys to,
As Mary and Elizabeth, Jhesus and John, 1575
And Joseph and Zakarye also.

And evyr Oure Lady abod stylle þus,
Tyl John was of his modyr born;
And þan Zakarye spak, iwus,
Þat had be dowm and his spech lorn. 1580
He and Elizabeth prophesyed as þus,
They mad *Benedictus* them beforn;

1558–60] *These lines begin the alternative ending and are written at the foot of f.*
74v with the note si placet; *for the passage omitted here see Appendix 3.* 1571
Thre] *MS*.iij

And so *Magnificat* and *Benedictus*
Fyrst in þat place þer made worn.

Whan all was don, Oure Lady fre   1585
Toke here leve than aftere this
At Elizabeth and at Zakarie,
And kyssyd John and gan hym blys.

Now most mekely we thank ȝou of ȝour pacyens,
And beseke ȝou of ȝour good supportacyon;   1590
If here hath be seyd ore don any inconuenyens,
We asygne it to ȝour good deliberacyon,
Besekynge to Crystys precyous passyon
Conserve and rewarde ȝour hedyr comynge.
With *Aue* we begunne, and *Aue* is our conclusyon;   1595
Ave regina celorum to Oure Lady we synge.

1592 deliberacyon] *Half the -o- and the mark of suspension have been trimmed
away at the edge of the leaf.*

Notes

The notes to the play are intended to function in a number of ways. The first is to explain those passages where for some reason the text is obscure. In this I am only too aware of the twin dangers of explaining what will be obvious and ignoring what is incomprehensible. The second is to provide a context of thought for the play. I have quoted freely, mainly from *Meditationes* and *Legenda Aurea*, to give an idea of how the story was viewed in the later Middle Ages. Less often I have referred to vernacular works to show similarities and differences in the treatment of the story, and from vernacular sermons and instructional works to explain or comment on individual points. The third purpose is to demonstrate actual dependences, where the playwright is basing his text closely on another work, in order if possible to give some idea of the way in which he wrote. The fourth purpose is to indicate the action of the play where it is not clear in the text; and the fifth briefly to show the kind of associations that the liturgical pieces have.

For the short titles used in the notes, full bibliographical references will be found in the Bibliography.

The following abbreviations are used throughout:

EETS OS/ES	Early English Text Society Ordinary Series/Extra Series
MED	*Middle English Dictionary*
NQ	*Notes and Queries*
OED	*Oxford English Dictionary*
PL	*Patrologia Latina*

1sn The name of the expositor may have been suggested by the marginal notes that appear in some manuscripts of Nicholas Love's *Mirrour* or possibly by the explicits (e.g. *Explicit contemplacio pro die Mercurio*). The nature of the contemplation in the plays (i.e. that of the humanity of Christ) is of the kind that Love describes in his opening remarks. This kind is however common enough for the name to have arisen from elsewhere.

The contemplation is for ordinary people; of the humanity of God, not of his divinity. It is common to divide contemplation into two or three types; see for example *St Edmund's Mirror*, (*Religious Pieces*, pp. 21–49) where the third division is itself divided into contemplation of the manhood (41–6) and of the godhead (46–9). This form of contemplation is also that associated with pilgrim tours of the Holy Land, visiting the sites associated with the events of Christ's life, especially his Passion; and both result, as do the plays, in an evocation of human actions and motives beyond that found in the gospels.

1 *congregacyon*. The word means simply 'an assembly of people' (here 'an audience') without any necessary religious association.

3–5 Either: 'so that the speaking of their speeches may be solemn and deliberate, and that no awkwardness [of delivery] make this play difficult to follow'; or: 'so that the setting forth of the doctrine may be serious and careful and that no error obscure the meaning'.

9 *þe modyr of mercy*. A common epithet for Mary, perhaps because of its occurrence, *mater misericordiae*, in the frequently used antiphon of Mary *Salve Regina*; see *Horae*, p. 62; the English translation in Maskell, III, p. 74; *Prymer*, p. 34; and the adaptation in B.L. MS Addit. 37049, f. 29v. Fabri records its frequent use on his pilgrimage; e.g. I, pp. 313, 347, 466, 555.

10 There is no biblical warrant for the names Joachim and Anna but they were early established through their appearance in the apocryphal gospels and, through them, the liturgy and later writings; see *Missal*, Conception of Mary, 669, St Anne's day, 825–6; *Breviary*, St Anne, III 539–56 (lections from the apocryphal gospels); *Legenda*, pp. 585–8; *Vita Christi*, pp. 11–12.

9–16 This stanza enumerates the five sections of the play: (1) how Mary was conceived by Joachim and Anne; (2) afterwards offered in the temple (briefly compiled); then (3) married to Joseph, and so, following (4) the Annunciation, (5) the meeting with Elizabeth, and after that a brief conclusion.

16 The word 'process' is very common in Love, 'the processe of the Incarnacioun' (p. 37), 'the forseide proces', 'the whiche processe' (p. 99). It also occurs in marginal notes. It is, however, also common in dramatic contexts; e.g. *Killing of the Children*, ll. 20 and 49, *Conversion of St Paul*, ll. 13 and 163; *Processus Talentorum, Towneley* XXIV.
   The scribe appears to have been going to write, 'þis is þe processe of oure play'.

17–25 In this stanza the rhyme scheme changes from the common Marian octave to a nine-line stanza, rhyming *ababcdddc*. Taken with the apparent rounding-off of the introduction in l. 16, this may point to an addition. It adds nothing to the subject matter but a request for silence and a blessing; cf. ll. 262–70 where a similar change takes place.
   Theatrically there is nothing awkward about the re-starting, which could mark a movement or turning to another part of the audience. The request for silence is a common enough opening, not restricted to tyrannical ranters.

20–1 The sense seems to be: 'I entrust you to that Lord, who is always omnipotent, to maintain you in goodness . . . – we may see him in heaven'. Perhaps a wish, 'may we see him . . .' was intended.

24 *towre* is a commonplace expression for heaven and does not necessarily imply a particular type of structure for the heaven scaffold.

25   At the foot of f. 37v are some further notes relating to the genealogy of Mary. They should be seen in relation to those at the foot of the previous leaf.

f. 37   Barpanter
Asmaria   } genuit Joachym

Ysakar
Nasaphat   } genuit Anna

Joachym   } genuit Maria, mater Jhesu Christi; sponsa Joseph
Anna   } fabro.

Cleophas &   } genuit secunda Maria, mater Symonem et Judam,
Anna   } Jacobum minorem & Joseph iustum; sponsa Alpheo.

Salome &   } genuit tertia Maria, mater Johannem euangelistam
Anna   } & Jacobum maiorem; sponsa Zebedeo.

Emeria fuit soror Anne que habebat quondam filiam Elizabeth que nupta fuit Zakarie de quo peperit Johannem Baptistam, precursorem domini. Elyud, Eminen filia, beatus Geruasius episcopus.

f. 37v   Est Ysakar Anne pater; Melophat sic quoque mater vel Nasaphat Quinque sunt Anne: Mater Samuelis
Vxor Raguelis
Uxor Tobie
Mater beate Marie
Anna prophetissa

These genealogies should be compared with those in *Reynes*, pp. 191–5.

26sn   *Ysakar*. The name appears in the *Nativity of Mary* as Issachar; the priest is not named in *Legenda* and appears as Ruben in *Pseudo-Matthew*. These three possibilities all appear in later versions of the story. The *Breviary* use of Ysachar (III 548) no doubt added weight to the first.

Ysakar's speech is not in any of the sources but is a compilation from a variety of places. It serves to emphasise the exceptional importance of the high office of priesthood, the coming feast, and its nature; all of which prepare for the seriousness of Joachim's rejection.

26–7   From Leviticus xxi, 6: 'For they offer the burnt offering of the Lord, and the bread of their God, and therefore they shall be holy'. It is used at the mass on Corpus Christi day (*Missal*, 458–9).

34–5   *Festum Encenniorum*. In the *Nativity of Mary* this is *Encaeniorum festivitas*, in the *Legenda* it is *in festo encaeniorum* (p. 587). It is described as one of three during the year (p. 587; cf. Exodus xxiii, 14). Both *Speculum Sacerdotale* (p. 91) and *Stanzaic Life* (pp. 167–8) describe the feasts and their origins, associating them with the Ember days or regular days of fasting in the Church's year. Isidore gives the meaning of *Encaenia* as 'nova templi dedicatio' (VI xviii 12), 'the new dedication of the temple'.

þe newe fest is no doubt to be explained by Isidore's further comment: 'Graece enim καινὸν dicitur novum. Quando enim aliquid novum dedicatur, encaenia dicitur' ('In Greek καινὸν means "new". When therefore anything is dedicated anew it is called *encaenia*'). It is not suggested elsewhere that this new feast is more important than the others.

40   *regal sacerdocium* 'a kingly priesthood'. The phrase occurs in *Legenda* (p. 587) but in relation to the line of Christ's descent which makes him descendant of priests and kings, and hence those who are called Christians after Christ are called 'genus electum et regale sacerdotium' ('a chosen race and kingly priesthood'). The phrase 'genus electum, regale sacerdotium' originates from 1 Peter ii, 9, also describing ordinary Christians.

41   This group, as a fourfold means of cleansing from sin, is listed in *Speculum Sacerdotale* in the Ember days section, 'prayingis, fastyngis, almes dede and wakyngis' (p. 90).

42–3   Joachim's origins in Galilee and Nazareth show that Mary is of the tribe of David just as Joseph is. 'Joachim namque ex Galilaea et civitate Nazareth sanctam Annam ex Bethlehem duxit uxorem' (*Legenda* p. 587). The *Legenda* complicatedly explains the descent of Mary and Christ to show that Christ is the inheritor through Joachim of the kingly line and through Anne of the priestly line (pp. 585–7).

46   *Protevangelium* and the Middle English lives of St Anne all picture Joachim as a wealthy man. *Pseudo-Matthew* shows him as a shepherd, but a wealthy one (ch. 1); and Mézières as a priest (pp. 86–7).

47   The explanation of the name Joachim is given by Isidore as 'ubi est praeparatio' ('where there is readiness') (VII vi, 75). *Pseudo-Matthew* emphasises his fear of God (ch. 1).

50–3   His righteousness and the threefold division of his goods are next to each other in the *Legenda* (p. 587). The threefold division also occurs in *Pseudo-Matthew* (ch. 1), and most later accounts, though not always in the same order.

54–7   There is no doubt that Joachim's remarks are aimed at the parish priest, but this certainly need not imply a clerical audience. The simple view of responsibility was that the parish priest was responsible for the chancel and the parish for the nave of the church. Some of the actual complexity is briefly shown in A. H. Thompson, *The English Clergy and their Organization in the later Middle Ages* (Clarendon Press, Oxford 1947), p. 117. *curat* is here one who has 'cure of souls', or parishioners in his care.

58–61   None of the early versions contains Joachim's preparatory fear of rejection. In *Protevangelium*, after his rejection, he goes to check if he is the only one; in *Legenda* he is *confusum* (p. 587); in *Cursor Mundi* he cannot understand why he is rejected and questions Ysacar about it (ll. 10246–84).

64–5   The *Legenda*, drawing on the *Nativity of Mary*, has the vowing of the hoped-for child to God, but neither has the separate vows; Joachim's of a male child and Anne's of a female (ll. 71–3). The *Breviary* does mention male or female (III 548).

68   The explanation is in the *Breviary* (III 545) Anna 'id est gratia', but her comment is an addition.

70   Presumably Isaiah vii, 14 'Virgo concipiet et pariet filium'.

73   *foot-mayd* is an unusual word. *MED* has, besides this use, one from a glossary, translating *pedisequa*, and two later uses.

75   Two turtle doves is a common sin offering in the Old Testament

associated with the poor, but the connection here is more likely to be with the offering at the presentation of Christ in the temple (Luke ii, 24, quoting Leviticus xii, 8). It is also possible that the birds are connected with Joachim and Anne because of their traditional association with marital fidelity.

81   Proverbial; see Whiting S515, though its import is the opposite of the proverb quoted by Whiting from *Towneley* XXIV l. 397.

85   Putting the praise into the mouths of the fellow-members of his tribe, increases the bitterness of Joachim's shame and the audience's awareness of it.

89   The threefold repetition of words in moments of extreme emotion becomes characteristic of Joachim and Anne.

97sd   *Benedicta sit beata Trinitas* is a sequence used in the services of both *Missal* and *Breviary*. It is associated almost exclusively with masses of the Trinity; see *Missal* 453 (Trinity Sunday), 736* (Votive Mass of the Trinity); *Breviary* II 502 (Commemoration of the Trinity).
    In as much as the playwright uses elements from the liturgy to give the impression of a solemn temple service, it is possible that the censing would have followed the general lines of the censing of an altar before mass (*Missal* 581). The order of events would seem to be that the choir sings the sequence while the censing is proceeding and possibly while Ysakar and his ministers make their offering. Ysakar then turns to the 'congregation' and invites them to offer. This has little to do with the order of the Ordinary of the Mass (i.e. the part leading up to the communion service); see below, note to l. 110. For the offering see *Lay Folks Mass Book*, pp. 231–44 and *Ancient Liturgy*, pp. 78–81.

101–5   Many of the elements of Ysakar's speech are in *Legenda* (p. 587) though the order is considerably altered.

102   *ware* is probably plural, being at a distance from its subject *Neyther*.

105sd   'And he rejects Joachim's offering'; *refudit* is either a spelling of *refutit*, or *refundit* with a missing mark of abbreviation. Either could mean 'rejects'.

106   It seems best to take this as a statement leading into l. 107 rather than a command, even though Joachim is clearly still there.

108   'And he draws back weeping.'

110   These sung lines are taken from early in the Ordinary of the Mass (*Missal* 580). Two or more of the lines appear frequently in the liturgy. The blessing is not exactly similar to any that I have found. The whole effect is to re-emphasise the solemn liturgical nature of the episode without locating it precisely in the present.

110–16   'With the minister singing:
	Our help is in the name of the Lord,
Choir:	Who made heaven and earth.
Minister:	Blessed be the name of the Lord:
Choir:	From this time, now and for evermore.
Bishop:	May the divine majesty and one God bless you, + Father, + and Son + and Holy Spirit,

Choir: Amen.
Making the sign of the cross solemnly with his hand; and the tribes shall
withdraw from the temple.'

121–4   Close to *Legenda* (p. 587), where however Joachim's reaction is
described rather than being put into his own mouth.

129   'But since God allows this, we must needs bear it'; with a play on the
two meanings of 'suffer'.

130   *sherherdys*, implying responsibility for shearing as well as safe-
keeping, is otherwise unrecorded and may well be an error for *shepherdys*.

132   Proverb-like, though not recorded in Whiting.

133–212   This section is marked off in the manuscript with a thick grey line
in the left margin before l. 135 (f. 39v) and another in the right margin after
l. 212 (f. 41). In the right margin before l. 135 is the word *pastores* and it seems
to draw attention to the section as a separate scene or at least one which
theatrically takes place in a different location, though Anne's prayer is not
differentiated from it. The marks and note are later than the writing of the
manuscript. Lettering *a, b, b, c, d*, marks the order of speeches at ll. 135, 139,
141, 143 and 145. It was probably a result of the correction from *ij pastor* to
Joachym at the foot of f. 39v (l. 139).

133   *In 3ow is lytel pryde*. The phrase seems a little awkward in the middle of
fairly colloquial speech. *Pryde* here perhaps means 'ostentation, show'; cf.
Cursor Mundi, l. 15212.

136   The multiplying of the sheep performs the same function, though
more obliquely, as the sparrows in *Protevangelium* (ch. 3) and *Pseudo-
Matthew* (ch. 2); that of setting Joachim and Anne's childlessness against
natural fecundity. It does not, however, have the bitterness of the earlier
versions.

141   An expression of trust in God; cf. Luke i, 52 'Deposuit potentes de sede
et exaltauit humiles', part of the *Magnificat*; see below, ll. 1513–14.

143   This proverbial expression is repeated by the angel, l. 226; see Whiting
S507, and for similar proverbs, references at B325.

144   'We shall pray for you in our own simple way.'

149–72   Joachim's prayer is not in the *Legenda*.

150   Cf. the steps of Adam and Even which remained burnt into the ground
when they were driven from paradise; see *Legends of the Holy Rood*, ed.
Richard Morris, EETS OS 46 (London 1881), pp. 22, 23 and 66.

151   *setys sefne*. Perhaps the throne of God beyond the seven planets.
'Celum empireum, fixum et inmotum in quo est tronus Salamonis et locus
Dei et spirituum' ('The empyrean heaven, fixed and unmoving, in which the
throne of Solomon and the place of God and the spirits is'), John Pecham's
sphere in B.L. MS Arundel 83, f. 123v; or simply the seven heavens:
'Heuenes beþ seuene, inempnede in þis manere: *aereum, ethereum, olimpium,
igneum, firmamentum, aqueum, empireum celum* . . .; *Celum empireum* . . . is þe
hiest wonynge place of God . . . And þerfore heuen is specialliche iclepid
God his owne sete', *On the Properties of Things*, pp. 447 and 454–5.

151–64   The line of thought is: I am the worst (151–2); you have shamed me (153); for which I thank you, since it is a sign that you are with me and therefore I need not fear (154–7). But I am afraid I have done something wrong. If so, punish me and not Anne (158–60). Only prayer will help, so I pray you to remember our vow and look after Anne in your mercy (161–4).

155   Apocalypse iii, 19: 'Such as I love, I rebuke and chastise'; Proverbs iii, 12: 'For whom the Lord loveth, he chastiseth'. Cf. *Paston Letters and Papers,* ed. Norman Davis, 2 vols. (Oxford 1971, 1976) I, p. 44 'Qhom God vysyteth, him he louyth'.

159–64   Joachim's humane care for Anne also serves to draw her into the audience's attention and prepares for the switch to her location.

164–5   The word *mercy* is echoed across the place from one location to the other and links the two.

168   *3e*; MS. *he.* The simplicity of the emendation is spoilt by the abruptness of the change from singular to plural form; but the change must take place somewhere in ll. 167–8, and for an almost exact parallel cf. l. 1396.

169   *þe . . . I take to borwe* 'I take you as my witness'; presumably because of the barren women who became mothers through God's might; see the angel's speech (ll. 181–7).

171   Anne's words echo Joachim's at l. 158.

172sd   This is the first mention of the heaven location. *Exultet celum laudibus* is a hymn for Lauds at the feast of the Apostles (*Breviary* II 368). It is referred to, and possibly sung, at the end of the *Conversion of St Paul* (p. 23). 'Let the heaven rejoice with praises, the earth resound with joys, they sing in solemn festival to the glory of the archangels.' The inappropriate *apostolorum* of the original has been altered to *archangelorum.* For the substitution of words more appropriate to a place or time, see Fabri I, 557. This particular hymn has a great many forms; see the entries in *Analecta Hymnica* under *Exultet celum laudibus.*

174   The brightness of the angel's appearance is emphasised in *Legenda,* p. 587.

175–200   The angel's speech is an almost literal translation of *Legenda,* pp. 587–8. Alterations are mainly for the sake of rhyme. Those which are altered for other reasons are: l. 180, cf. 'ut mirabilius denuo aperiat, et non libidinis esse, quod nascitur, sed divini fore muneris cognoscatur' ('so that he may open it [the womb] afterwards more wonderfully and it may be known that it is not from lust that [the child] is born but as a divine gift'); l. 196, cf. 'ita et mirabiliter ex ea altissimi filius generabitur, cujus nomen erit, Jesus' ('thus wonderfully from her the son of the highest shall be born, whose name shall be Jesus').

For Sara and Isaac, see Genesis xviii and xxi; for Rachel and Joseph, see Genesis xxx; for Samson, Judges xiii, and for Samuel, 1 Kings i. Samuel's mother, Anna, is the first of the five referred to in the marginal note *Quinque sunt Anne* on f. 37v (see note to l. 25).

191–3   The source here is considerably altered. It reads: 'Haec, ut vovistis, erit ab infantia domino consecrata et adhjuc ex utero matris suae spiritu sancto plena nec forinsecus inter populares sed in templo domini semper morabitur' ('As you vowed, she shall from infancy be consecrated to the Lord and even from her mother's womb be filled with the Holy Spirit, nor shall she dwell abroad among the people but always in the temple of the Lord'). The omissions do not alter the sense very much, however.

The five joys seem to be used here merely as padding. They were a frequent object of devotion and celebration. They are usually listed as the Annunciation, the Nativity, Resurrection, Ascension and Assumption, but the number sometimes rises to fifteen (see, for example, *Lydgate* I, pp. 260–7).

198   *þe Gylden Gate* was the eastern gate of Jerusalem through which Christ passed on Palm Sunday and at which Joachim and Anne met; see Fabri, I, 458.

212   The singing of shepherds is a traditional feature of all the plays. The end of the *pastores* section is here marked by a line; see note to ll. 133–212.

213–16   Anne's words reflect the *Legenda* (p. 588).

217–18   The angel's words to Anne, except for the direction to go to the Golden Gate, are not reported in the *Legenda*. The *Nativity of Mary* has a speech for Anne quite unconnected with this one.

222   Perhaps suggested by *Legenda*, 'domum redierunt divinum promissum hilariter exspectantes' ('They returned home joyously awaiting the divine promise'), p. 588.

225   The 'salvation' of the angels, or rather their restoration, is given as the third reason for the angelic greeting at the Annunciation in the *Legenda* (p. 216), 'lapsus angelici reparandi' ('restoring the fall of the angels').

226   The angel repeats the shepherd's words (l. 143), thus rounding off the reconciliation of Joachim. The words are slightly changed; *gras*, or mercy, is hoped for by the shepherd, *gladnes* is promised by the angel.

236sd   The delayed return of the angel to heaven enables him to oversee the meeting of Joachim and Anne.

238   Anne's creeping to Joachim on her knees is not in *Legenda* where the manner of their meeting is not described. In *Pseudo-Matthew* (ch. 3) Anne runs to meet him and embraces him. The visual arts usually show the moment of their meeting when they are both standing. The word 'creep' is sometimes used simply to mean 'kneel' (as at l. 1052), but *to-hym-ward* suggests movement.

241   *kusse of clennesse*. Some awareness of the debate over the Immaculate Conception seems to be implied by this, but Contemplacio's words at ll. 256–7 state that the conception and birth of Mary are not being played. Only by a rather forced punctuation of ll. 256–7 can the meeting of Joachim and Anne be linked with the conception.

In the *Legenda* (p. 588) the conception seems to take place later; *Protevangelium* (ch. 4–5) leaves the time in doubt, and in *Pseudo-Matthew* (ch. 3) Anne says to Joachim that she has conceived, the angel's words to Joachim showing that it had occurred before their meeting. Fabri, a Dominican, comments somewhat scornfully on the idea of the Immaculate Conception, II p. 72.

244   Anne's words hark back to her own earlier ones, l. 69.

255   'the holy meeting of both Joachim and Anne'.

256–7   The *Legenda* goes straight from the meeting at the Golden Gate to Mary's presentation in the temple with only a brief reference to Mary's birth. The treatment of Mary's presentation and her life in the temple also is very brief in both the *Nativity of Mary* and the *Legenda*.

258–9   There is a very faint hint of Lydgate's *Life of Our Lady* here; cf. 'And thenne anon, in her tendre age/Vnto the Temple, deuoutely they hir bryng' (I, 185–6), but it is too commonplace to be a borrowing.

261   Cf. note to l.9.

262–70   Cf. note to ll. 17–25.

270sd   Three years old is Mary's age in all the sources. In Mézières also she is dressed in white (pp. 85–6).

273–4   Cf. ll. 63–5 and 71–3.

275–6   The significance of the number three is here made apparent; cf. l. 79.

277   'the younger that she is admitted [to the temple], the better it seems to me to be.'

278   Joachim is still showing a proper fear of God, cf. ll. 49 and 158.

282–3   Since the angel did not say this and it does not appear in any source, it seems that either it is a part of the common tradition of Mary as queen of heaven, or the word is used to mean someone pre-eminent, which was certainly foretold by the angel. Cf. however the annoyance of the maidens with Mary in *Pseudo-Matthew* (ch. 8), when they mockingly call her 'queen of virgins'.

The marriage imagery used here is appropriate to the consecration of a nun, where a form of marriage service was performed; see Maskell III, pp. 336, 347–8. See also the *Servitio includendorum* of the Sarum Use in *York Manual* 108★–9★. There is also a useful note discussing the resemblances by Raymond St Jacques, *Notes and Queries* 27 (1980), pp. 295–7.

287–94   Mary's reply establishes from the beginning her humility, of which her action at the Annunciation was taken to be the supreme example. The ideas of serving and marriage are interwoven in the service for the consecration of a nun. Mary's desire to serve the Mother of God echoes the promise made by Anne (l. 73) and looks forward to her own petition (ll. 521–4).

294sd   'And she shall kneel to God.'

296   *Pseudo-Matthew* has 'thirty years' (ch. 6), which Mézières follows (p. 36), as a gauge of her maturity of speech.

298–306   The emphasis upon the loving attention of Joachim and Anne is not in the sources. In the *Legenda* there is no mention of what they were doing, and in the *Nativity of Mary* (ch. 6) they are changing out of their travelling clothes while, unknown to them, Mary climbs the steps.

302   *wys.* The reading 'wys husbond' is not a collocation used in the plays and does not sound like Anne's normal mode of speech. It seems to be

confirmed by 'wys fadyr Joseph' (1554), but 'wise' is never spelt without final -e in the play, and I have therefore assumed that wys is the aphetic form of iwys in both cases.

307   The officiating priest is made the same bishop Isakar who rejected Joachim's offering. There is no warrant for this in the sources or similar use in the later versions but it makes good dramatic sense and in any case the events are only about four years apart. Note the similarity (by contrast) of ll. 309 and 103. The name is only used here (307sn).

310   Isakar's remark could mean no more than 'You are sweet', but given the later emphasis upon grace it should probably be seen as more significant (see especially ll. 1279–80 and 1286–7).

310sd   'Joachim kneeling to God, saying thus:'

311–12   Frequent reference to God as Trinity leads naturally to the Trinitarian emphasis in the Annunciation.

321–2   The play on 'father' is also used by Mézières, 'trium annorum de domo patris carnalis ad domum eterni Dei Patris' ('at three years old from the house of her fleshly father to the house of God the eternal Father', (p. 50). See also Meditationes (p. 513) and cf. Nativity of Mary (ch. 7) quoting Psalm xxvi, 10.

323–5   The extra-metrical blessings give a formal naturalness to the scene.

330   The exemplary conduct of Mary is again stressed.

330sd   'And embracing them she shall kiss her father and mother.'

335–46   A very delicate balance is kept here between exemplary conduct (ll. 335–8), didactic observation (ll. 339–43) and naturalness. It is necessary in gauging its dramatic effect to remember Mary's age.

348   'Make your way carefully to this place.'

350–1   fyftene grees. The fifteen steps of the temple are not mentioned in Protevangelium, but are in Pseudo-Matthew and from there in later accounts. They are referred to (though not the number) in Jacques de Vitry's History of Jerusalem (pp. 43–4) but are not usually mentioned by pilgrims to Jerusalem. Fabri refers to them as ruinous and the doorway blocked, II, pp. 126–7. They presumably derive ultimately from the seven and eight steps of the temple described in Ezechiel xl.

352   The interpretation of the Gradual Psalms in terms of the return to Jerusalem from the Babylonic captivity is one among many interpretations and is usually only a basis for a spiritual interpretation, as here; see, Bede, In Psalmorum Librum exegesis, PL 93, 1084–92. It is common to assign the fifteen psalms to the fifteen steps (as some manuscripts of Pseudo-Matthew, Nativity of Mary and the Legenda do). The Bede exegesis goes further and says, 'they are called psalms of the steps because in going up to the temple they were sung one psalm per step'. Mézières too describes the singing by the priest of one psalm at each step (p. 35). The spiritual meaning of the psalms as a whole is the amendment of life as a way to salvation, or steps to the perfect love of God (Cassiodorus, Expositio Psalmorum, PL 70, 901–61).

354   'and thus from the beginning to the end of the fifteen psalms'.

355–444   Each of the next fifteen stanzas consists of a brief spiritual application, a translation and a text of the first line of one of the Gradual Psalms. The translations in common with many other biblical translations of the time are often concerned more with literalness than comprehensibility. The added considerations of rhyme and metre have caused a number of minor additions to be made. One translation at least includes a gloss (see l. 412).

I have not found a single source for the expositions and it is likely that they were made specially for the play. They have occasional similarities with a number of commentaries and explanations. The psalms are Vulgate cxix–cxxxiii (AV cxx–cxxxiv). They form a frequent section in primers as a separate devotion; see *Prymer*, II, pp. xi–xxxviii; and Maskell, III, pp. 95–6.

It should not be forgotten that the psalms are spoken by Mary and often through their spiritual applications have a relevance to her situation as well as, didactically, to the audience; see Introduction p. 16.

361–2   'The second is truly study and humble inquiry into how I shall know the will of God.'

367–8   'The third is happiness of mind in that we may hope that we shall all be saved thus.' *thus* is suspiciously like a necessity of rhyme, cf. l. 380.

374   See the note to l. 151.

382   This line partly translates the second verse of the psalm: 'Cum exurgerent homines in nos: forte vivos deglutissent nos'. *Dicat nunc Israel* is not translated.

392   *Lorde-is grace*; MS. *lorde is as gracy*. The reading of the manuscript seems to me to be simply a muddle, and there are a variety of ways by which the confusion may have arisen. The emendation is merely the simplest Gordian cut.

398   *For hym þat* . . . 'On account of him [God] who . . .'

409   'The tenth is strong forbearance in the face of bodily temptation.'

412   *Þou seynge God* is the interpretation of the name 'Israel' interpolated very awkwardly into the translation. Augustine refers to it in his commentary on Psalm cxx, 4, 'Be thou then Israel, What meaneth Israel? It is interpreted, Seeing God'. Isidore has the same interpretation (VII vii, 6).

415   For the idea that confession should be self-accusing, see *Ancrene Riwle*, p. 135 and *Jacob's Well*, pp. 180–3.

416   'The sufferings of which are very great [lit. "painful"]'.

424   *lokynge abowte* is an odd translation of *elati*, 'raised up'; but presumably the playwright wished to suggest a general contrast to eyes cast humbly down; and the rhyme perhaps confirmed the phrase.

433   The fourteenth psalm is related to the company of Christ and the apostles in the *Quest of the Holy Grail* (Penguin Books 1969), p. 67.

436   *in on* 'in unity'.

439–40   Cassiodorus in his commentary (957–61) emphasises unity and divine love in this last of the psalms. The emphasis in l. 439 is therefore perhaps on the *on acorde* 'with complete unity'.

449–50   The *Nativity of Mary* also sees this as a miracle and a sign of future greatness (ch. 6).

451–76   The *Legenda* contains only a very brief account of Mary's life in the temple (p. 589) and the main source for this section is the *Meditationes*, either in its original Latin form or in the English translation by Nicholas Love.

451–2   Cf. *Meditationes*, 'feci me doceri legem Dei mei' ('I had myself taught the law of my God'), p. 513.

453–68   The brief statement in the *Meditationes* naturally develops into a piece of regular religious instruction. Arising from Matthew xxii, 37–40, it was normal to divide the ten commandments into two tables (corresponding to those which Moses carried), one relating to God and one to man. The contents of each were subsumed under the two commandments of love God and love thy neighbour (see, *Lay Folks' Catechism*, p. 60, *Religious Pieces*, pp. 26–7). The three commandments of the *Meditationes* have been turned into two with the third tagged on as an afterthought (ll. 469–70).

455–6   cf. Luke x, 25–8.

459–60   A commonplace eloquently expressed in the section on Love in *Ancrene Riwle* (especially pp. 176–7) and frequent in lyrics and drama.

462–4   The attributes of the three persons of the Trinity.

466–8   *Meditationes* (p. 513), where the order is the same; cf. Luke x, 27.

469–70   A gloss on the *Meditationes* 'Hate your enemy' (p. 513). A partly similar gloss also appears there a few lines later, 'nisi suos inimicos, id est vitia et peccata habuerit odio' ('if it [the soul] did not hate its enemies vice and sins'), p. 513.

472–5   The order given here, prayer, food, physical work, is not drawn from any of the earlier versions or their derivatives.

473   MS. *For with prayȝer with grace and mercy.* The manuscript reading makes no sense to me. In view of the emphasis on the importance of prayer for grace in *Meditationes*, it seems likely that *with* has replaced some word like 'come'. Cf. *Meditationes*, 'propterea petebam sic gratiam et virtutes . . . nullam gratiam, donum vel virtutem habui a Deo sine magno labore, continua oratione, ardenti desiderio etc . . . nulla gratia descendit in animam, nisi per orationem et corporis afflictionem' ('therefore I sought thus for grace and virtues . . . no grace, gift or virtue I had from God without great labour, continual prayer, ardent desiring etc . . . no grace descends into the soul except through prayer and bodily suffering'), p. 513.

477   Fellow maidens in the temple are mentioned in many of the versions from *Pseudo-Matthew* onwards, but no numbers or names are specified at this point. In the main text of Mézières, Mary is to be accompanied by two (p. 86), but fifteen are mentioned in the description of 1385 (p. 110). Mary is sent home after her marriage with five maidens named, in *Pseudo-Matthew*, Rebecca, Sephora, Susanna, Abigea and Cael (ch. 8); see below, note to l. 910.

481–3   This does not appear to be a ready-made group of five. Meditation, Contrition, Compassion and Cleanness (Purity) are commonplace words and ideas, but *Fruyssyon*, the enjoyment of God's love through communion with him, is not. The first four could perhaps be seen as prerequisites of the last, but I have not found a source for this idea. In the Wycliffite *Lanterne of Light*, 'fruition' is the last of the four rewards of the souls in heaven (p. 26). All are clearly attributes of Mary; 'compassion', her fellow feeling for others, and 'purity' obviously so; 'contrition' fits her own view of herself as sinful, and 'meditation' is appropriate to her life in the temple. As for 'fruition', in the *Legenda* it is said of Mary 'et visione divina quotidie fruebatur' ('and she enjoyed daily a vision from God/of God'), p. 589.

490–6   Like the five maidens, the seven allegorical priests do not appear in other versions and like them are not an obviously ready-made group. Again there is a mixture of commonplace and unusual. The purpose of the priests (ll. 491–2) is confession, teaching in general, tending Mary, and teaching her God's law and how to read the Bible, and the names given to them fit this purpose: 'Discretion' (sound judgement), 'Devotion' (piety), 'Dilection' (spiritual love), 'Deliberation' (consideration, thought), 'Declaration' (exposition), 'Determination' (investigation, definition, conclusion). *Divinatio*, however, is almost always connected with evil in the Bible; the exception is Proverbs xvi, 10 where the meaning is 'oracular utterance, divinely wise words'. Something like this is almost certainly the meaning here, perhaps a kind of divine foreknowledge. The number seven is not unexpected in view of the tradition that she was taught by the Holy Ghost, but in a more conventional treatment the gifts of the Holy Ghost might have been expected. There are occasional similarities between the two groups of seven. For the endowing of Mary with the gifts of the Holy Ghost in the temple see Lydgate, *Life of Our Lady* I, ll. 365–78, and for the view that the seven priests and the seven gifts are related see *NQ* 27 (1980), pp. 295–7.

500   The Latin blessing here is metrical, cf. ll. 323–5.

500sd   'And he shall withdraw with his ministers. All the maidens shall say: Amen.' Though the plural 'they shall withdraw' (MS. *recedent*) is possible, it seems unlikely and the mistake is an easy one.

503–9   The playwright ingeniously interweaves the Trinity with their blessings by making Joachim's by the Father (503–4), Anne's by the Son, the wisdom of God (505–6; and cf. l. 463), and Mary's by the Holy Ghost (509).

508sd   'Here Joachim and Anna shall turn back home.'

510sd   'to the virgins'.

513–25   Cf. *Meditationes*, p. 513. The playwright has altered the order of the seven petitions to make the fifth of the *Meditationes* into the seventh. The order does not appear to have been changed elsewhere. It is a simple but effective way of again stressing the divine plan of salvation through Mary.

514   *þi love and þi lawe*; cf. *Meditationes* 'dilectionis praeceptum' ('the commandment of love').

518   *þe ordenaryes of þe temple*; cf. *Meditationes* 'mandatis et ordinationibus Pontificis templi' ('commandments and ordinances of the high-priest of the temple'). *ordenaryes* of the play could mean 'ecclesiastical authorities' or 'rules'.

519–20   Cf. *Meditationes* 'ut templum et universum populum suum ad servitium suum conservaret' ('that the temple and all its people may be maintained in his service').

524   'oculos, linguam, manus, pedes, genua, ('eyes, tongue, hands, feet, knees') of *Meditationes*, becomes the commonplace *my wyttys fyve*.

525   '. . . and otherwise it should not be disputed about.'

528   Cf. Canticles v, 2: 'Ego dormio et cor meum vigilat' and its interpretation in *Rolle*, I p. 50.

528sd   *manna . . . lyke to confeccyons*. The word *confeccyons* no longer helps to specify the appearance of the manna, as seems to have been intended. Manna is usually represented in the form of sacramental wafers (as it was often interpreted), as in the fifteenth-century glass at Great Malvern (Rushforth, p. 184 and pl. 87). Cf. also *Mary Magdalen* ll. 2007 and 2018sd, 2065–7. In the Paris *Resurrection* manna falls from heaven as Christ ascends with the saved from hell. It is described as being like large coins, gold and silver (*Staging of Religious Drama*, p. 65). The shower of wafers ('waffrons') in York at the entry of Henry VII in 1485 was probably also intended to represent manna (REED *York* 142).

    þe hefne syngynge. Possibly *Jhesu corona virginum* is sung, as it is later at 560sd.

531   *aungelys mete* is a common phrase for manna (see for example *Minor Poems* I, pp. 169–70, ll. 8–12 and 33–40). The phrase is adapted from the 'panem angelorum' of Psalm lxxvii, 25. Cf. *Passion Play* (I, l. 753).

535–6   'We shall teach you the whole of Our Lord's gentle law, because my words reveal signs of diffidence in you' or '. . . on account of my words signs of diffidence appear in you'.

539–40   Cf. *Mary Magdalen* 'fode of most delycyte' l. 2038, and *The Killing of the Children* 'Wiche is in tast celestialle of savoure' l. 12.

541–2   All the early versions record that Mary received food from angels; *Pseudo-Matthew* (ch. 6) adds that angels were often seen speaking with her, and the *Legenda* (p. 589) that she was daily visited by them.

545–50   Playing with the letters of a name was a not uncommon poetic trick. Mézières does it with a greeting to Mary in the prose for the mass of the Presentation (pp. 80–2), as well as with a pseudonym of his own, Frater Rostagnus, in the Office (pp. 55–7). It is common to use each letter of Mary's name as a starting point for listing her virtues or attributes, as here. See also Woolf *Lyric*, pp. 291–3; Gray *Lyrics* no. 57; Brown *Lyrics XV*, no. 31. The device sometimes develops extraordinarily heavy alliteration.

547   *auerte* 'averter, turner aside' or the Latin imperative *averte* 'turn aside!' used as a noun. Perhaps the scribe has merely omitted the last letter of the word, but *MED* records no use of it.

548   *regyon* could refer to either heaven or earth. 'Queen of heaven' is one of her frequent titles, see l. 1398.

549   'Innocent through the descent from Jesse'. Jesse trees frequently lead to Mary and Christ at the top. It is often pointed out that though the genealogy of Christ that is given in Matthew (i, 1–16) leads to Joseph, Mary was also a descendant of Jesse (see for example *Mirk's Festial* p. 215, and note to ll. 42–3 above).

550   'advocate most worthy of trust'. Mary's advocacy to God on the

behalf of man was a commonplace. *antecer* seems to be either a telescoping of *antecessour* or, more probably (given the ease of confusion of *t* and *c*), a version of *ancetre*, 'ancestor'. There is no obvious connection besides alliteration between the two halves of the line.

551–2   An idea borrowed from Philippians ii, 10 'ut in nomine Iesu omne genu flectatur caelestium terrestrium et infernorum'.

555   That is, the Annunciation. The playwright gives the impression of the knowledge of future events already existing in heaven, though to what extent this affected the audience's reaction to the discussion in the Parliament of Heaven is not clear.

557   That is, at the Council of the Trinity, see below ll. 1233–46.

560sd   'Here let her kiss the ground.' This seems to be a set-piece with music. The angels descending to the kneeling Mary and ascending again to heaven while the choir sings *Jhesu corona virginum*. *Jhesu corona virginum* is a hymn for the nativity of a virgin or martyr (*Breviary* II 448). The line *Sponsisque reddens praemia* ('giving rewards to your brides') is perhaps intended to echo the giving of presents to Mary.

561–4   Only *Pseudo-Matthew* (ch. 6) and *Meditationes* (p. 514) of the earlier versions have the sending of food to Mary by the priests; but it appears in many later versions.

562   *his servyce indede* 'food from his own table'.

567–73   *Pseudo-Matthew* (ch. 6) and *Meditationes* (p. 514) both contain the giving of the food to the poor, but no other version has Mary giving it to her fellow-maidens.

568   'God's plenty is always nearer at hand for his servants than we think'. See Whiting G231 (rather than G228 where this is placed).

574   The seven works of mercy, one of the numerical arrangements for teaching basic Christian behaviour, were drawn from Matthew xxv, 35–6 and Tobias i, 20: Feed the hungry, give drink to the thirsty, shelter the stranger, clothe the naked, visit the sick, comfort those in prison, bury the dead. They are listed in *Lay Folks' Catechism*, pp. 70–1, for example.

577   The metre of Contemplacio's speech changes to two quatrains and a nine-line stanza.

586   The *Legenda* (p. 589) has fourteen as the age at which maidens were expected to marry; *Protevangelium* (ch. 8) has twelve and *Pseudo-Matthew* (ch. 8) varies in different manuscripts between twelve and fourteen. Strictly speaking the line ought to mean that Mary was seventeen (fourteen years *after* her presentation in the temple), though this is clearly not the playwright's real intention (see ll. 600, 602, 623). The *Legenda* deals with the Betrothal at some length; *Meditationes* mentions it only very briefly (p. 514).

590–2   It is in this prologue speech that the Parliament of Heaven is mentioned for the first and only time. For the Salutation (Annunciation) see above l. 12.

593sd   *Abysakar*. *Protevangelium* has 'Zacharias', *Pseudo-Matthew* 'Abiathar'. He is not named in the *Legenda* or *Nativity of Mary*. The *Life of St*

Anne (1) has 'Abathar/Abaythar' who is at first a priest who wishes to marry Mary to his son (ll. 403–8) and later the bishop (l. 460). 'Isachar' is the bishop of Juda (l. 506). The N. town proclamation has 'Abyacar (l. 118) and this part of the episode is drawn from the pageant material (see below, note to l. 594). The version used here is a confusion of these traditional names, no doubt affected by the name of the bishop earlier in the play.

594   With this line the blend of pageant and *Mary Play* material begins. The most obvious difference is in the metre: octaves in the *Mary Play* material, thirteeners in the pageant. The Betrothal is the first episode in the play to be represented in the Proclamation. It is described in three stanzas (ll. 118–56) and consisted of two pageants. For a discussion of the blending of pageant and play, see Introduction p. 3.

597   The statement made here hardly fits with Abysakar's concern for the law as something outside himself which must be kept.

600   *for what Þat ȝe owe* 'at all costs' (lit. 'for all that you own').

608–12   Joachim here confirms that, contrary to all the early versions, Mary is at home and not in the temple. The fact that Mary was settled in the temple at l. 576 and is now at home may be a result of the intrusion of the pageant material; but it is doubtful, especially in view of the break created by Contemplacio, whether it would appear awkward in performance.

613–17   Joachim and Anne are willingly subject to the law as later Mary is (l. 629). It is later still an essential part of Christ's establishment of the New Law.

630–2   As in the *Legenda* (p. 589) Mary immediately and briefly rejects the bishop's demand.

637–62   Mary tells the story of her own conception and presentation in the temple because there was no previous representation of these episodes in the pageant series. In its new position in the *Mary Play*, it briefly repeats the material of the previous episodes. There is no parallel speech in any of the early versions, though the idea of her twofold objection to marriage is in the *Legenda*, 'tum quia parentes sui eam domini servitio mancipassent, tum quia virginitatem suam domino ipsa vovisset' (p. 589).

639   *here frute was do* 'their time of childbearing was past'.

676–84   His quandary is similar to that in the *Legenda* (p. 589) except that there it is between breaking a vow and breaking the law; as it is here in the *Mary Play* material.

685–708   This is the first of the *Mary Play* material. It repeats the previous stanza but is closer to the *Legenda* where *Vovete et reddite* is quoted (from Psalm lxxv, 12). Ll. 685–708 are written on the verso of a leaf previously left blank (f. 48v) before the opening of this episode; see frontispiece.

708sd   *Veni creator spiritus* is one of the best-known of Latin hymns. It is the hymn at Terce at Pentecost (*Breviary* I mviii), and is sung in the Sarum Use while the priest is preparing for the Mass (*Missal* 577–9). It is associated with a request for guidance in deliberations.

713   An angel brings the advice in *Protevangelium*; in the *Legenda* the advice is given by a voice. Again the *Mary Play* is closer to the *Legenda* (see below, l.

804sn). The incident does not occur in *Pseudo-Matthew*. The presence of the angel is too slight a resemblance to suggest dependence on *Protevangelium*. The idea of the choosing by the flowering of a rod is ultimately derived from Numbers xvii, 1–9, where Aaron is chosen by the flowering of the rod of the house of Levi. This was frequently seen as a prefiguration of Mary and the birth of Christ.

719   *Protevangelium* (ch. 8) has 'widowers of the people'; *Pseudo-Matthew* (ch. 8) has 'everyone [of the tribe of Judah] who has no wife', the *Legenda* has all those of the house of David that were 'unmarried and fit for marriage' (p. 589).

721   The word *ȝard* is used throughout the pageant material, and *wand* or *rod* in the Marian, see Vriend, p. 54. None of the early versions calls for *white* rods.

724   The 'sign' in the *Nativity of Mary* (ch. 7) and the *Legenda* is to be the blossoming of the rod and the dove settling on it; though the *Nativity* mentions the flowering only in the foretelling. In *Pseudo-Matthew* (ch. 8) it is to be only the dove coming from the rod. In the choosing of Aaron it is simply the flowering of the rod that decides (Numbers xvii, 5 and 8).

731–47   The summoning of the kinsmen of David is a natural dramatic development for which there is no immediate parallel in the early versions. The messenger calls for *all* the kinsmen of David; cf. note to l. 719 above.

747   Between ll. 747 and 748 a passage has been interpolated for Joseph and the four kinsmen of David. It explains the nature of the bishop's summons, which otherwise Joseph knows without having been told (ll. 751–5). The other effect of the interpolation is to emphasise Joseph's old age. For the text see Appendix 1.

748sn   *Joseph* replaces a speaker's name *Primus generacionis David*, perhaps suggesting a change of mind on the part of the scribe as to which material to add. The next pageant stanza, spoken by *Primus generacionis David* (ll. 776–88), could well have followed here.

748–75   This is another section of *Mary Play* material.

748   *Benedicite* could be pronounced with any number of syllables between five and two. The commonest colloquial pronunciation was *Benste*.

752   *maydon*. This is one of the traditions of Joseph's life. He is a widower with children in one of the other main traditions (*History of Joseph*, ch. 2–3). *Protevangelium* (ch. 9) reflects this as do *Pseudo-Matthew* (ch. 8), *Cursor Mundi* (ll. 10750–56) and *Life of St Anne* (1) (l. 565).

759–63   These lines emphasise, without overdoing, Joseph's age. Fabri is annoyed with the painters, who overdo the age of Joseph, showing him as a decrepit mannikin, I, pp. 516–17. The internal rhymes of ll. 758–63 are little touched by the stress and therefore appear as an undertone rather than a dominant feature.

763   The general sense needed for this and the preceding line seems to be: I am old and weak and walking is a trial to me; so, provided my staff lasts, I wish to get on with this journey. The main difficulty lies in the meaning of *to wore*. Block's suggestion 'were to, i.e. arrived' (p. 402) is attractive but does

not fit very well with Joseph's remarks about his staff. If the journey is over, the strength of the staff is irrelevant. There is no reason, however, why the phrase should not mean 'started, under way', since it is the journey that is 'to' not the destination. One other possibility is that *to wore* is a form of the word 'towards'. The meaning would be little affected whichever were chosen. I have assumed that a somewhat jingly rhyme is intended in l. 763, even though the phrase *holde I* is not of a type that is used elsewhere in the play. I have therefore emended *wole* to *wolde*.

765   *our* is perhaps unexpected here but gives good sense: 'the coming of us all together'.

770   This is the first mention of the sign of the dove sitting on the rod. See note to l. 724 above. The earlier reference comes in a pageant stanza.

771sd   'Here they bring their rods.'

772   The manuscript reading makes sense but seems to make Joseph's frustration of the divine plan too absolute, and, taken with *I ley a grote*, too casual. The omission would be an easy one to make and the emendation fits well with Joseph's personal reluctance to take part.

777   The offering *and* the rod which were asked for by the bishop in ll. 738 and 742 have here become one. In the *Mary Play* material, represented by l. 766, there seems only to have been a rod.

793–801   Joseph's hiding follows the *Legenda*. *Protevangelium* (ch. 9) and *Pseudo-Matthew* (ch. 8) have quite different reasons for the non-appearance of the sign.

796   An unusual use of *Goddys toure* for the temple, but particularly appropriate if the scaffold is doubling for heaven. Cf. *Goddys hous* ll. 299, 370, 452.

798–801   Joseph deliberately over-does his age and decrepitude, or is panicked into it.

802   This quatrain continues the rhyme-scheme of ll. 772–5 and in the *Mary Play* the two may have formed a single octave, perhaps divided in two by a stage direction.

803   The second prayer occurs in *Pseudo-Matthew* (ch. 8) and *Legenda* (p. 589). In the former the advice is given by an angel. In the *Legenda* it is implied but not stated that it is the Voice which again replies. The words of the Voice are very close to the passage in the *Legenda*. There is a distinction between pageant (the Angel) and *Mary* (Vox) material; see above, note to l. 713.

808–9   Joseph's hesitation is here drawn out longer than in any of the early versions, linking with his later reluctance to accept the divine decision.

810   Once again the playwright uses an extra-metrical line for colloquial effect. In *Pseudo-Matthew* the high priest shouts loudly at Joseph 'Veni Ioseph et accipe virgam tuam, quia tu expectaris' ('Come, Joseph, and receive your rod, for we are waiting for you'), ch. 8.

819   *sterrys seven*. The seven planets; see note on l. 151.

820–1   'that he receives truly this poor offering, that is so insignificant, in his honour.'

827   'As it pleases you.'

828   The precise significance of this line is not clear. If it originally followed from l. 814, without the intervening thirteener, it could have been a continued protest by Joseph suddenly overtaken by the event of the flowering rod. As it is it seems as though he tries to offer the rod and finds it too heavy. As he does so, it flowers. The interpolation of the pageant stanza has upset the sense.

831   The *Mary Play* material may well have run straight from this line to l. 871.

831sd   'And they all cry: . . .'

835   The sign, since it is described in a thirteener, accords with the angel's words.

850   *rave* in the sense of 'go wild with passion, act passionately'; cf. *rage* at l. 870.

851ff   The traditional lore of the unequal marriage is made use of skilfully, as it frequently is in the Mary and Joseph relationship in the plays. See also Appendix 2, especially ll. 49–56. Joseph's reluctance to accept Mary appears in *Protevangelium* and *Pseudo-Matthew* but his objections are quite different. It does not appear in the *Nativity of Mary* or the *Legenda*.

855   'If I rebuke her she will patch my coat, trick me and find fault with me.' The first image is perhaps connected with the proverb 'a little clout may (make) loathly a large piece' (Whiting C321), in the sense of: 'she will make things worse'. It may on the other hand simply mean 'she will falsely conceal her wrong-doing [the tear in his coat]'. The second image takes the commonplace *bleren eies* 'to delude, trick' and enlivens it by attaching the biblical mote and beam to it, thus: '[she will] make me bleary-eyed [so as not to see what is going on *or* with weeping] and pick out a speck' pretending that that is what is wrong but implying the existence of the beam in her own eye (cf. Matthew vii, 3).

871   It is worth noting that this quatrain continues the rhyme scheme of the last *Mary Play* stanza (see l. 831). It is quite possible that the two quatrains formed a single octave perhaps divided by a stage direction. As it is, the reluctance of Joseph concludes with ll. 862–3 and then without warning starts up again at l. 877. The business of the flowering rod is also repeated (ll. 835 and 872).

872–3   The rod is described now as blossoming *and* with a dove sitting on it; cf. the earlier descriptions in ll. 724 and 835.

874sd   'And here let them sing: Blessed be the holy Trinity.' *Benedicta sit beata Trinitas* is primarily a sequence for masses of the Holy Trinity; see above, note to 97sd. The Sarum Use contains a Trinity mass as the nuptial mass but substitutes *Alma chorus domini* for *Benedicta* as the sequence (*Missal* 835*–8*). York however retains it (*Manual* 30). There is therefore appropriateness both to thanksgiving to the Trinity and to the coming betrothal in this sequence.

875–6   The bishop's words are reminiscent of the marriage service in English: 'Wil tow have þis woman to þin wif, and loue here, and worschipe here, and holde hire and kepe here . . .' (Maskell I, p. 53), but it is difficult to know how familiar this would have been since normally in service books only the vows of the man and woman are given, and were presumably delivered, in English. These vows do however have similarities with the priest's words (*Missal* 831*–2*, Maskell I, pp. 56–7). Joseph's rejection is that much more striking if following words that were recognisably those of the marriage service of the church.

877   This rejection is from the *Mary Play* and is natural as a first reaction. Coming after the previous rejection and agreement (ll. 841–70) it seems awkward and repetitive. The adaptability of theatrical presentation is such, however, that handled skilfully the repeated rejections of Joseph become a naturally developing series culminating in near panic as the solemnity of the marriage is brought home. In both versions, pageant and Marian, Joseph's obedience to God is stressed (ll. 862–3 and 881–2).

883   The lay-out of the versified marriage service in the manuscript allows for Joseph repeating the bishop's words in short sections. The version in the Sarum Missal is as follows: 'I N. take the N. to my weddyd wyfe, to have & to holde, for better for wurs, for rycher for porer; in sykenesse & in helth tyll deth vs departe, & therto I plyght the my trouth' (*Missal* 831*). The play version is sufficiently similar to have the ring of truth and reality.

893–4   *Missal* 833*: 'With thys ryng I the wedde and tys gold and siluer I the geue; and wyth my body I te worscype, and wyth all my wordly catell I the honore'. Much of the normal wording is, of course, inappropriate.

900   Cf. ll. 865–6.

903   Both *terme-tyme and tyde* means no more than 'always', but it is not an alliterative tag that I have found elsewhere.

905   *Þe hyʒe names of oure Lord* refers to the following sequence, *Alma chorus domini*, which consists entirely of names of God.

907   'Now let the gracious choir sing the highest names of the Lord'. *Alma chorus* is the sequence for the nuptial mass in all uses but York. It is also the sequence of the mass on Thursday and Saturday of the week following Pentecost (*Missal* 439–40 and 450), and is used as an office hymn (*Breviary* II 236, III 618).

910   In *Pseudo-Matthew* five maidens are sent with Mary: Rebecca (Reutha, Retram), Sephora (Sophera, Sephiphora), Susanna, Abigea, Cael (Agabel, Zahel); (ch. 8). In the *Nativity of Mary* and the *Legenda* there are seven, unnamed. The vernacular versions have various combinations of these. See the note to ll. 768–771 in Lydgate's *Life of Our Lady*, p. 676. In the *Mary Play*, from which this stanza comes, the maidens mentioned were presumably the five given to Mary at her Presentation in the Temple (see ll. 481–4).

916   The blessing is extra-metrical, cf. ll. 323–5.

921–4   A reintroduction of the maidens as something new. Again, this is repeated because the first is in a Marian section (l. 910) and the second in pageant material.

926–8   For the names see the note to l. 910 above.

943   Joachim and Anne have remained in the background for most of the

episode but now come forward for their final farewells. None of their speeches is in Mary material and it may be that they did not appear in the *Mary Play*.

947–8   The formal farewell reaches its height in Gabriel's farewell to Mary (ll. 1376–9 and 1396–1403).

984–5   In none of the early versions does Mary remain in the temple as she appears to do here. It is of course possible that there is missing *Mary Play* text in which she returned to her parents' house, cf. ll. 910–13 above.

986   This emphasis on poverty is not in the sources though it is traditional.

990–3   The reference to Christ's choosing poverty is odd since strictly speaking Joseph at this point does not know; unless it merely means that God has chosen a poor man to be the husband of the virgin devoted to his temple.

996   In the play Mary remains in the temple having already taken leave of her parents (ll. 974–81). In the earlier versions she either returns home to her parents with the maidens from the temple (*Nativity of Mary* and *Legenda*), or she goes with Joseph and the maidens to his house (*Protevangelium* and *Pseudo-Matthew*). See note to ll. 984–5 above.

1002–25   This section in praise of the psalter seems to be original, or rather perhaps draws together material from a wide range of current teaching. *The Myroure of Oure Ladye* (pp. 36–7) has a section on the value of the psalms, drawn from Augustine, but it only occasionally overlaps with this. Cassiodorus too draws on Augustine (*PL* 70, 9–11). The *Myroure* makes the general point (again drawn from Augustine) that all the Old and New Law is contained in the Psalms.

In the *Meditationes* it is said that Mary was better read in the psalms than anyone ('in carminibus Davidicis elegantior', p. 114). The psalter was frequently used in the Middle Ages as a book of private devotions, and the psalms are basic to the liturgy.

1009   Cf. 'the propertye of these psalmes deuoutly songe is to dryue away fendes & all euel spirites', *Myroure*, p. 36.

1016–17   Cf. 'An other cause is for example of penaunce & hope of mercy to synners, whyle we se that Dauyd whome our lorde chose after hys oune harte felle so depe in synne, & by penaunce rose agen to so moche mercy and grace', *Myroure*, p. 36.

1019   Cf. 'For oure lorde god hathe made a drynke by hys seruante Dauid whiche is swete to taste . . . This drinke is these psalmes, that ar swetely harde when they ar songe. . . .' *Myroure*, p. 37; and 'Dona michi, queso, deus meus, vt per hec sacrosancta verba psalterii celesti melle anima mea saginetur' ('Grant me, I ask, my God, that through these sacred words of the heavenly psalter, my soul may be fed with honey') *Rolle*, I, p. 398.

1028   'Thou hast blessed thy land, o Lord'. Mary in her reading reaches Psalm lxxxiv, 1, the psalm containing the verse which is the basis for the Parliament of Heaven which follows, *Misericordia et veritas obviaverunt sibi etc*. Verse 1 also interweaves the liturgy at the end of the period after Trinity Sunday with that of the beginning of Advent, and so again appropriately leads to the Annunciation, the advent of Christ; see *Missal* 24.

Significant readings of this sort are used also of Mary at the Annunciation, when she is sometimes said to have been 'perauenture redynge the prophecie of ysaie touchynge the Incarnacioun', Love, p. 25.

1032   The hiring of a house seems to be unique to this play, though it could be seen as part of the preparation of the 'bridal' referred to in Cursor Mundi, ll. 10825–32.

1037   After this line the journey to Nazareth with the maidens takes place; see note to l. 996.

1042   The nine months is used here as it is (though more elegantly) at the beginning of The Winter's Tale (I, ii, 1–3) to introduce the idea of pregnancy; though there it indicates the presence and here the absence of the possible father.

1056   conclaue, an unusual word in English, is familiar from the fourteenth-century Latin carol of the Annunciation, Angelus ad virginem. It is possible that like the psalm at l. 1028 this looks forward to the Annunciation. It is, however, also used of the sealed tomb in the N. town Proclamation (1. 419). Vita Christi quotes Bernard's use of the word describing the room in which Mary was at the Annunciation, 'in thalamo et conclavi domunculae suae' (p. 20). The basic idea is of a lockable, hence a private, room.

1060–91   In the manuscript an older arrangement shows through in Contemplacio's speech in the 1us before l. 1060 and the 2 to the left of l. 1076, both in red. It seems that the speech was originally divided between two speakers representing either the prophets and patriarchs or the angels and archangels. For the former, see Alan J. Fletcher, 'The "Contemplacio" Prologue to the N-Town play of the Parliament of Heaven', Notes and Queries 27 (1980), pp. 111–12; and for the latter, see W. W. Greg, Bibliographical and Textual Problems in the English Miracle Plays (London 1914), p. 125 and footnote 1. There are good arguments on both sides but the scale seems to tip in favour of the patriarchs and prophets.

1060   The length of time that mankind had been in hell was calculated variously. The Meditationes has 'more than the space of five thousand years' ('ultra spatium quinque millium annorum'), p. 511; the York Harrowing of Hell XXXVII has 'Foure thowsande and sex hundereth ƺere' (l. 39); the Charter of the Abbey of the Holy Ghost has 'foure þousande sex hundred & foure ƺer' (Rolle I, p. 345). The close correspondence between the Charter and the play was noted by Hemingway, English Nativity Plays, pp. 239–41. This is the first of the signs of a close relationship between the two.

For other computations see Legenda, p. 40; Vita Christi, p. 10; Stanzaic Life ll. 57–61, drawing on Higden's Polychronicon; Gospel of Nicodemus II ch. 12, and Hemingway's note (pp. 242–3).

1064   The emphasis is from the beginning on the mercy of God.

1067   It is unlikely that this line is also intended to be the words of Isaiah. They are certainly contained in ll. 1068–9.

1068–9   Isaiah lxiv, 1 'Utinam dirumpere caelos et descenderes'; Charter, p. 347, 'wolde god, he seyd, þou woldest bresten heuene & come adoon'.

1070   The length of Christ's life is the same in the Charter (p. 345), but the age was traditional.

1071–2 The bread and wine of the Eucharist, see *Vita Christi*, p. 675. Christ's death on the cross was a ratification of the institution of the sacrament at the Last Supper.

1073 Christ's death on the cross is seen as the only way of salvation for man. Contemplacio, as a character both within and outside the limits of the action, already displays knowledge of the solution to the problem of the salvation, in the narrative context of a prayer for a solution to be found.

1076–7 Jeremiah xlv, 3 'Ve mihi misero, quoniam addidit dominus dolorem dolori meo'; *Charter*, p. 347, 'wo me wrecche, he seiþ, þat god haþ eked more sorowe to my sorowe'.

1076ff A number of alterations by a later hand seem to be a half-hearted attempt to up-date or clarify the passage; see textual notes.

1083 Traditionally the fall of man was a result of the deceit of the devil. Christ coming to earth as man and thereby concealing his godhead was often seen as a fittingly deceitful reply; see for example *Piers Plowman* B XVIII, ll. 355–8.

1084 This line begins a series of translations of quotations from Jeremiah and Lamentations which also appear in the *Charter*. Whereas they are often given in full in the *Charter*, in the play they frequently appear as extracts only.

1084–5 Cf. Jeremiah ix, 1; *Charter*, pp. 347–8.

1088 Cf. Lamentations ii, 13; *Charter*, p. 348.

1089 Cf. Lamentations v, 16; *Charter*, p. 348.

1091 The repeated cries of the suppliants again become a feature of the play echoing the cries of Joachim and Anne and the bishop (ll. 165 and 830).

1092sn The *Virtutes* or Powers, together with the angels and archangels, form the lowest of the hierarchies of the angels in the Gregorian order. The nine orders were divided into three hierarchies: seraphim, cherubim and thrones; principates, potestates and dominations; powers, archangels and angels. This is the arrangement in *On the Properties* (I, pp. 70–84). They are also described in *Legenda* (St Michael, pp. 644–6), where the care of angels for the salvation of man is described (650). Their 'offyse' is ministering to man and it is the angels in the *Meditationes* who plead for him (p. 511). Here the name, *Virtutes*, seems to be used as representative of the whole hierarchy, and to refer to three speakers, one from each of the orders.

1099 See note to l. 1091. Perhaps the three speakers were intended to divide here and then build cumulatively to the end of the line.

1100–3 Lucifer, who fell from heaven through his sin and became a devil in hell, then tempted man to sin. One difference between the two was that man repented and Lucifer did not; see *Þe Deuelis Perlament* ll. 345–8 in *Hymns to the Virgin and Christ*, ed. F. J. Furnivall (EETS OS 24, 1868), p. 52; *Middle English Sermons*, p. 315.

1106–7 The creation of man was usually seen as a means of restoring the full complement of heaven; see *Meditationes* 'ut nobis ex ipso nostrarum contingeret restauratio ruinarum' ('so that for us from him [man] the restoration of our fall may occur'), p. 511; and Augustine, *Enchiridion* ch. 29.

1108–10   Psalm xi, 6. Augustine in his commentary on the psalm says that it was spoken by God the Father promising to send his son, and is here clearly a sign of his initial move towards mercy (I, p. 103). 'By reason of the misery of the needy, and the groans of the poor, now will I arise'. The following lines (ll. 1111–13) translate the Latin.

1114   Much is made of the need for reconciliation in the *Charter*, not just between God and man, but between all parts of creation (p. 351). The idea of the *right* time is in Bernard (col. 387), and *Meditationes* (p. 511) where it is clearly associated with Galatians iv, 4–5, 'But when the fulness of time (*plenitudo temporis*) was come, God sent his Son, made of a woman, made under the law: That he might redeem them who were under the law: that we might receive the adoption of sons'.

1115–17   The naming of three petitioners perhaps derives from the original division of Contemplacio's speech, and to some extent supports the association with patriarchs, prophets and angels.

1118   *exorte*. This use is the only one quoted in *MED*. The word derives from the Latin p.p. *exortus*. *Exortum est in tenebris* (from Psalm cxi, 4) is an antiphon for second vespers at the Nativity (*Breviary* I cxciv) 'To the righteous a light is risen up in darkness: the Lord is merciful, and compassionate and just', and the first two words are used in the macaronic Christmas carol 'Nowel syng we bothe al and sum' (Greene no. 29). It is possible that the word occurred to the playwright's mind because of that kind of association with Christ's birth and the coming of grace.

1119–1250   The debate of the four daughters of God derives ultimately from an Annunciation sermon of St Bernard (*PL* 183, 383–90). It is used at the beginning of the *Meditationes* and the *Vita Christi* and frequently elsewhere. The closest parallel to its use in the play is in the *Charter*, though it is closer in its use of the same biblical quotations than in its wording. See Introduction, p. 18 and Hemingway, *English Nativity Plays*, pp. 238–47. The fullest study of the debate is in Hope Traver, *The Four Daughters of God* Bryn Mawr dissertations (Philadelphia, 1907).

1123–4   *Charter*, p. 349, 'þou seydest þat what-tyme þat man ete of þat appul, þat he shulde dieye & gon to helle'.

1126   This sounds like a statement in logic of the kind that Augustine refers to in *Enchiridion* ch. 14, 'Accordingly in the case of these contraries which we call good and evil, the rule of the logicians, that two contraries cannot be predicated at the same time of the same thing, does not hold' (p. 184). Here, of course, it is stressing that God's nature cannot contradict itself.

1127   *Charter*, p. 349, '*Quia veritas domini manet in eternum* for whi goddys treuþe schulde dwellen eueremore wiþouten ende' (Psalm cxvi, 2).

1133   *Charter*, p. 349, '*Ecce enim veritatem dilexisti*, . . . þou hast ȝit eueremore loued wele me þat am þi douȝtre' (Psalm l, 8).

1135–6   *Charter*, p. 350, '*O pater misericordiarum & deus totius consolacionis, qui consolaris nos in omni tribulacione nostra*' (2 Corinthians i, 3–4). The play is closer to the Bible than to the *Charter*'s translation, and in the word *counsell* may have been influenced by the sound of the original.

1139 Emphasis on man's repentance; see note to ll. 1100–3.

1141–2 'It seems to me there should be no objection [to the granting of their request] since their prayers are made in so exceptional a way.'

1145 *Charter*, p. 350, '*Quoniam dixisti, in eternum seruabo illi misericordiam*, forwhy, scho [Mercy] seyde, þou seydest þat þou schuldest kepe to hym þi mercy wiþouten ende . . .' (Psalm lxxxviii, 29).

1147 'My truth and my mercy with him . . .' (Psalm lxxxviii, 25). Not quoted in *Charter*.

1153 *Charter*, p. 350, '*Quia iustus dominus & iusticias dilexit*, for whi, lord, scho [Justice] seiþ, þou art riȝtful & þou louest riȝtfulnesse' (Psalm x, 8).

1154–5 The idea that because God is infinite so man's punishment should also be infinite is not an argument that appears in Bernard, *Meditationes*, or the other English versions. It is implied in *Charter* (pp. 349–50) in Truth's words and Righteousness' (p. 350). It is picked up and answered by Mercy later (l. 1168).

1156 This line is perhaps based on '*Dominum qui se genuit dereliquit, & oblitus est dei creatoris sui*' (cf. Deuteronomy xxxii, 15), as it is quoted in the *Charter* (p. 350).

1157 Grosseteste lays stress on the free will of man's choosing to serve the devil, and of its legal results (*Castle* ll. 241–54, 401–8). Augustine discusses the position of the bond-slave in *Enchiridion* ch. 30.

1159 Cf. Genesis iii, 5 'scit enim Deus quod in quocumque die comederitis ex eo, aperientur oculi vestri, et eritis sicut dii scientes bonum et malum.'

1162 *Charter*, p. 350, '*Quia iusticia eius manet in seculum seculi*' (Psalm cx, 3).

1165 '[Mankind] of necessity can never make satisfactory amends [on his own]'; cf. Augustine *Enchiridion* ch. 30, p. 197.

1167 Mercy in the *Charter* (p. 350) responds by stressing the necessity of God remaining merciful, because if he did not he would be unjust and untrue to himself and therefore Right and Truth would also be lost. The argument here takes a rather different line.

1168 Cf. ll. 1154–5.

1169 *Charter*, p. 350, '*Quia misericordia eius super omnia opera eius*, for why only goddis mercy is abouen al his werkes' (Psalm cxliv, 9).

1170 'Though he abandoned God by sinning against him, yet he never abandoned his belief in him.' As the devils also are said to believe in God, the distinction here may depend upon that made by Augustine between believing that he is God which the devils also do, and believing *in* him, that is loving him, which men only do (Augustine *Commentary on the Psalms* (Psalm 130) VI, p. 73). See also *Lay Folks' Catechism* ll. 245–53 and note.
    Mercy is here taking up the words of Righteousness at ll. 1156–7.

1171–2 Mercy finally takes up Righteousness' demonstration of man's presumption and answers it. Her final point, that man cannot make amends (ll. 1165–6), is answered by the Son, but obliquely (ll. 1200–10), and taken up in the Council of the Trinity when Righteousness reiterates the idea in different words (ll. 1223–4).

1174   *Charter*, p. 350, '*Et misericordia eius ab eterno & vsque in eternum*, & goddis mercy was wiþouten begynnyng & schal ben wiþouten endyng' (Psalm cii, 17).

1175–6   Cf. *Meditationes*, p. 512, 'Parcite vobis a verbis istis; virtutum non est honesta contentio' ('Refrain from these words; the strife of virtues is not proper'), quoting from Bernard. The Latin words have clearly affected the English.

1177   *Charter*, p. 351, '*Pax domini exsuperat omnem sensum* &c., Goddis pees ouergoþ eueriche maner witt' (Philippians iv, 7).

1178–9   *Charter*, p. 351, 'Þouȝ it be so, sche seiyt, þat Truþe seiþ a grete skile . . . neuerþeles me þenkeþ þat Mercy seiþ alþerbest . . .'

1180–2   Cf. *Charter*, p. 351, 'for why as longe as man soule is in helle, þer schal ben discord bytwene ȝou þre . . . so þat pees schal ben amongys ȝou forsaken. Þere schulde also, ȝif man were stille in helle, ben a discord bytwene god & man . . .'

1183–6   Cf. *Charter*, p. 351, '& þerfore doþ after my conseil, seide Pees, & praye we alle to-geders to god þat is prince of pees . . .'

1185   'Place both your arguments in [the hands of] our Lord.'

1186   *Meditationes* refers to the Son as *Rex* but Love calls him 'souereyne wisdome' (p. 16).

1188   Cf. *Charter*, p. 351, '& ordeyne sich a weye þat he miȝt kepen vs stille alle foure . . .'

1196   l. 1186 begins the shift from God's wisdom, to wisdom as an attribute of the Son, and hence to another name for him, as here.

1197   The Trinity is undoubtedly on the stage but it is uncertain at what point they appear. The debate begins before God the Father (and makes reference to him) and is now handed over to him for judgement. It seems possible that the Father is only at this moment joined by the Son and Holy Spirit, which gives added point to Peace's remark 'here is vnyte'. God has been present all along but he is now perceived differently, to prepare for the Incarnation. It is however possible that all could have been present from l. 1108 (or even earlier) onwards. 'Unity' as well as 'Trinity' is used for God in *Knyghthode and Bataile* (ed. R. Dyboski and Z. M. Arend, EETS OS 201, 1936) ll. 24–6.

1199   *Charter*, p. 351, 'þe fadur of heuene . . . seyde *Ego cogito cogitaciones pacis & non affliccionis* &c., I þenke, he seyde, þouȝtis of pees & not of wickednesse' (Jeremiah xxix, 11). The play parts company with the *Charter* here mainly because there the Council of the Trinity precedes the debate of the four daughters.

1200–6   The summing-up and the solution is ultimately drawn from the *Meditationes*, generally quoting Bernard; 'Haec dicit; Perii, si Adam non moriatur. Et haec dicit: Perii, si non misericordiam consequatur. Fiat mors bona, et habeant utraeque quod petunt' ('This one says: I perish if Adam

does not die; and this one says: I perish if he is not granted mercy. Let there
be a good death, and they may each have what they seek'), p. 512.

It is here treated somewhat differently, partly at least because of the
accumulation of material from other treatments of the episode. If Adam
(man) had not died then God's justice and truth would have been compromised because of the warning given to Adam and Eve in paradise. On the other
hand if God did not release Adam (man) then his mercy would not exist and
his peace would be eternally broken. The idea of the second death is brought
in prematurely at l. 1204 to balance mention of Adam's death. The death is
then defined in ll. 1207–8.

1206   The balancing of death with death is picked up again in l. 1212. The
episode in *Vices and Virtues* is rounded off by a series of balances of this kind
(ed. F. Holthausen, EETS OS 89, 1888), pp. 117–19.

1207–12   Cf. Augustine *Enchiridion* ch. 49, pp. 210–11.

There is no mention at this point of the love which makes the victim
willing to undertake the 'mors bona' in *Meditationes* (and Bernard), p. 512.
But see below, ll. 1220–1.

1214   Cf. *Meditationes*, p. 512, 'Placuit sermo' ('these words pleased').

1215–22   Between this and the previous line the search of heaven and earth
is carried out. The search is described in *Meditationes* (p. 512) and this
description is paraphrased in the speeches of Truth and Mercy.

1216   *in sothe*. Truth again plays on her own name, as at l. 1191.

1216–17   *Meditationes*, p. 512, 'Nemo mundus a sorde, nec infans unius
diei' ('No one is pure of sin, not the infant of one day'; cf. Job xiv, 4–5 in the
Septuagint).

1219–21   *Meditationes*, p. 512, 'Sed a misericordia perlustratur caelum, et
neminem invenit, qui sufficientem ad hoc habeat charitatem' ('And the
heaven was passed through by Mercy and she found no one who possessed
love sufficient for this').

1223–6   Of all the sources only Love's translation gives Righteousness
(*Justicia*) a part to play. Mercy searches heaven, Truth searches the region
between heaven and the clouds, 'Riȝtwisnesse went doun to Erthe and
souȝte among the hiȝe hilles and in to þe depe pytte of helle/whether there
were eny man that myȝte take this good and innocent deth; but there was
none founden clene of synne/no/not the child of one dayes birthe'
(pp. 17–18). Rather than being influenced by this, however, it seems more
likely that the playwright wanted a speech for Justice to give one each to the
four daughters, and so made use of the remarks in the *Meditationes* which
follow the report of Mercy's unsuccessful search: 'Omnes enim servi sumus,
et qui cum bene fecerimus, dicere debemus illud Lucae: Quia inutiles servi
sumus . . . qui majorem charitatem haberet, ut animam suam pro servis
inutilibus poneret . . .' ('We are all servants, who when we do good ought to
say this with Luke: "that we are unprofitable servants" . . . who has the
greater love that he will lay down his soul for unprofitable servants . . .'),
p. 512.

1227   *Meditationes*, p. 512, 'Non est qui faciat bonum, non est usque ad
unum' (Psalm xiii, 3; lii, 4), which is understood here as Love understands it

'Wete ȝe not wele/that the prophete that seide there is none founden that may done good; afterward he putteth to more and seith/til it come to oon: this oon may be he that ȝaf the sentence forsaide of mannis sauacioun' (p. 18).

This is the only use of the spelling *god* for 'good'. It is possible that the scribe thought the word was 'God'.

1229   *Meditationes*, p. 512, 'Sed qui dedit consilium, feret auxilium' ('But he who gave the advice, let him bring the help').

1231–2   *Meditationes*, p. 512, 'Paenitet me fecisse hominem. Poenitentiam me agere oportet pro homine quem creavi' ('It pains me to have made man' [Genesis vi, 7]. 'It is necessary for me to do penance for man whom I have made'). The verse from Genesis is frequently associated with God's anger against man; see Block p. 38, l. 105 and *York* VIII, ll. 15–16.

1233   The 'counsel of þe holy trinite' has already met in the *Charter* (pp. 348–9) before the debate.

1235–7   Wisdom was the quality normally associated with the Son, power with the Father, love/goodness/gentleness with the Holy Spirit; see *Religious Pieces*, pp. 28–9, 47–8, 63; Block p. 181, ll. 89–92. Love has 'the persone of the fader is propurly dredeful and myȝty; the persone of the sone is al wyse and witty; and the persone of holy gost moste benigne and goodly' (p. 18). Cf. *Wisdom* ll. 1–16 (*Macro Plays*, p. 114), and ll. 462–4 above.

1236   Cf. Love's remark that as man has forfeited his bliss by 'vnwitte and foly', he should be saved by 'sothefast wisdome' (p. 19). See also Christ's explanation in the *Doctors in the Temple* pageant (Block p. 182, ll. 115–28); and l. 1159 above, and note.

1237   Wisdom as an attribute of God finally merges in the play with the Son as a person of the Trinity.

1239   The idea originates with Anselm *Cur Deus homo* 'and if God only *can*, and man only *ought* to make this satisfaction, then necessarily One must make it who is both God and man' (*Documents of the Christian Church*, ed. Henry Bettenson (OUP, 1943), p. 194). *Cursor Mundi* has:

> Man for man to suffer pine,
> Godd to quell þe wiþerwin;
> Man to dei, godd for to rise,
> Moght nan tak elles þis emprise.   (ll. 9799–9802)

The *Charter* makes use of the idea very much in Anselm's words (p. 349).

1240   The idea of humanity as clothing is so common as to make it unlikely that the image is still a living one here; see, for a similar example, *Castle* l. 547. *Piers Plowman* makes complicated use of it in the arms that Jesus wears, *humana natura* (*Piers Plowman* B XVIII, ll. 22–6).

1243   Cf. Athanasian Creed v. 23, 'Spiritus Sanctus a Patre et Filio: non factus nec creatus nec genitus, sed procedens' (*Breviary* II 47); 'The holi gost cometh bothe of ye fader and of ye sone: not maad ne maad of nought but comyng forth' (Maskell III, p. 258).

1245   Cf. *Religious Pieces*, p. 28 'Lufe [ordaynes vs] to þe Haly Gaste, till whaym es appropyrde gudnes'; p. 48 'And forþi þat þis worde Gaste sownnes sumwhate into fellenes, For-þi es swetnes, lufe, and gudenes appropirde to þe Haly Gaste'.

1249–50   Psalm lxxxiv, 11. It is the text of Bernard's Annunciation sermon and the basis of the debate in heaven. It is quoted in almost every version of it.

1250sd   'And here they shall all kiss each other.'

1251–74   God's instructions, which in the *Meditationes* are all delivered by the Father, are here divided between the three persons of the Trinity; no doubt to demonstrate the point made in the *Meditationes* and elsewhere, that the work of the incarnation was undertaken by the whole Trinity. 'Scire namque debes, quod excelsum incarnationis opus totius Trinitatis fuit, licet sola persona Filii fuerit incarnata' ('For you must know that the highest work of the incarnation involved the whole of the Trinity, even though only the person of the Son was incarnate'), p. 514. See also *Vita Christi*, pp. 22–3.

1251–8   This speech is very closely modelled on Luke i, 26–7, which perhaps accounts for the slightly awkward syntax; see Introduction, p. 19.

1253   Mary has returned to Nazareth; see l. 1035 above.

1251   'God' seems the most likely reading despite the considerable awkwardness of delivery, not only because of the Latin, *a Deo*, but also because 'good' (adj.) is invariably spelt *gode* or *good* in the plays (see l. 1227 for the single spelling *god* for the noun 'good').

1255   *se* often translates the Latin *ecce* (as below l. 1318), and though there is no *ecce* in the source, it seems likely that the meaning 'lo' is what is required here.

1259   A translation of *Ave* (= *A ve*, lit. 'from woe') *gracia plena*; see note to l. 1282–3.

1261–2   Cf. *Meditationes*, p. 514, 'Sed nec sic volavit, quin praeveniretur a Deo, et sanctam ibi Trinitatem invenit, quae praevenit nuntium suum' ('But he did not fly quickly enough to arrive before God, and he found the Holy Trinity there before its messenger'). In the play the Trinity does not descend until Mary has consented (1355sd).

1263–4   Cf. *Meditationes*, p. 514, 'et dic ei, quod filius meus concupivit speciem suam, et sibi eam elegit in matrem' ('and say to her, that my son has desired her beauty and chosen her as his mother').

1265–6   Cf. *Legenda*, p. 216, the third reason for sending Gabriel, 'Quia enim incarnatio non tantum faciebat ad reparationem humani lapsus, sed etiam ad reparationem ruinae angelicae' ('Because the Incarnation was not made only to restore the fall of man but also to restore the angelic fall').

1267–74   The Holy Spirit's speech is derived mainly from the forthcoming conversation between Gabriel and Mary. Only perhaps the stress on unity might be derived from the *Meditationes*.

1275–8   The speed of angels' flight is commented on in *On the Properties*: 'Peyntoures peyntiþ angelis with feþires and winges, to tokene here swift passinge and meuynge' (I, p. 81).

1279   It is difficult to be sure whether the playwright intended *Maria* to be included, but in view of his later comments on the greeting, it seems more likely that he did not (see ll. 1563–6). Its inclusion was probably a slip by the scribe and possibly corrected by him.

1280–1   Gabriel speaks and translates the first part of the greeting, then gives a translation of the second part, *benedicta tu in mulieribus* (Luke i, 28), followed by commentary on the whole.

1282–3   The two commonest plays made upon the greeting: *Ave* as the reversal of the name *Eva*, and the interpretation *A ve* (see note to l. 1259 above). The three are neatly joined here. For some examples of *Ave/Eva* see Hemingway, p. 248 (note to l. 217). The carol with the refrain '*Ave fitt ex Eva*' ('*Ave* is made from *Eva*') puts it in its popular form (Greene, no. 238); *Myroure* (pp. 235–6 and 295) and *Missal* (763★), '*et ex Eva formans ave/Evae verso nomine*', shows its use in a liturgical context.

For *Ave/a ve* see for example *Horae* p. 136 and note 5, and *Reynes* p. 300; and for both, *Missal* 670 and *Vita Christi* p. 20.

1284–91   Gabriel's whole speech is an ingenious linking of all the parts of the greeting through a series of expositions: *Ave*, 1284, leading to *gracia plena*, 1286, leading to *Dominus tecum*, 1289, and finally to *benedicta tu in mulieribus*, 1291. The *Myroure* has a similar though not nearly so ingenious commentary (pp. 78–9).

1292–8   Mary appears to be worried by three things: first, she is puzzled by the strangeness of the message; second, she is perturbed that the angel is in the form of a man; third, she is confused as a humble person at the great honour conveyed in the greeting. The first and third of these are normal comments on her behaviour, but the second is unusual. The *Nativity of Mary*, the *Legenda* and the *Meditationes* all say that she is used to the sight of angels – as indeed she is in the play – and that it is the unusualness of the message that perturbs her. *Vita Christi*, quoting Chrysostom, says that though used to the sight of angels, Gabriel frightened her by his splendour (p. 21). Orm, however, makes the same point as the play, that she was used to the sight of angels but was nevertheless worried 'forr þatt he comm/Inn aness weress hewe' ('because he came in the form of a man', ll. 2181–2).

The difficulty with a play is to know how the distinction was made. Was it made in costume between the albs of the earlier visits and the feathers and tights or bare legs of this one? The latter is not unparalleled pictorially as a costume for Gabriel, but it is certainly not common. Most appropriate in time and place are the late fifteenth-century (nave) and early sixteenth-century (transepts) roof bosses in Norwich cathedral; see C. J. P. Cave, *Roof Bosses in Medieval Churches* (Cambridge 1948) pl. 158, and 'The Roof Bosses in the Transepts of Norwich Cathedral Church' *Archaeologia* 83 (1933) plates XVI (9) and XIX (3 & 6), and M. D. Anderson, *Drama and Imagery in English Medieval Churches* (Cambridge 1963) pl. 10 (b–d). It is, as all commentators are agreed, her humility which is disturbed above all.

1300   Commentators frequently mentioned the homeliness of Gabriel's first use of Mary's name to calm her perturbation (e.g. *Vita Christi* p. 21). The word *dred* is neatly picked up from Mary's speech.

1300–22   Very closely modelled on Luke i, 30–7. Expansions occur at ll. 1310–12 which (a) stress her vow of virginity and (b) ensure that the audience understands that she does not *doubt* the words of the angel as

Zacharias had done (see below ll. 1442–6). The commentators emphasise this and the *Legenda* compares Mary with Zacharias (pp. 218–19).

   Sanctum 'holy one' translated as *Holy Gost* (l. 1316) is a curious specifying rather than an expansion. It should perhaps be emended to 'holy one', since the scribe could easily have accidentally repeated *Holy Gost* from l. 1314.

1324–47   The play here departs from the gospel narrative to include the episode of the anxiety over Mary's reply. The *Legenda* (p. 219) quotes a short passage from one of Bernard's sermons on the *Missus est* (*PL* 183, 83), and Rosemary Woolf has drawn attention to the importance of another section of the sermon (*Mystery Plays*, pp. 167–8). It is upon this that the *Meditationes* account is based. But it is clearly Love's translation that the playwright draws upon, changing an invitation to meditate into an urgent plea to Mary herself. For Love's text compared with the play, see Block, p. lviii. This section was almost certainly an addition to the original play.

1326   The *Meditationes* and Love have 'Holy Trinity' here. Changing to *Holy Gost* brings it into line with ll. 1268 and 1314.

1328–31   Not in the sources and apparently premature in that Mary has not yet consented.

1330   *fraternyte*. Christ's taking on of human nature makes him the brother of man. Cf. *Meditationes*, p. 516, 'Hodie etiam factus est unus ex nobis, et frater noster' ('Today he is made one of us, and our brother').

1333   Does the playwright use *vertu* rather than *heuene* (Love) because of the *Virtutes* who make the first plea to God? Or is it merely for convenience of rhyme?

1337   Bernard 'patres scilicet tui' *PL* 183, 83 ('namely your own ancestors') perhaps suggested this line which is not in Love, but Bernard is talking of those in hell not those who are still alive.

1344   *persevere* 'recipient'.

1348–9   Cf. *Meditationes*, p. 515, 'Et qualiter etiam Domina stat timorate ac humiliter, facie pudorosa . . . Et, ut in suis revelationibus continetur, profunda devotione genuflexit, et junctis manibus dixit: Ecce ancilla . . .' ('And how the Lady stands fearfully and humbly, with modest look . . . And, as is said in her revelations, she knelt with deep devotion, and with clasped hands said: Behold the handmaid . . .').

1350–1   Luke i, 38.

1352–5   The repeated thanks here and the farewells later (ll. 1376–81, 1396–1401) are a common rhetorical device especially used in devotions to God and to Mary; see for example the sequences of the Mass for Mary on Christmas Day (*Missal*, 769*–75*).

   The hailing of Mary under her many titles is partly a result of the devotion to the *Ave Maria*. For particularly exuberant examples, see *Minor Poems* I, pp. 134–7, and *Lydgate* I, pp. 299–304. Comments on a number of her titles appear in *Vita Christi*, pp. 12–27.

1355   A commonplace image sometimes elaborated in view of Mary containing in her body Christ, the light of the world.

1355sd   Pictorial representations of the Annunciation commonly show a beam of light from God in heaven to Mary, often bearing a dove, occasionally a child. It seems most likely that the beams referred to here were stage properties representing light. The three beams are obviously symbolic of the unity of the Trinity, and the three persons of the Trinity standing at intervals seem to be intended to link heaven and Mary by means of the triple beams. The early sixteenth-century sculpture at Barnack, Northants., has the Trinity, the beams and Mary, but I know of no representation that pictures the scene quite in the way described here. For pictorial representations of the Annunciation see Gertrud Schiller, *Iconography of Christian Art* (London 1971), plates 65–124.

'And in this way all three [of the Trinity] enter her womb.'

1356–61   The *Legenda* and *Meditationes* both describe the perfection of Christ's body at the moment of conception. *Legenda*, p. 220, 'Statimque filius Dei in utero illius conceptus est perfectus Deus, perfectus homo et in ipsa prima die conceptionis tantae sapientiae ac potentiae exstitit, quantae in xxx anno fuit' ('Immediately the son of God was conceived in her womb, perfect God, perfect man, and in this first day of conception appeared as wise and strong as he was at thirty'); Love, 'and not as othere children/conceyued and born by kynde/ben schapen/membre after membre/and after þe soule shed in to the body; but anone at the firste instaunce he was ful schapen in all membres and alle hole man in body and soule; but neuertheles ful lite in quantite' (p. 31). See also *Life of St Anne* (3) ll. 437–48; *On the Properties* I, p. 298 (and pp. 294–7 for normal human development); and *Vita Christi* p. 25.

1363   The painlessness of the birth of Christ is a commonplace, that of the conception unusual. It may have been borrowed from the birth or perhaps simply refer to the gentleness of the act of conception. It is usually the absence of stain or corruption that is stressed; see *Legenda*, p. 218; Lydgate's *Life of Our Lady* II, ll. 521–7 and *Speculum Sacerdotale*, pp. 40–1.

1376–81   See note to ll. 1352–5. For *dowtere, modyr, sustyr, Meditationes* has 'filiam', 'matrem', 'sponsam', the normal group (cf. *Horae* p. 137). *pleyngefere* ('play-fellow') is unusual; *turtyl* ('turtle-dove'), *chawmere* and *bowre* are commonplace.

1381   'God's speedy messenger'. 'Angel' is interpreted as meaning 'messenger'; see Isidore VI, ii, 43 and VII, v, 1 and 6.

1385–7   *Myroure* refers to all the angels' foreknowledge of the Incarnation (p. 5); Love to Gabriel's alone, 'to whom as Seint Bernard seith/was made special reuelacioun of cristes incarnacioun' (p. 14).

1390   *mene passage.* The meaning may be 'in the intervening pregnancy' but a more general meaning, like 'time', seems more likely. 'my' for *mene* seems unlikely since there is no other use of the form in the N. town plays or recorded in *MED*; cf. Happé p. 665.

1396–1401   See note to ll. 1352–5. Another series of common epithets are contained in Gabriel's commendations.

1398   Cf. *Middle English Sermons* (p. 324) 'Þan she seid not, "Loo, here Goddes moder," or els, "Loo, here þe qwene of heven, ladie of erthe, and emperish of hell"; but mekely she answered and seid, "Loo, here þe hondemayde of oure Lord."'

1400   'By means of your body [that] bears the child [that] shall restore our happiness'; Kittredge's suggestion put forward by Manly (*Specimens* I, p. 93) seems the best solution, though not an ideal one.

1401   *modyr of mercy*, see note to l. 9.

1403   This seems to be an absolute phrase, 'heaven and earth united'.

1403sd   'With the angel singing this sequence: Hail Mary full of grace the Lord is with thee, fair virgin'; see *Missal* 871, 770★–1★.

 And þan Mary seyth has been deleted in red by the scribe since in the manuscript this episode is followed by *Joseph's Doubts about Mary*. None of the stage direction is underlined.

1404ff   For a discussion of this section see Introduction, pp. 3–4 and Appendix 2. It is also discussed in *Aspects of Early English Drama*, ed. Paula Neuss (Cambridge 1983), pp. 26–9.

1405–6   Mary is frequently associated with light but this brilliance is like a transfiguration. See Lydgate's *Life of Our Lady* I, ll. 281–7; *Myroure*, p. 213.

1409–10   The power for virtue of the appearance of Mary is commented on in Lydgate's *Life of Our Lady* I, ll. 288–94; *Myroure*, pp. 224–5; and Fabri I, pp. 512–13.

1413   *cosyn Elyzabeth*. In genealogies of Mary, Elizabeth is indeed her cousin, daughter of Anne's sister Ismeria/Emeria; see the *Legenda*, p. 586 and the note to l. 25 above. The phrase is taken from Luke i, 36 'Elisabeth cognata tua'.

1414   In *Meditationes*, too, Mary asks Joseph to accompany her (p. 516). He is not mentioned as going with her in Luke (i, 39).

1415   Mary's reason in *Meditationes* (p. 516) is 'ad congratulandum eidem, ac etiam serviendum' ('to rejoice with her and also to serve her').

1418–20   Luke's 'in montana' ('into the hills') is often taken to refer to a place name in the Middle Ages, as it seems to be here. Joseph's fifty-two miles is just one of many distances given – cf. *Meditationes* 'quatuordecim vel quindecim milliaria', p. 516. Love has 'sixty myle and fourtene or there aboute' (p. 37).

1422   *I wole*. 'go' understood.

1425   Luke's 'cum festinatione' (i, 39) was interpreted as Mary's desire not to be seen long in public; *Meditationes*, p. 516, *Legenda*, p. 885.

1429   Cf. *Rosarium* 'it [pilgrimage] ow to be done wiþ gret hastyng & deuoute' (p. 80, l. 10).

 helpyngys are presumably acts of charity of the sort described in the *Rosarium*, p. 80 ll. 23–7. I have not found the word used elsewhere in quite this way.

1430   The reading *i-cast* is uncertain. There are forms of the past participle with *i-* elsewhere in the manuscript (Block p. 149 *i-fownde* l. 90, *i-nvm* l. 83) but both here and in the *Passion Play* (I, l. 85, *i-schrewe*) the suggested forms are not past participles. Their unfamiliarity may have been a reason for the scribe to mis-read them.

1433sd   'And thus they shall cross around the *platea*.' This is the only place in the *Mary Play* where the *platea* or open playing-space is mentioned. See Introduction, pp. 20–1.

1434–46   Based on the *Legenda* (p. 357) occasionally translating, paraphrasing and re-ordering. Cf. Luke i, 5–23, and, for the organisation of the temple, 1 Paralipomenon xxiv. For a discussion of the speech, see 'A Reconsideration of Some Textual Problems in the N-town Manuscript (BL MS Cotton Vespasian D VIII)' *LSE* (1977), pp. 35–9.

1436   *after . . . apere* 'to be present according to the drawing of lots'. For the emendation of MS. *let* see Block, p. 116 and 'A Reconsideration', p. 36.

1437   *for here mynistracyon* 'because of their duties'.

1438   *havynge dominacyon* 'being in a position of authority'.

1442   'During his period of duty, at the time of the censing [of the altar].'

1445–6   'He, considering his unworthiness and age, did not believe [him], so, lo, the malady of dumbness sealed his lips.' For a discussion of the emendation of MS. *hese juge* or *jnge* see 'A Reconsideration', pp. 36–7.

1447   *Thei.* It is not clear who this refers to, but in *Cursor Mundi* (l. 10996) Zachary is taken home by the people waiting for the service in the temple.

1452   A translation of *Deus sit in principio*, a common prayer for God's blessing at the beginning of any enterprise.

1457–8   Mary's humility is deliberately re-emphasised by her continuing readiness to go to Elizabeth. Cf. *Legenda*, p. 885, 'ecce quomodo intravit superior ad minorem, domina ad servam, regina caeli et terrae ad famulam et ancillam' ('behold how the greater went to the lesser, the lady to the servant, the queen of heaven and earth to the attendant and hand-maid')

1460–1   Mary's colloquial and homely greeting is a further enacting of her humility.

1462–75   Expanded from Luke i, 41–5. For commentary on the episode see *Meditationes*, p. 516.

1464   *Meditationes*, p. 516, 'Cum enim Virgo salutavit Elisabeth, repletus est in utero Joannes Spiritu sancto, repleta est etiam et mater: nec prius repletur mater quam filius, sed filius repletus replet et matrem' ('When the Virgin greeted Elizabeth, John in her womb was filled with the Holy Spirit, and the mother was filled also; the mother was not filled before the son, but the son being filled, filled the mother'). It goes on to point out that it is Mary's *words* which confer the Holy Spirit.

1466   Pictorially the children are occasionally visible in their mother's wombs and John is shown kneeling. See Schiller, I, plates 16 and 133.

1469–70   'Benedicta tu inter mulieres et benedictus fructus ventris tui', Luke i, 42 – the second part of the *Ave Maria*. The first part of Elizabeth's blessing overlaps with the latter part of Gabriel's, 'Benedicta tu in mulieribus'. The latter is usual in devotional use; see below, l. 1564.

1476   Once again the speeches drop into the conversational and homely.

1481   Cf. ll. 1324–7, 1348–51 above.

1482   Cf. ll. 1356–9 above.

1488–9   The story of John's conception is in Luke i, 5–23; but see above ll. 1442–6. *hym* (l. 1489) is Zacharias. The reference hints at, but does not prove, his presence in the scene; see below, l. 1550.

1492   *For* seems as though it must mean 'therefore' and is perhaps a colloquially abbreviated form of it. *MED* gives no example of this and perhaps emendation to *Therfor* or *For þis þis holy psalme* is desirable; but cf. *fore* l. 1232.

1493–1537   The *Magnificat* (Luke i, 46–55) was frequently translated; see, for example, *Stanzaic Life*, pp. 251–88; *Prymer*, p. 54; Maskell III, pp. 64–5 and 245–6; *Myroure*, pp. 158–63 (with commentary). None of these is related to the play version, nor is that in *Towneley* XI (pp. 98–9). Much of the translation is literal (a not uncommon feature of Middle English biblical translation, see Gradual Psalms ll. 355–444, above), and affected by the needs of rhyme and metre. Some is adaptation rather than translation. The Latin text is the same as that in *Breviary* II 221; but see l. 1522 below.

1495–9   Elizabeth's first line is not a translation but rather an explanation of the circumstances of Mary's joy. Her second is badly affected by awkward literalness, simple awkwardness and some mistranslation (*þe helth of þi God* for 'in God my salvation').

1500   *So ferforthe for þat* 'To such an extent that'; cf. Maskell 'lo, forsothe, of this' (p. 245), *Prymer* 'for, lo, of þis' (p. 54). *in þes* is added perhaps merely for the rhyme (see l. 1507 below).

1503   *and also myghtyest*; a mistranslation or more probably an adaptation for the sake of rhyme. Cf. Maskell (p. 65) 'he that is miȝti'.

1507–8   Both *of þes* and *now is he cum* are added primarily to provide rhymes; but they also inevitably produce an undercurrent of specific reference to the Annunciation and so act, however fitfully, as a kind of commentary.

1511   *þore* is 'power' or 'might'. The other translations also have trouble with this line; e.g. Maskell (p. 246), 'He dide myȝt in his arme'; *Prymer* (p. 54) 'He made myȝt in his arm'.

1512   It seems likely that *dyspeyre* is catching the sound and not the meaning of the Latin *disspersit*; cf. *Prymer* (p. 54) 'he scateride proude men with þe þouȝt of his herte'.

1516   The need for a rhyme for the Latin plural in *-es* no doubt caused the repeated addition of the word, *þes*, as well as its generally appropriate meaning. *heyth* is 'height'.

1520   The translation is again doubtful; cf. Maskell (p. 245) and *Prymer* (p. 54) 'and he hath lefte riche men voide'. The splendid phrase *fellyth to voydnes* seems to mean 'strikes down to emptiness' or 'oblivion'.

1522   The *Breviary* text has 'recordatus misericordiae suae', the Vulgate 'memorari misericordiae suae'.

1523   *to cum* seems to be added purely for the sake of rhyme. A meaning 'in the future' seems unlikely. *for hese þat be* ('for those that are his') is also added, but makes sense in the context.

1527   *in clos* 'in secret'; i.e. by types, figures, prophecies in the Old Testament, which were only revealed in the New.

1528   Only Maskell (p. 246) avoids 'world/worlds' for *secula*: 'and to his seed for euere'. The playwright is making use of dialectal variation for rhyme in *sa* ('so').

1529–30, 1534–5   The *Gloria Patri* and *Sicut erat* are liturgical additions; see for example, *Horae*, p. 58.

1529–33   The rhyme scheme is altered to round off the set-piece with l. 1533, an extra line, linked with the following quatrain. The rhyming is again a little forced; *to ken* is merely a tag (perhaps 'to be mentioned, bear in mind').

1537   The Latin again is adapted in rather a feeble way.

1538   Liturgically the Magnificat is often called a psalm and was normally placed with the other canticles at the end of the liturgical psalter.

1539   I have not been able to find a source for Mary's claim.

1540–1   Cf. *Myroure* p. 157, '*Magnificat*, Thys ys owre ladyes songe, and yt ys sayde euery daye at euensonge . . .' See also *Prymer*, pp. 29–30, *Horae*, p. 58, Maskell III, pp. 64–5, *Breviary* II 221. It is also used at other times e.g. *Missal* 307–8, Feria 5 in Coena Domini; 357, Vigil of Easter.

1542–5   Cf. Luke i, 56; and *Meditationes* (pp. 516–17), 'Et stetit ibidem Domina quasi mensibus tribus, ministrans et serviens ei in omnibus quae poterat humiliter, reverenter, et devote, quasi oblita se matrem Dei esse, et totius mundi reginam' ('And the lady stayed there about three months, helping and serving her in everything that she was able, humbly, reverently and devotedly; as if forgetting she was the mother of God and queen of all the world').

1546–9   As the *Meditationes* does, the section again lays stress on Mary's humility. For *trone* and *tabernakyl* see note to ll. 1352–5.

1550   It may seem somewhat odd that Joseph and Zacharias have said nothing all this time, but there is nothing really to show that Zacharias appears before this moment. The colloquial tone of Joseph's speech breaks the stylised atmosphere as Mary's has done at l. 1542.

1554   For comment on *wys*, see note to l. 302.

1555   See above ll. 1446 and 1490.

1555–7   For affliction as a sign of God's concern, see note to l. 155.

1558–60   These lines are at the foot of f. 73v. See Appendix 3 for another possible ending, and Introduction, pp. 4 & 5 for a discussion of it.

1563–6   This division of the *Ave Maria* into its chronological parts is the same as that in *Lay Folks' Catechism* (pp. 12–13). It forms an appropriate rounding-off of the series of episodes, bringing the historical actuality of the biblical scenes into a present actuality of the Church's devotions.
     The *Ave gracia plena dominus tecum* is the same as the form in l. 1279; the second part is translated in l. 1281. The first part of Elizabeth's greeting overlaps with this second part of the angel's, *Benedicta tu inter mulieres/in*

mulieribus (cf. 1. 1469), so that only the second part is used: *et benedictus fructus ventris tui*. In devotions *Maria* is added after *Ave*, and *Jhesus* at the end of the whole, giving the normal form of the *Ave Maria* in use during the Middle Ages. See *Myroure*, p. 79 and *Lay Folks' Catechism*, p. 108 (note to l. 207) for some comments on the additions.

1567   The basic form of *Oure Ladyes sawtere* is the repetition of one hundred and fifty *Ave Maria*'s with a *Pater Noster* after every ten. The strings of beads made for this devotion are a frequent legacy in wills of the fifteenth century. For a brief contemporary description of the devotion see Mirk, p. 299, ll. 24–6. A more developed form of the devotion is in *Horae*, pp. 142–7. The *sawtere* is discussed in the Introduction to the *Horae*, pp. xxxv–vii, and in a note (to l. 220) in *Lay Folks' Catechism*, pp. 109–10. Felix Fabri has a long discussion of it, I, pp. 634–7.

1567–8   The note in *Lay Folks' Catechism* referred to above (note to ll. 1563–6) gives a pardon of thirty-four years and thirty weeks for the saying daily of 'oure ladyes psalter'.

1569–88   These stanzas are perhaps part of the same additions as ll. 1324–47.

1573–6   There is need of a verb such as 'dwelt in', or if *hous* is the subject, 'held'. It may simply have been forgotten in the long parenthetical list of names. Cf. Love, 'A lord god/what house was that/or what chambre/and what bedde in the whiche dwelleden togidre and resteden so worthi moderes with so noble sones/that is to saie Marie and Elizabeth/Jesu and John! And also with hem dwellynge tho worschipful olde men/ȝacharie and Joseph' (p. 39).

1579–84   Cf. *Meditationes*, p. 517.

1582   Luke i, 68–79. *Benedictus Dominus Deus Israel* is another of the canticles placed at the end of liturgical psalters. It is associated particularly with Lauds; see *Breviary* II 35, *Horae* pp. 44 and 110.

1583–4   Cf. Love 'And so in that hous thise two noble and worthy Canticles/that is to sayen *Magnificat* and *benedictus*/weren first spoken and made' (p. 40).

1585–8   Cf. *Meditationes*, p. 517.

1595   This could refer to the beginning of his speech (l. 1562) or simply to *Ave* as an initial greeting and therefore suggest that the play has come round full circle. If this latter were the case one might have expected the word or a translation of it to be prominent in Contemplacio's opening speech.

1596   *Ave regina celorum* is the antiphon used in processions at the Nativity of the Blessed Virgin Mary and at the entrance to the choir on the Monday after Easter and first Sunday after Trinity (see *Processionale ad Usum Sarum* 1502 (reprinted Boethius Press, 1980) ff. 93, 121v–22 and 169). It would be particularly appropriate for a processional ending to the play.

Appendix 1

The following section of text occurs on an interpolated bifolium (ff. 51–2) referred to as quire E. It is in a different hand from the main text, probably of the early sixteenth century. It is just possible that the same hand was responsible for the series of letters showing the order of Episcopus' speeches in this same episode (see textual note to ll. 594, etc). In as much as the text is written mainly in Marian octaves, it may have its origin in parts of the *Mary Play* that were omitted when the blending of pageant and play material took place. On the other hand, it may be an independent composition later than either. The stanza form, though Marian, is unusual in the play since every quatrain is linked together by rhyme. Moreover, the final rhymes, *Mary/asay*, suggest carelessness or error, since they are presumably intended to join the two quatrains (ll. 13–16 and 17–20) by linking up with *wey/sey* in ll. 14 and 16.

The passage probably owes its inclusion to the inconsistency that Joseph talks about the wedding as the reason for the summons by the bishop (l. 751) without this having been previously mentioned. To avoid this in the interpolation, *Quartus generacionis David* explains, perhaps as hearsay (*as it is told*, l. 18), that the summons involves Mary and her marriage. This section also introduces Joseph in a slightly more deliberate way and adds a little to the emphasis on his age.

The addition of this section, whether original or not, suggests a continued interest in the performance of the play.

f. 51

Joseph

In gret labore my lyff I lede,
Myn ocupasyon lyth in many place,
For febylnesse of age my jorney I may nat spede;
I thank the, gret God, of thi grace.

Primus generacionis David

What chere, Joseph, what ys the case
That ye lye here on this grond?

5

Joseph
    Age and febylnesse doth me enbrace,
    That I may nother well goo ne stond.

Secundus generacioni[s David]
    We be comandyd be the beschoppys sond,
    That euery man of Dauyd kynrede   10
    In the tempyll to offyr a wond;
    Therfor in this jorney let vs procede.
Joseph
    Me to traveyll yt is no nede;
    I prey you, frendys, go forth your wey.
Tertius generacioni[s David]
    Yis, com furth, Joseph, I you rede,   15
    And knowyth what the buschop woll sey.
Quartus gener[acionis David]
    Ther ys a mayd whos name ys clepyd Mary,
    Doughter to Joachym, as it is told;
    Here to mary thei woll asay
    To som man dowty and bold.   20
Joseph

1 *The passage is preceded by a large* ✠ *indicating its position on f. 53*   9 *sn Secundus generacionis David] the last word and part of the second lost at edge of leaf*   13 *sn Joseph] corrected from* tertius generacionis *which is deleted*   15 *sn] as 9 sn*   17 *sn as 9 and 15 sn*   18 it is told] *MS.* I have herd; have herd *deleted and* t is told *added above*   20 man] *MS.* many   20+ *sn Joseph] roughly written low in right margin*

Notes to Appendix 1

1–3 Joseph seems already to be on a journey such as he took in relation to his work as a carpenter; cf. *Pseudo-Matthew*, ch. 10.

4 Like Joachim (l. 154) and Elizabeth (l. 1556), Joseph gives thanks to God for his sufferings.

9 The others of the tribe of David have already heard the bishop's announcement, so the messenger presumably leaves as Joseph comes in.

11 *wond* is the word used in the *Mary Play*, as opposed to ʒarde in the pageants.

17–20 The rhymes *Mary/asay* are presumably intended to link this quatrain with the previous one, which they do in only a very rough and ready way.

Appendix 2

In the reorganisation of the Marian material, the pageant of *Joseph's Doubts about Mary* has been inserted into the *Mary Play* between the end of the Annunciation and the beginning of the Visit to Elizabeth. It is written throughout in the hand of the main scribe. It seems that some lines from the *Mary Play* describing Joseph's return home have been incorporated into the pageant (ll. 14–20). This cannot be proved, but a false start by the scribe (*how hast*, the first words of l. 21, follow l. 12), combined with a longer line in ll. 14–20 and a different tone, provides some evidence. Besides this, the rhyme scheme of the quatrain, ll. 17–20, fits with that of the quatrain which in the manuscript begins the Visit to Elizabeth (ll. 1432–35); and this same quatrain (ll. 17–20) is preceded in the manuscript by a paragraph mark with a dot, a common sign of Marian material (see Introduction p. 3). The pageant is included in the Proclamation. It is written in a variety of stanza forms, but mainly thirteeners and a ten-line stanza rhyming *aabaabbcbc*.

There is no gospel position for Joseph's Doubts in relation to the Visit to Elizabeth. The episode is developed from Matthew i, 18–24, but the Visit occurs only in Luke (i, 39–56). *Protevangelium, Pseudo-Matthew* and the *Nativity of Mary*, like Matthew, contain only Joseph's Doubts. *Meditationes* (ch. 5 and 6), Comestor (coll. 1538–9), *Vita Christi* (pp. 28ff. and 35ff.), the *Pepysian Gospel Harmony* (pp. 3–4), *Chester* VI and *York* XIII all contain both, and place Joseph's Doubts after the Visit. In *Towneley*, Joseph's Doubts is part of the Annunciation and precedes the Visit which is a separate pageant. There is no doubt that the most common position for Joseph's Doubts is following the Visit, not preceding it, as the reorganisation has placed it.

ff. 67–70v

f. 67　　*Joseph*
　　　　　　How, dame, how! Vndo ȝoure dore, vndo!
　　　　　　Are ȝe at hom? Why speke ȝe notht?

1] *large red numeral* 12 *in right margin*

Susanna
   Who is ther? Why cry ȝe so?
   Telle us ȝour herand; wyl ȝe ought?
Joseph
   Vndo ȝour dore, I sey ȝow to.   5
   For to com in is all my thought.
Maria
   It is my spowse þat spekyth us to,
   Ondo þe dore; his wyl were wrought.

   Wellcome hom, myn husbond dere,
   How haue ȝe ferd in fer countré?   10
Joseph
   To gete oure levynge, withowtyn dwere,
   I haue sore laboryd for þe and me.
Maria
   Husbond, ryght gracyously now come be ȝe,
   It solacyth me sore sothly to se ȝow in syth.
Joseph
   Me merveylyth, wyff, surely, ȝour face I cannot se,   15
   But as þe sonne with his bemys qwan he is most
                          bryth.

Maria
   Husbond, it is as it plesyth oure Lord, þat grace of
                          hym grew;
   Who þat evyr beholdyth me, veryly,
   They xal be grettly steryed to vertu.
   For þis ȝyfte and many moo, good Lord, gramercy.   20

Joseph
   How hast þu ferde, jentyl mayde,
   Whyl I haue be out of londe?
Maria
   Sekyr, sere, beth nowth dysmayde,
   Ryth aftyr þe wyl of Goddys sonde.
Joseph
   That semyth evyl, I am afrayd,   25
   Þi wombe to hyȝe doth stonde.
   I drede me sore I am betrayd,
   Sum other man þe had in honde
f. 67v   Hens sythe þat I went.

12] *below the beginning of this line* how hast *has been deleted*   14 se] ȝw *deleted*
after se

Thy wombe is gret, it gynnyth to ryse,   30
Than hast þu begownne a synfull gyse.
Telle me now in what wyse
   Thyself þu ast þus schent.

Ow, dame, what þinge menyth this?
With childe þu gynnyst ryth gret to gon.   35
Sey me, Mary, þis childys fadyr ho is,
I pray þe telle me and þat anon.
Maria
   The Fadyr of hevyn and ȝe it is,
   Other fadyr hath he non.
   I dede nevyr forfete with man, iwys;   40
   Wherfore I pray ȝow amende ȝour mon,
      This childe is Goddys and ȝour.
Joseph
   Goddys childe? Þu lyist in fay!
   God dede nevyr jape so with may;
   And I cam nevyr ther, I dare wel say,   45
      Ȝitt so nyh þi boure.

But ȝit I sey, Mary, whoos childe is this?
Maria
   Goddys and ȝoure, I sey iwys.

Joseph
   Ȝa, ȝa, all olde men to me take tent
   And weddyth no wyff in no kynnys wyse   50
   Þat is a ȝonge wench, be myn asent,
   For doute and drede and swych servyse.
   Alas, alas, my name is shent!
   All men may me now dyspyse
   And seyn, "Olde cokwold, þi bowe is bent   55
   Newly now after þe Frensche gyse".

f. 68   Alas and welaway!
   Alas, dame, why dedyst þu so?
   For þis synne þat þu hast do,
   I the forsake and from þe go   60
      For onys, evyr and ay.

Maria
   Alas, gode spowse, why sey ȝe thus?

62 Alas] s *omitted and added above line;* sey ȝe] so *deleted after* ȝe

Alas, dere hosbund, amende ȝour mod.
It is no man but swete Jhesus;
He wyll be clad in flesch and blood   65
    And of ȝour wyff be born.

Sephor
Forsothe þe aungel þus seyd he:
Þat Goddys sone in Trynité
For mannys sake a man wolde be,
    To save þat is forlorn.   70

Joseph
An aungel? Allas, alas, fy for schame!
Ȝe syn now in þat ȝe to-say,
To puttyn an aungel in so gret blame.
Alas, alas, let be, do way!
It was sum boy began þis game   75
Þat clothyd was clene and gay,
And ȝe ȝeve hym now an aungel name.
Alas, alas and welaway,
    Þat evyr this game betydde!
A, dame, what thought haddyst þu?   80
Here may all men þis proverbe trow,
Þat many a man doth bete þe bow,
    Another man hath þe brydde.

f. 68v *Maria*
A, gracyous God in hefne trone,
Comforte my spowse in þis hard cas;   85
Mercyful God, amend his mone,
As I dede nevyr so gret trespas.

Joseph
Lo, lo, serys, what told I ȝow?
Þat it was not for my prow
    A wyff to take me to.   90
An þat is wel sene now;
For Mary, I make God avow,
    Is grett with childe, lo.
Alas, why is it so?
To þe busshop I wole it telle   95
Þat he þe lawe may here do,
With stonys here to qwelle.

72 þat ȝe] to *deleted after* ȝe   89 it was] þat it *deleted after* was

Nay, nay, ȝet God forbede
Þat I xuld do þat vengeabyl dede
   But if I wyst wel qwy;   100
I knew never with here, so God me spede,
Tokyn of thynge in word nor dede
   Þat towchyd velany.
Nevyrþeles, what forthy?
Þow she be meke and mylde,   105
Withowth mannys company
She myght not be with childe.

But I ensure myn was it nevyr.
Thow þat she hath not don here devyr,
   Rather than I xuld pleynyn opynly,   110
Serteynly ȝitt had I levyr
Forsake þe countré forevyr
   And nevyr come in here company.
For and men knew þis velany,
In repreff þei wolde me holde;   115
And ȝett many bettyr than I,
Ȝa, hath ben made cokolde.

f. 69   Now, alas, whedyr xal I gone?
I wot nevyr whedyr nor to what place.
For oftyntyme sorwe comyth sone   120
And longe it is or it pace.
   No comforte may I haue here.
Iwys, wyff, þu dedyst me wronge,
Alas, I taryed from þe to longe!
All men haue pety on me amonge,   125
   For to my sorwe is no chere.

Maria
God, þat in my body art sesyd,
Þu knowist myn husbond is dysplesyd
   To se me in þis plight;
For vnknowlage he is desesyd,   130
And þerfore help þat he were esyd,
   Þat he myght knowe þe ful perfyght.
For I haue levyr abyde respyt,

99 vengeabyl] *MS.* vegeabyl   102 Tokyn] nevyrþeles *deleted before*
Tokyn   108/109 nevyr/devyr] -vyr *of both appears to have been added*
afterwards

To kepe þi sone in priuité,
Grauntyd by þe Holy Spyryt,   135
    Þan þat it xulde be opynd by me.

Deus
Descende, I sey, myn aungelle,
Onto Joseph for to telle
    Such as my wyl is.
Byd hym with Mary abyde and dwelle,   140
For it is my sone ful snelle
    Þat she is with, iwys.
Angelus
Almyghty God of blys,
I am redy for to wende
Wedyr as þi wyl is,   145
To go bothe fer and hynde.

Joseph, Joseph, þu wepyst shryle;
Fro þi wyff why comyst þu owte?
f. 69v *Joseph*
Good sere, lete me wepe my fylle;
Go forthe þi wey and lett me nowght.   150
Angelus
In þi wepynge þu dost ryght ylle;
Aȝens God þu hast myswrought.
Go chere þi wyff with herty wylle,
And chawnge þi chere, amende þi thought,
    Sche is a ful clene may.   155
I telle þe God wyl of here be born,
And sche clene mayd as she was beforn,
To saue mankynd þat is forlorn.
    Go, chere hyre þerfore, I say.

Joseph
A, lord God, *benedicite*!   160
Of þi gret comforte, I thank the,
    Þat þu sent me þis space.
I myght wel a wyst, pardé,
So good a creature as she
    Wold nevyr a don trespace;   165

· 147 shryle] *MS.* shyrle

For sche is ful of grace.
I know wel I haue myswrought.
I walk to my pore place
And aske forgyfnes I haue mysthought.

Now is þe tyme sen at eye,   170
Þat þe childe is now to veryfye
      Which xal saue mankende,
As it was spoke be prophesye.
I thank þe, God, þat syttys on hye,
      With hert, wyl and mende,   175
Þat evyr þu woldyst me bynde
To wedde Mary to my wyff;
Þi blysful sone so nere to fynde,
In his presens to lede my lyff.

Alas, for joy I qwedyr and qwake;   180
Alas, what hap now was this?
f. 70   A, mercy, mercy, my jentyl make,
Mercy, I haue seyd al amys!
All þat I haue seyd here I forsake,
Ȝour swete fete now lete me kys.   185
Mary
      Nay, lett be my fete, not þo ȝe take;
My mowthe ȝe may kys, iwys,
      And welcom onto me!
Joseph
      Gramercy, myn owyn swete wyff;
Gramercy, myn hert, my love, my lyff!   190
Xal I nevyrmore make suche stryff
      Betwyx me and þe.

A, Mary, Mary, wel þu be,
And blyssyd be þe frewte in the,
      Goddys sone of myght!   195
Now, good wyff, ful of pyté,
As be not evyl payd with me,
      Þow þat þu haue good ryght,
As for my wronge in syght
To wyte þe with ony synne.   200
Had þu not be a vertuous wythe,
God wold not a be þe withinne.

I knowlage I haue don amys;
I was never wurthy, iwys,
   For to be þin husbonde.   205
I xal amende aftere thys,
Ryght as þin owyn wyl is,
   To serve þe at foot and honde,
And þi chylde bothe to vndyrstonde,
To wurchep hym with good affeccyon.   210
And þerfore telle me, and nothynge whonde,
The holy matere of ȝour concepcyon.

f. 70v   *Maria*
At ȝowre owyn wyll, as ȝe bydde me.
Ther cam an aungel hyght Gabryell,
And gret me fayr and seyd "*Aue*";   215
And ferthermore to me gan tell
God xulde be borne of my bodé,
Þe fendys powsté for to felie,
Þorwe þe Holy Gost, as I wel se;
Þus God in me wyl byde and dwelle.   220

Joseph
Now I thank God with spech and spelle,
Þat euyr, Mary, I was weddyd to the.
Mary
It was þe werk of God, as I ȝow telle;
Now blyssyd be þat Lord so purveyd for me!

214 aungel] *MS.* aunge   217 God xulde] *repeated but not deleted*   223 þe
werk] of *deleted after* werk

Notes to Appendix 2

2sn   Susanna is one of the maidens left with Mary at the end of the Betrothal
(ll. 923–35). The section describing them there is from pageant material.

8   'Open the door; we should do what he wants'.

13–20   The greater elaboration of the language and the mysterious
brightness of Mary's face seem more akin to the tone of the *Mary Play* than to
that of the pageant. In this edition, these lines have also been included in the
main text (ll. 1404–11). They were probably not an original part of this
pageant.

21   Joseph's words seem to be a response to Mary's 'How haue ʒe ferd . . .?' (l. 10).

Mary always addresses Joseph, as her husband, in the plural pronoun. He addresses her in the singular, as the normal form to a wife, except at ll. 15, 185 and 212. The plurals in the latter two are explicable in as much as he is in the first asking her pardon, and in the second asking her about the conception. The plural in l. 15 could be explained by the wondrous light, but it seems more likely that it is simply a part of Joseph's normal usage in the *Mary Play*.

23–4   Mary is not hiding the meeting with Gabriel, 'Goddys sonde', and seems to be already responding to Joseph's suspicions.

25–35   Joseph's apprehensions grow audibly from 'þi wombe to hyʒe' (l. 26), to 'Thy wombe is gret' (l. 30), to 'With childe þu gynnyst ryth gret to gon' (l. 35).

42   The last words of Mary's reply appear also in *York* XIII, 'Sir, Goddis and youres' (l. 103), and *Towneley* X, 'Syr, godys and yowrs' (l. 195). Its appearance here probably bears witness to the remembering of a striking phrase rather than to direct influence. The N. town playwright seems to have thought it good enough to add a couplet in order to repeat it (ll. 47–8).

44   As Rosemary Woolf says, Joseph in his denial momentarily presents a picture of a Christian Jupiter (Woolf, *Mystery Plays* p. 170).

49ff.   Though commonplace, the complaints of unequal marriage lead to some very effective audience addresses in the plays.

55–6   Whiting B482; but this is the sole example. It presumably means that previously he could have 'drawn the bow' himself, but that now someone else has done it for him. *Frensche*, because of their proverbial proclivity towards sexual activity; see Whiting F617.

64–6   Mary's explanation does not seem to square with her remarks at ll. 133–6. It should perhaps be seen as forced out of her by her anguish. It does not explain enough to satisfy Joseph.

67–70   Sephor, the third of the maidens, presents a neat summary of the reasons for Mary's conception, though it is not clear how she knew. In *Pseudo-Matthew* it is more naturally explained by the maidens, 'But if you wish us to tell you what we suspect, no one but the angel of the Lord has made her pregnant' (ch. 10).

75–7   Cf. *Pseudo-Matthew*, ch. 10.

81–3   See Whiting B604.

95–7   The Mosaic law punishment for adultery (cf. John viii, 5); cf. Block p. 206, ll. 201–4.

98–103   Joseph's basic good nature and Mary's virtue both come through in Joseph's words.

120–1   Whiting S518; but again it is the only example.

127   'God, who art in possession of my body'. The expression was a legal one often of an overlord's rights (see *OED* sv. Seize *v*. I 1 (b)).

133–6 'For I would prefer to put up with the delay, to keep your son, conferred by the Holy Spirit, in secret, than that it should be revealed by me'. The meaning seems a little forced. Perhaps *respyt* should be *despyt* 'humiliation, scorn'. The reason behind it is once again Mary's humility; cf. *Meditationes*, p. 517.

137–46 The angel descends from God, but unfortunately the lack of stage directions makes it impossible to be sure of the staging of the pageant.

149 Joseph does not at first realise that it is an angel; implying that he does not immediately look up.

166 An echo of Gabriel's message.

169 'And ask forgiveness in that I have misjudged'.

170–3 Joseph in *York* XIII (ll. 61–4) has already dismissed the idea that the prophecy (Isaiah vii, 14) could possibly refer to Mary. In Matthew, the prophecy is specifically linked with this episode (i, 23).

186–8 Mary's humility and her humanity both appear.

194 Joseph anticipates (in its present manuscript position) Elizabeth's greeting; cf. the main text l. 1470.

211–12 Cf. *Meditationes*, p. 517, 'Quaesivit Joseph de hac conceptione mirifica, quae ei Domina diligenter narravit' ('Joseph asked about the marvellous conception and the Lady told him the whole story').

Appendix 3

Towards the end of the Visit to Elizabeth, at the foot of f. 73v, there is a marginal note indicating an alternative ending to the *Mary Play*:

⁜ his mercy

	come I pray ȝow specialy	
si placet	iwys ȝe are welcome Mary	Elizabeth
	for þis comfortabelest comynge good God gramercy	
		Contemplacio

The cross surrounded by dots links the passage, through a similar mark in the right margin, to the end of the last of Elizabeth's speeches on the page. It is this ending which is set out in the main text, with the three additional lines of Elizabeth's leading on to the complete speech of Contemplacio. This ending concludes the *Mary Play* by leaving Mary and Joseph at the house of Elizabeth and Zacharias. Contemplacio's speech then describes the birth of John the Baptist, adds the *Benedictus* to the liturgical pieces springing from the episodes in the play (ll. 1581–4), and finally describes Joseph and Mary's departure. This ending coincides, occasionally in some detail, with the episode as it appears in *Meditationes* ch. 5. It consists of Marian octaves with the exception of the three introductory lines and ll. 1569–88 which are a mixture of quatrains and a non-Marian octave and were fairly certainly additions to the original play.

Another possible ending is that set out below. Mary and Joseph leave Elizabeth and Zacharias, who themselves go to the temple. Contemplacio's speech follows, but without ll. 1569–88 which contradict what has happened. There is no reliance here on *Meditationes* which is also contradicted. All the material which is additional to the main text is in non-Marian octaves except for the opening quatrain.

I have chosen to use the first of these endings in the main text because of the play's frequent dependence on *Meditationes* and because this ending's devotional tone seems to me to fit better with the rest of the play. It seems likely that neither represents the original ending of the play which perhaps consisted simply of Contemplacio's speech, ll. 1561–8 and 1589–96. The revisions may

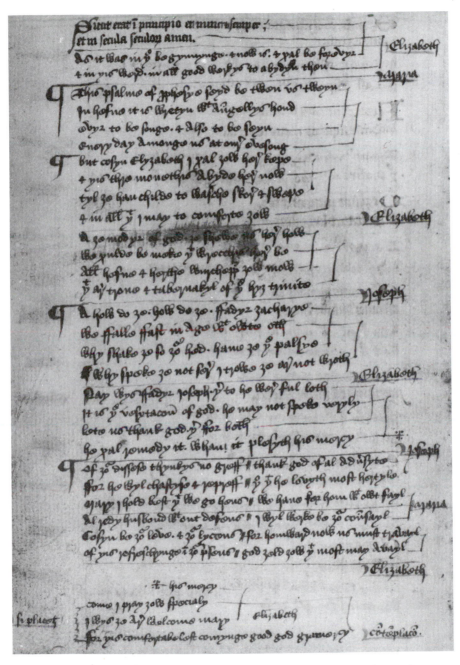

f.73v.   The alternative endings. Note also the more elaborate script used for the Magnificat at the head of the page. (See Appendix 3 and Introduction pp. 4–5.) Photograph reproduced by permission of the British Library (BLMS Cotton Vespasian D VIII).

have been two contrasting attempts to fill out a rather abrupt conclusion, both of which the scribe managed to include in his manuscript; or they may have been the result of an awareness of the value of leaving open the choice of ending.

f. 73v–4

f. 73v *Joseph*

    Of ȝour dissese thynkys no greff,
    Thank God of al aduersyté;
    For he wyl chastyse and repreff
    Þo þat he lovyth most hertylé.

    Mary, I hold best þat we go hens;   5
    We haue fer hom withowt fayl.
Maria
    Al redy, husbond, without defens,
    I wyl werke be ȝour counsayl.
    Cosyn, be ȝour leve and ȝour lycens,
    For homward now us must travayl.   10
    Of þis refreschynge in ȝour presens,
    God ȝeld ȝow þat most may avayl.

f. 74 *Elizabeth*

    Now, cosynes bothe, God ȝow spede
    And wete ȝow wele withowtyn mo!
    ȝour presens comfortyth me indede,   15
    And þerfore now am I ryght wo
    That ȝe, my frendys and my kynrede,
    Þus sone now xul parte me fro.
    But I pray God he mote ȝow lede
    In every place wherso ȝe go.   20

Here Mary and Elizabet partyn, and Elizabeth goth to Zakarie and seyth:

    Good husbond, ryse up I beseke ȝow,
    And go we to þe temple now fast
    To wurchep God with þat we mow,
    And thank hym bothe – this is my cast –
    Of þe tyme þat is comynge now.   25

14 withowtyn] wo *deleted after* withowtyn   19 lede] sp *deleted at beginning of word and* l *added above*

For now is cum mercy and venjauns is past:
God wyl be born for mannys prow
To brynge us to blysse þat ever xal last.

Contemplacio
Lystenyth, sovereynys, here is a conclusyon;
How þe *Aue* was mad, here is lernyd vs: 30
Þe aungel seyd: *Ave gracia plena dominus tecum*
Benedicta tu in mulieribus;
Elyzabeth seyd: *et benedictus*
Fructus uentris tui; thus þe Chirch addyd *Maria* and
                                         Jhesus her.
Who seyth Oure Ladyes sawtere dayly for a ȝer þus,   35
He hath pardon ten thowsand and eyte hundryd ȝer.

Now most mekely we thank ȝou of ȝour pacyens,
And beseke ȝou of ȝour good supportacyon;
If here hath be seyd ore don any inconuenyens,
We asygne it to ȝour good deliberacyon,   40
Besekynge to Crystys precyous passyon
Conserve and rewarde ȝour hedyr comynge.
With *Aue* we begunne, and *Aue* is oure conclusyon;
Ave regina celorum to Oure Lady we synge.

40 deliberacyon] *Half the -o- and the mark of suspension have been trimmed away at the edge of the leaf*

Notes to Appendix 3

1–4   This is the fullest expression of trust in the mercy of heaven-sent tribulation; cf. l. 155 above and note.

5ff   This section seems to spring from the playwright's sense of what would have happened naturally, rather than drawing on a particular tradition.

17   For Mary's relationship with Elizabeth, see notes to ll. 25 and 1413.

26–8   Elizabeth's words nicely round off the play with trust in the new time of grace. *mercy* and *venjauns* are aspects of the New and Old Laws.

29–44   See main text, ll. 1561–8 and 1589–96.

Glossary

Note to the Glossary

The Glossary is intended to contain examples of every English word and spelling used in the main text and appendices. If there are more than four examples of a word or spelling, two line references are given, followed by 'etc.'. Where there are four or fewer examples, one to four references are given, without an 'etc.'. Where it seemed to me important, and where it was possible, I have listed all examples. No line references are given for very common words unless there is a less common variant in the text. References to the Appendices consist of a line number followed by *A1, A2*, or *A3* respectively. References to different forms of an individual word are separated by a semi-colon; *e.g.*: '**hey, hy(e), hy3(e)** ... 449, 1275, 1515; 1098; 1382; 458, 713 etc.; 26*A2*; ...' means that there are examples of the form **hey** in lines 449, 1275 and 1515; of **hy** in line 1098; of **hye** in line 1382; of **hy3** in lines 458, 713 and a number of others (at least five in all); and **hy3e** in line 26 of Appendix 2.

Verbs are listed under their infinitives where such a form exists in the text.

In the alphabetical sequence, initial *i* and *j*, *g* and *3* are treated as separate letters, but initial *þ* is combined with *th*, and *u* with *v*. Medial *u* and *v* have their normal alphabetical positions. The very few words beginning with *y* have been given their normal alphabetical position, but medial and final *y* have been treated as *i*.

The series of meanings given towards the beginning of each entry is intended to cover all the varieties found in main text and appendices. Occasionally glosses are given for individual words or phrases. No glossary can give enough information about any one word, and to enable a reader to gain easy access to further information, every entry is followed by the relevant headword in the *Middle English Dictionary* (*MED*), as far as that has been published (up to **to** *prep* at the time of writing). Thereafter, there are occasional references to the *Oxford English Dictionary* (*OED*), if a connection between the fifteenth–century and the modern form is not obvious.

a, ha *interj.* ah!, oh! (expressing horror, surprise, etc., or invocation) 89, 91 etc.; 133 (**a, ha** *interj.*)

a (reduced form of various prepositions in unstressed position) **a Godys sake** 1416 (perhaps confused with **a Godys name** in God's name)

a *see* **haue**

a(n) *indef. art.* a, an (**a** *indef.art.*)

abhomynabyl *adj.* abominable 1160 (**abhominable** *adj.*)

abyde, abydyn *v.* dwell, live, remain, stay, await, wait 119, 124 etc.; 1537; *3sg. pr.* **abydyth** 1327; *pl. pr.* **abyde** 53; *imp. sg.* **abyde** 100, 210; *imp. pl.* **abydyth** 988; *3sg. pa.* **abod** 1570, 1577 (**abiden** *v.*)

abydynge *vbl. n.* home, place of rest 477 (**abiding** *ger.*)

abyl *adj.* able 751 (**able** *adj.*)

abyl *v. sg. pr. subj.* enable 294 (**ablen** *v.*)

abod *see* **abyde**

abought, abowte *adv.* about 1476; 424 (**aboute(n** *adv.*)

above *adv.* above 345; (as *adj.*) 660; (as *n.*) 1314 (**above(n** *adv.*)

above *prep.* above 374, 376, 1169 (**above(n** *prep.*)

abowt *prep.* around 174 (**aboute(n** *prep.*)

abowte *see* **abought**

absens *n.* absence 160 (**absence** *n.*)

abuse *v.* appear falsely 103 (**abusen** *v.*)

accusatyff *adj.* self-accusing 415 (**ac(c)usatif** *adj. & n.*)

acorde *n.* unanimity of feeling, agreement 1348; **with on acorde** with complete harmony 439 (**accord** *n.*)

acorde *v. 2pl. pr.* agree, become reconciled 1183 (**accorden** *v.*)

adde *v. 1sg. pr.* add 1286; *3sg. pa.* **addyd** 1566; *p. p.* **haddyd** 1077 (**adden** *v.*)

adrad *p.p.* afraid 173 (**adreden** *v.*)

aduersyté *n.* adversity, trouble, affliction 2A3 (**adversite** *n.*)

aduocat *n.* intercessor, mediator 550 (**advocat** *n.*)

affeccyon *n.* will, inclination 210A2 (**affeccioun** *n.*)

afrayd *p. p.* afraid 25A2 (**affraien** *v.*)

after(e), aftyr *prep.* after, according to 681, 782; 143, 226 etc.; 620, 826 etc. (**after** *prep.*)

after(e) *adv.* afterwards 560sd; 592, 1449 (**after** *adv.*)

agast *p. p.* fearful 1427 (**agasten** *v.*)

age *n.* age, old age 262, 275 etc.; **tendyr age and 3yng** childhood 258; **grett age** old age 1271 (**age** *n.*)

ageyn, a3en *adv.* (back) again 91, 93, 234, 803; 118, 236sd, 566; in return 459 (**ayen** *adv.*)

a3en *prep.* against 617, 694 (**ayen** *prep.*)

a3en-comynge *vbl. n.* return 996 (**ayen-coming** *ger.*)

a3ens *prep.* against 629, 845, 862, 152A2 (**ayen(e)s** *prep.*)

agyd *p. p.* aged, old 799 (**agen** *v.*)

ay *adv.* ever 229, 404, 61A2 (**ei** *adv.*)

al *adv.* altogether, completely 137, 251, 270sd, 183A2 (**al** *adv. & conj.*)

al, all(e) *n.* all 1258; 17, 23 etc.; 107, 117, 692, 709 (**al,** *lim. adj. & n.*)

al, all(e) *adj.* all 174, 197 etc.; 32, 36 etc.; 263, 542, 1519 (**al** *lim. adj. & n.*)

alas, allas *interj.* alas (exclamation of grief, pity etc.) 53A2, 57A2 etc.; 71A2 (**alas** *int.*)

allmyght *adj.* almighty 530 (**al-might** *adj.*)

almes, helmes *n.* alms 41; 176 (**almes(se** *n.*)

almyghty *adj.* almighty 956, 971, 1113, 143A2 (**al-mighti** *adj.*)

almost *adv.* almost 801 (**al-most** *adv.*)

alon(e) *adv., adj.* alone, unaided 385, 1229; 90, 298, 558, 910 (**al-on(e** *adv. & adj.*)

also *adv.* also 183, 286 etc. (**also** *adv.*)

alway, alwey *adv.* all the time 1490; 560sd (**al–wei, –wei(e)s** *adv.*)
am *see* **be**
amen *interj.* amen 25, 324 etc. (**amen** *interj.*)
amend(e) *v.* remedy, relieve, improve 168; 353, 1087, 206*A2*; *sg. pr. subj.*
  amende 148; *imp. sg/pl.* **amende** 41*A2*, 63*A2*, 154*A2* (**amenden** *v.*)
amys *adv.* wrong 183*A2*, 203*A2* (**amis** *adv.*)
amonge *adv.* **evyrmore amonge** continually 924 (**among(es** *adv.*)
amonge *prep.* among 103, 106 etc. (**among(es** *prep.*)
an *see* **haue**
and, an *conj.* and, if 2, 3, etc.; 91*A2*; as if 296 (**and** *conj.*)
angelys *see* **aungel**
anguysch *n.* hardship, suffering 547 (**angwisshe** *n.*)
any, ony *adj., pron.* any 1019, 1591; 1190, 1394 (**ani** *lim. adj.*)
anodyr, another *pron.* another, the second 53; 1360 (**other** *pron.*)
anon, anoon *adv.* at once, immediately 730, 1361, 1462; 615 (**an–on** *adv. &
  conj.*)
another *adj.* another, a second 1204, 83*A2* (**other** *adj.*)
ansuere, answere *n.* answer 685; 285, 1327 etc. (**answere** *n.*)
answere *v.* answer 1298; *2pl. pr.* **answere** 296 (**answeren, –ien** *v.*)
antecer *n.* precedessor, forebear 550 (probably a spelling of **ancetre** but
  possibly **ancessor** or **antecessour** *n.*)
apace *adv.* quickly, promptly 1261 (**apas** *adv.*)
ap(p)ere, aper *v.* appear, come (into sight) 542, 1436, 1457; 262; 1295; *3sg.
  pa.* **apperyd** 1443, 1488 (**ap(p)eren** *v.*)
applyed *p. p.* applied, used 355 (**ap(p)lien** *v.*)
ar(e) *see* **be(n)**
archaungelys *n. pl.* archangels 1096 (**archangel** *n. 1.*)
ardent *adj.* passionate, fervent 1225 (**ardaunt** *adj.*)
areste *n.* ?dwelling, residence 624 (**arest(e** *n.*)
aryse *v.* come about, arise 62 (**arisen** *v.*)
arme *n.* arm 1511 (**arm** *n.*)
arn, art *see* **be(n)**
as *adv., conj.* as, like; when 1462 (**also** *adv.*; **as** *conj.*)
asay *v.* try, endeavour 19*A1* (**assaien** *v.*)
ascende *v.* ascend 350; *1sg. pr.* **ascende** 1403 (**ascenden** *v.*)
aschamyd *p. p.* embarrassed, shy 775 (**ashamed** *ppl.*)
aseyth *n.* satisfaction, atonement 1165 (**asseth** *n.*)
as(s)ent *n.* **be myn asent** ?if you take my advice 51*A2*; (mutual) agreement,
  approval 1246, 1327, 1343 (**assent** *n.*)
asygne *v.* *1pl. pr.* entrust 1592; *p. p.* **assygnyd** allotted, entrusted 859
  (**assignen** *v.*)
aske, haske *v.* *1sg. pr.* ask 1313; 521; *3sg. pr. subj.* **aske** 1267 (**asken** *v.*)
aspy *v.* detect, discover 802 (**aspien** *v.*)
assygnacyon *n.* direction, order 700 (**assignacioun** *n.*)
ast *see* **haue**
at(t) *prep.* at 41, 84 etc.; 930; of 979; from 1301; according to 1392; to 1421
  (**at** *prep.*)
auerte *n.* ?averter, turner aside 547 (?error for 'averter'; *MED* has only three
  examples of the verb **averten**, none of **averter**)
aungel(le) *n.* angel 175, 218 etc.; 137*A2*; *n. poss.* **aungel** 77*A2*, **aungelys**
  1293; *n. pl.* **angelys** 1008, **aungelys** 542, 1096, 1106, 1295; **aungellys**
  533, 1117, 1266; *n. pl. poss.* **aungelys** 531, (?)**aungellys** 1539 (**aungel** *n.*)

autentyk *adj.* reliable, worthy of trust 550 (**autentik** *adj.*)

autere *see* **awtere**

avayl *v.* help, be of use 12*A3* (**availen** *v.*)

avyse *n.* opinion, advice 692, 697, 1228 (**avis** *n.*)

avow *n.* vow 163, 170 etc. (**avou(e** *n.*)

avow *v. 1sg. pr.* vow 63 (**avouen** *v.*)

away, awey *adv.* away 582, 760, 1009; 1011 (**awei** *adv.*)

awe *n.* fear, great reverence 519 (**aue** *n.*)

awey *see* **away**

awtere, autere *n.* altar 512; 97sd (**auter** *n.*)

babe *n.* child, babe 347, 447, 1400 (**babe** *n.*)

bad *see* **bydde**

bale *n.* misfortune, grief 172; *n. pl.* **balys** sufferings 1080 (**bale** *n. 1.*)

bar *see* **bere**

bare *adj.* without offspring, childless 101 (**bar** *adj.*)

bar(r)eyn, barrany *adj.* barren, childless 181, 187 etc.; 179, 304; 101, 195; (as *n.*) **barreyn** 106 (**barain(e** *adj.*)

barynes *n.* sterility, childlessness 168 (**barainnesse** *n.*)

be, by *prep.* by 10, 41, etc.; 449, 1066, 1330, 1385, 1386 (**bi** *prep.*)

be(n), bene *v.* be 4, 14 etc.; 283, 752 etc.; 679, 853; *1sg. pr.* **am** 30, 50 etc.; *2sg. pr.* **art** 104, 152 etc.; *3sg. pr.* **is** 9, 16 etc., **ys** 5*A1*, 17 *Al,* **his** 1211; *pl. pr.* **ar(e)** 1283; 99, 166 etc.; **arn** 101, 405; **be** 38, 39 etc.; **ben** 17, 263 etc.; *sg. pr. subj.* **be** 71, 94 etc.; *imp. sg.* **be** 902, 966; *imp. pl.* **beth** 228, 298, 338, 596; *pr. p.* **beyng(e)** 270sd; 1365, 1482; *sg. pa.* **was** 10, 181 etc.; *pl. pa.* (?) **ware** 102; **were** 187, 304 etc.; **weryn** 1437, **wern** 647, **wore** 643, **worn** 1584; *sg. pa. subj.* **were** 87, 174 etc.; **wore** 693, 774 etc.; *p. p.* **be** 48, 752 etc.; **ben** 117*A2* (**ben** *v.*)

becawse, bycause *conj.* because 60; 642 (**bicause** *conj.*)

bedde *n.* bed 868 (**bed** *n. 1.*)

bedyght *p. p.* set, placed 467 (**bidighten** *v.*)

befalle *v. sg. pr. subj.* befalls, happens 214 (**bifallen** *v.*)

before, beforn *adv.* before, first, in front 236, 761 etc.; 157*A2* (**bifore(n** *adv*)

bef(f)ore, beforn, byf(f)ore *prep.* before, in front of 254, 914; 1262; 512, 1582; 162; 1334 (**bifore(n** *prep.*)

begynne *v.* begin 97, 471 etc.; *1sg. pr.* **begynne** 1492; *sg. pa.* **began** 547, 1241, 1359, 1402; *pl. pa.* **begunne** 1595; *p. p.* **begownne** 31*A2* (**biginnen** *v.*)

begynnyng(e) *vbl. n.* beginning 260; 1452, 1536 (**biginning(e** *ger.*)

behest *v. pl. pa.* promised, vowed 651 (**bihesten** *v.*)

behynde, byhynde *adv.* behind 773, 795; 806 (**bihinde(n** *adv.*)

beholde *v.* see 299, 301; *3sg. pr.* **beholdyth** 1323sd, 1409; *imp. sg.* **beholde** 1277; *sg. pa.* **beheld** took notice of 1499 (**biholden** *v.*)

beleve *v. 1sg. pr.* believe 321; *sg. pa.* **belevyd** 1445, 1474 (**bileven** *v.*)

bemys *n. pl.* beams (of light) 1355sd, 1407 (**bem** *n.*)

bende *v.* bend, submit 935; *pl. pr.* **bende** 551; *p. p.* **bent** prepared 739, bent 55*A2* (**benden** *v. 1.*)

benyngne *adj.* meek, gracious 596 (**benigne** *adj.*)

benyngnyté *n.* meekness, good will 1349 (**benignite** *n.*)

benyson *n.* blessing 499 (**benisoun** *n.*)

bere *v.* carry, give birth to 70, 190 etc.; bear leaves 724; *3sg. pr.* **beryth** 835,

1400; *2pl. pr.* **bere** 1467; *?3pl. pr.* **beryth lyff** are alive 999; *sg. pa.* **bar** 218; *p. p.* **bore, born(e)** 195, 196 etc.; 291, 638, 657, 1578; 217*A2* (**beren** *v. 1.*)

beschoppys *see* **busschop**

besech(e), beseke *v. 1sg. pr.* entreat, beseech 692; 76, 329 etc.; 21*A3*; *lpl. pr.* **besech** 588, **beseche** 581, **beseke** 1590; *pr. p.* **besekynge** 1593 (**bisechen** *v.*)

besy *adj.* engaged, diligent 580 (**bisi** *adj.*)

besyly *adv.* attentively, eagerly 495 (**bisili** *adv.*)

besynes *n.* work, occupation 484 (**bisinesse** *n.*)

best *adj., adv.* best 20, 803 etc. (**best** *adj.* and *adv.*)

bestad *p. p.* settled 211 (**bisteden** *v.*)

bestys *n. pl.* animals 134, 142, 210 (**best(e** *n.*)

betake *v. 1sg. pr.* entrust, commend 80 (**bitaken** *v.*)

bete *v.* beat 82*A2* (**beten** *v. 1.*)

beteche *v. 1sg. pr.* entrust, commend 19 (**bitechen** *v.*)

bethwen, betwen *prep.* between 885; 270sd, 280, 1181, 1538 (**bitwene** *prep.*)

betydde *v. sg. pa.* came about, happened 79*A2* (**bitiden** *v.*)

betrayd *p. p.* deceived, betrayed 27*A2* (**bitraien** *v.*)

bettyr, betyr *adj.* better 277, 116*A2*; 949 (**bettre** *adj.*)

betwyx *prep.* between 192*A2* (**bitwix(e** *prep.*)

by *see* **be** *prep.*

bydde *v.* require, command, request 682; *3sg. pr.* **byddyth** 470, 601; *2pl. pr.* **bydde** 213*A2*; *imp. sg.* **byd** 733, 140*A2*, **byddyth** 1149; *sg. pa.* **bad** 563 (**bidden** *v.*)

byddyng(e) *vbl. n.* command 718, 932; 779, 935 (**biddinge** *ger.*)

byde *v.* tarry, await 220*A2*; *1sg. pr.* **byde** 1278; *3pl. pr.* **byde** 1339 (**biden** *v.*)

bynde *v.* oblige 176*A2* (**binden** *v.*)

byrth *n.* birth 1217 (**birth(e** *n.*)

blame *n.* reproach, shame 122, 73*A2* (**blame** *n.*)

blame *v.* blame, censure 677; **be to blame** are at fault 807 (**blamen** *v.*)

blede *v.* bleed 1072 (**bleden** *v.*)

blere *v.* make (my eyes) water 856 (see note) (**bleren** *v.*)

blys(se) *n.* joy, well-being, prosperity 233, 1273, 1415; 942, 989 etc. (**blis(se** *n.*)

blys(se) *v.* bless 1588; 109, 230 etc.; *3pl. pr.* **blysse** 1500; *imp. pl.* **blysse** 322, 337; *3sg. pr. subj.* **blysse** 915 (**blessen** *v.*)

blysful *adj.* blessed, beautiful 178*A2* (**blisful** *adj.*)

blyssyd *p. p.* blessed, devout, revered 39, 58 etc. (**blessed** *ppl.*)

blyssydnes *n.* state of happiness/bliss 1476 (**blessednesse** *n.*)

blyssyng(e) *vbl. n.* blessing 914, 968; 23, 182 etc. (**blessinge** *ger.*)

blyth *adj.* happy, joyful 837 (**blithe** *adj.*)

blome *v.* blossom, bear flowers 724 (**blomen** *v.*)

blood *n.* descent, race, blood 1080, 1393, 65*A2* (**blod** *n.*)

body, bodé *n.* body 191, 195 etc.; 217*A2* (**bodi** *n.*)

bodyly, bodely *adj.* physical (as opposed to 'spiritual') 470, 475; 476 (**bodili(ch** *adj.*)

boy *n.* lad, rascal, philanderer 75*A2* (**boie** *n. 1.*)

bold(e) *adj.* brave, excellent 20*A1*; **beth bolde** Don't be afraid! 298 (**bold** *adj.*)

bon *n.* **flesche and bon** the whole body 1363 (**bon** *n. 1.*)

book *n.* book 1004, 1018 (**bok** *n.*)

borwe *n*. **take to borwe** call as a witness, take as a surety 169 (**borgh** *n*.)

borwe *v*. rescue, release 1166; *imp. sg.* **borwe** 1080 (**borwen** *v*.)

bosom *n*. breast, womb 1355sd (**bosom** *n*.)

both(e), bothyn *adj., corr. conj.* both 656, 785, etc.; 96, 180, etc.; 728; **here botherys** of them both 255 (**bothe** *num*.)

bound(e), bownde *p. p.* under an obligation, in duty bound, committed 1000; 155, 315; 1218 (**binden** *v*.)

boure, bowre *n*. an inner room, (fig. the womb) 970, 46*A2*; 657, 1379 (**bour** *n*.)

bow *n*. bough, branch 873, 82*A2* (**bough** *n*.)

bow *v*. *1sg. pr.* bow, submit, be obedient 881; *pr. p.* **bowynge** 1349 (**bouen** *v*.)

bowe *n*. bow (fig.) 55*A2* (**boue** *n*.)

breffly *adv*. briefly, concisely 11 (**brefli** *adv*.)

breffnes *n*. shortness 257 (**brefnes(se** *n*.)

breke *v*. break, break open 693, 1068 (**breken** *v*.)

breste *v*. remedy, overcome 172 (**bresten** *v*.)

breth *n*. breath, words 1464 (**breth** *n*.)

bretheryn *n. pl.* brothers, fellow-men 436, 703, 1086 (**brother** *n*.)

brydde *n*. bird (fig.) 83*A2* (**brid** *n*.)

brynge *v*. bring 24, 91 etc.; *1sg. pr.* **bryng** 781; *3sg. pr.* **bryngyth** 528sd, 766; *imp. sg.* **brynge** 794; *imp. pl.* **bryng** 742; *sg./pl. pa.* **brought** 804, 502; *p. p.* **brought** 508, 509, **browght** 605 (**bringen** *v*.)

bryth *adj*. bright 1407 (**bright** *adj*.)

brothyrly *adj*. as between brothers, loving 433 (**brotherli** *adj*.)

bus(s)chop, busshop(p) *n*. bishop (used of the high priest of the temple) 608, 708sd, 936, 16*A1*; 560sd; 737, 779, 782, 867; 596, 620; *n. poss.* **beschoppys** 9*A1* (**bishop** *n*.)

but, bvtt *conj*. but, except 58, 63, etc.; 1412; unless 381; **but yf** unless 399; **but** but that 6 (**but** *conj*.)

bux(h)um, buxom *adj*. humble, obedient, submissive 848; 966; 596 (**buxom** *adj*.)

call *v*. call, summon, cry 318; *1sg. pr.* **call(e)** 347; 690; 711 (**callen** *v*.)

can, kan *v*. *1/3sg. and pl. pr.* can, know 63, 232, 298, 1223; 144, 802, 889, 1216; (also neg.) *1sg. pr.* **cannot(t)** 748, 1298; 1222, **kannot** 93, 808 (**connen** *v*.)

captiuité, captyvyté *n*. captivity (of hell) 393; 1081 (**captivite** *n*.)

care *n*. sorrow, hardship 508 (**care** *n*.)

care *v*. be sad, fear 157 (**caren** *v*.)

careful(l) *adj*. sorrowful, wretched 1075, 1081; 711; (as *n*.) those who are wretched 145 (**careful** *adj*.)

carnal *adj*. bodily, of the flesh 409 (**carnal** *adj*.)

carnalyté *n*. physical being, humanity 1358 (**carnalite** *n*.)

cas(e) *n*. situation, state of affairs, matter 690, 943; 5*A1* (**cas** *n*.)

cast *n*. intention, purpose 24*A3* (**cast** *n*.)

cast *v*. take (off) 758 (**casten** *v*.)

cawse *n*. reason, cause 636, 668, 765 (**cause** *n*.)

cawsyth *v*. *3sg. pr.* causes 1485 (**causen** *v*. 1.)

celestly *adj*. heavenly 1021 (**celestli** *adj*.)

certeyn *adv*. truly, assuredly 795 (**certain** *adv*.)

certyfyenge *v. pr. p.* affirming, officially notifying 32 (**certifien** *v*.)

cessacyon *n.* ceasing, interruption 1117 (**cessacioun** *n.*)

cety(e), cyté *n.* city, town 1419; 43; 1253 (**cite** *n.*)

charge *n.* obligation, responsibility 1244 (**charge** *n.*)

charge *v. 1sg. pr.* order, direct 108, 703; *3sg. pr.* **chargight** 739 (**chargen** *v.*)

chargyng *vbl. n.* command 783 (**charging** *ger.*)

charyté *n.* charity, love 25, 488 etc. (**charite** *n.*)

chast *adj.* sexually pure, chaste 289 (**chaste** *adj.*)

chast *adv.* chaste 634 (**chast(e** *adv.*)

chastyse *v.* punish 1203, 3A3 (**chastisen** *v.*)

chastyté *n.* chastity, sexual purity 631, 663, 897, 1058 (**chastite** *n.*)

chauncel *n.* chancel (of a church) 55 (**chauncel** *n.*)

chawmere *n.* private room, bedroom (fig.) 1379 (**chaumbre** *n.*)

chawnge *v. imp. sg.* alter, change (purpose) 154A2; *sg. pa.* **chaungyd** 753 (**chaungen** *v.*)

cher(e) *n.* mind, mood 154A2; comfort 126A2; **with mylde chere** humbly 726; **what cher(e)?** how are you? 1460; 5A1 (**chere** *n. 1.*)

chere *v. imp. sg.* comfort 153A2, 159A2 (**cheren** *v.*)

cherysch *v.* foster, take care of, protect 1206 (**cherishen** *v.*)

chese *v. imp. sg.* choose 627; *sg. pa.* **ches** chose 1157; *p. p.* **chosyn** 992 (**chesen** *v.*)

chyde *v. 1sg. pa. subj.* scolded, criticised 855 (**chiden** *v.*)

childe, chylde *n.* child 64, 71 etc.; 339, 626 etc.; *n. poss.* **childys** 36A2; *n. pl.* **childeryn** 1574, **childyr** 342 (**child** *n.*)

childely, chyldly *adj.* childlike, of a child 403; 1358 (**childli** *adj.*)

childhod *n.* childly form 1361 (**childhod** *n.*)

chirch *n.* the Church 1566 (**chirche** *n.*)

chosyn *p. p.* blessed, chosen (for heaven) 1338 (**chesen** *v.*)

clad, clothyd *p. p.* clothed, dressed 65A2 (fig.); 76A2 (**clothen** *v.*)

clay *n.* earth 1156 (**clei** *n.*)

claryfieth *v. 3sg. pr.* purifies, illumines 1015 (**clariffien** *v.*)

clene *adj.* pure, chaste 665, 673 etc. (**clene** *adj.*)

clene *adv.* handsomely, well 76A2 (**clene** *adv.*)

clennes(se) *n.* chastity, purity 482 (see note to ll. 481–3), 676, 681; 241, 663, 667 (**clennesse** *n.*)

clepe *v. 1sg. and pl. pr.* call, summon, name 34, 1457; *p. p.* **clepyd** called, named 50, 412 etc. (**clepen** *v.*)

cler(e) *adj.* bright, beautiful, pure, innocent 177; 625, 939, 980 (**cler** *adj.*)

clyne *v. 1sg. pr.* bow, submit 1348 (**clinen** *v.*)

clos *n.* **in clos** in a concealed/hidden way 1527 (**clos** *n.*)

clothyd *see* **clad**

clowte *v.* patch 855 (see note) (**clouten** *v. 1.*)

cokolde, cokwold *n.* cuckold 117A2; 55A2 (**cokewold** *n.*)

colde *adj.* lacking in animal spirits/physical powers 762 (**cold** *adj.*)

com(e), comyn, cum *v.* come, become 591, 798, 6A2; 448, 733 etc.; 364, 560sd; 36, 1523; *1sg. pr.* **com** 812; *2sg. pr.* **comyst** 796, 148A2; *3sg. pr.* **comyth** 386, 937, 560sd; *sg./pl. pr. subj.* **com** 703, **come** 198, 738; *imp. sg.* **com** 310, 793, **come** 347, 1034, **cum** 1074; *imp. pl.* **comyth** 98, 107, 810, **come** 1558; *pr. p.* **comyng(e)** 560sd; 25A3; *1sg. pa.* **cam** 45A2; *3sg. pa.* **cam** 214A2, **come** 1480, *pl. pa.* **come** 640; *p. p.* **com** 95, 175, **come** 83, 776, **cum** 1495, 1508 (**comen** *v.*)

comandyd *p. p.* commanded, ordered 9A1 (**commaunden** *v.*)

comaundementys *n. pl.* (the Ten) Commandments 453 (**commaundement** *n.*)

comendacyon *n.* praise 553 (**com(m)endacioun** *n.*)

comende *v. 1sg. pr.* **I me comende** I present my respects, I salute 501, 1396; *p. p.* **comendyd** praised 1297 (**commenden** *v.*)

comeryd *p. p.* engulfed (by), enveloped (in) 1090 (**combren** *v.*)

comfort(e) *n.* consolation, delight 201; 1116, 1135 etc. (**comfort** *n.*)

comfort(e) *v.* help, minister to, comfort 1485; 86, 1415, 1545; *imp. sg.* **comforte** 85A2 (**comforten** *v.*)

comfortabyl *adj.* inspiring, pleasing 1384; **comfortabelest** most acceptable 1560 (**comfortable** *adj.*)

comfortacyon *n.* consolation 1347, 1391 (**comfortacioun** *n.*)

comyng(e) *vbl. n.* coming 740; 765, 1485 etc. (**cominge** *ger.*)

company *n.* sexual union, company 106A2, 113A2 (**compaignie** *n.*)

compassyon *n.* pity, compassion 482 (see note to ll.481–3), 1075, 1138 (**compassioun** *n.*)

compiled *p. p.* written, related 11 (**compilen** *v.*)

comprehendyd *p. p.* contained, included 454 (**comprehenden** *v.*)

conceyte *n.* concept, matter (i.e. the play) 8 (**conceit(e** *n.*)

conceyve, conseyve *v.* conceive (a child) 1302; 223, 1444. 1489; *pr. p.* **conseyvenge** 1447; *1sg. pa.* **conceyvyd** 1481, **conseyvyd** 1487; *3sg. pa.* **conceyved** 1364; *p. p.* **conseyvid** 256, 1319, 1374 (**conceiven** *v.*)

concepcyon *n.* conceiving, conception 10, 188 etc. (**concepcioun** *n.*)

conclaue *n.* private room 1056 (see note) (**conclave** *n.*)

conclusyon *n.* ending, solution 13, 1163 etc. (**conclusioun** *n.*)

concorde *n.* harmony, unity 433 (**concord(e** *n.*)

confeccyons *n. pl.* ?sweetmeats, comfits 528sd (see note) (**confeccioun** *n.*)

confessyon *n.* confession (of sins) 379, 415 (**confessioun** *n.*)

confidens *n.* belief, trust 385 (**confidence** *n.*)

congregacyon *n.* gathering, audience 1 (**congregacioun** *n.*)

conseyve, conseyvyd, conseyvid *see* **conceyve**

conseyvynge *vbl. n.* conceiving (a child) 1484 (**conceivinge** *ger.*)

consente *v. 1sg. pr.* agree, assent 1191 (**consenten** *v.*)

consentynge *vbl. n.* consent, acquiescence 1481 (**consentinge** *ger.*)

conserve *v. sg. pr. subj.* preserve, keep safe 1, 1594 (**conserven** *v.*)

consyder *v.* take into account 1172; *pr. p.* **consyderynge** 257 (**consideren** *v.*)

consolacyon *n.* pleasure, encouragement, relaxation 478 (**consolacioun** *n.*)

contempt *n.* scorn, despising 397 (**contempt** *n.*)

content(e) *p. p.* satisfied 8, 541; 1193 (**contenten** *v.*)

contraryes *n. pl.* opposites, contrary decisions 1126 (**contrarie** *n.*)

contraryous *adj.* rebellious 1102 (**contrarious** *adj.*)

contraversy *n.* dispute, quarrel 1200 (**controversie** *n.*)

contryssyon *n.* remorse, sorrow for sins 482 (see note to ll.481–3), 1088 (**contricioun** *n.*)

contryte *adj.* remorseful, contrite 1116 (**contrit** *adj.*)

conuertyth *v. 3sg. pr.* transforms 393 (perhaps with future sense) (**converten** *v.*)

conversacyon *n.* way of life, conduct 1440 (**conversacioun** *n.*)

cosyn *n.* cousin 1270, 1318 etc.; *n. pl.* **cosynes** 13A3 (**cosin(e** *n.*)

cote *n. 1.* small cottage 774 (the meaning 'coat' is also possible; see next) (**cote** *n. 1.*)

cote *n. 2* coat 855 (**cot(e** *n. 2*)

counsel(l), counsayl *n.* meeting, advice 1195, 1233; 701, 1229, 8*A3* (**counseil** *n.*)

countré *n.* country, land 42, 1040 etc. (**contre(e** *n.*)

cowncell *v.* advise 690; *1sg. pr.* **counsell** 700; *3 sg. pr* **counsell** 1136 (**counseilen** *v.*)

cowpe *n.* cup, goblet 528sd (**cuppe** *n.*)

cowthe *adj.* familiar; **makyth cowthe** ?encourages 1015 (**couth** *adj.*)

creatour *n.* creator, maker 1132 (**creatour** *n.*)

creature *n.* created thing/person, person 8, 235 etc.; *n. pl.* **creatures** 1023, **creaturys** 434 (**creature** *n.*)

credyble *adj.* believable 1274 (**credible** *adj.*)

crepe *v.* move, go 238; *1sg. pr.* **krepe** 1052 (**crepen** *v.*)

cry(e) *v. 1sg. pr.* call, ask, cry out 1468; 559, 711, 1090; *pl. pr.* **cry(e)** 3*A2*; 830, 1099 etc.; *pr. p.* **cryenge** 1081; *p. p.* **cryed** 357, 417 (**crien** *v.*)

crysten *adj.* Christian 455 (**Cristen** *adj. & n.*)

crystyn *n.* **evyn crystyn** neighbour, fellow-man 457, 468, 515 (**even** *adj.*)

crowne *n.* crown (fig. of man's pre-eminence) 1089 (**coroune** *n.*)

curat *n.* priest with responsibility for those in his charge, parish priest 54 (**curat** *n.*)

cure *n.* care, charge 32 (**cure** *n. 1.*)

cursyd *p. p.* sinful, under God's curse 38, 104 (**cursed** *ppl.*)

cus *see* **kys** *v.*

custom *n.* custom, traditional practice 693 (**custum(e** *n.*)

custom *adj.* customary, regular 1389 (**custum(e** *n.*)

custommably *adv.* frequently, regularly 1014 (**custumabli** *adv.*)

day *n.* day 31, 337 etc.; **of o day byrth** one day old 1217 (**dai** *n.*)

dayly *adv.* every day, daily 472, 1295, 1567 (**daili** *adv.*)

dame *n.* mistress 138 (as a form of address) 1*A2* etc. (**dame** *n.*)

damesel *n.* girl, daughter, young woman 603; *n. pl.* **damysel(l)ys** 599; 923 (**damisele** *n.*)

dare *v. 1sg. pr.* dare 123, 124, 45*A2*; *2sg. pr.* **durste** 103 (**durren** *v.*)

date *n.* time, moment 201 (**date** *n.*)

declaracyon *n.* exposition (see note to ll.490–6) 496 (**declaracioun** *n.*)

declare *v.* relate, present 267 (**declaren** *v.*)

ded(e) *adj.* dead 835; 1023 (**ded** *adj.*)

deddly *adj.* fatal 1221 (**dedli** *adj.*)

dede *n.* deed, action, task 557, 647 etc.; *n. pl.* **dedys** 428, 574 (**dede** *n.*)

dede, dedyst *see* **do**

defende *v.* protect 503; *sg. pr. subj.* **dyffende** 351 (**defenden** *v.*)

defens *n.* **withowt defens** without denial 7*A3* (**defens(e** *n.*)

degré *n.* step 355; **in good degré** truly, correctly 605; **in þis degré** in this state of affairs 695; **in iche degré** in every way 716; **in ony degré** in any way 1394 (**degre** *n.*)

deye *v.* die 1124, 1207; *p. p.* **deyd** 1201 (**dien** *v.*)

deyté *n.* deity, godhead 557. 705 (**deite** *n.*)

deliberacyon *n.* consideration, judgement 494 (see note to ll.490–6), 1592 (**deliberacioun** *n.*)

deme *v.* judge, decide 1186; *1sg. pr.* **deme** 1200 (**demen** *n.*)

departe *v. 1pl. pr.* part 81 (**departen** *v.*)

depe *adv.* deeply, deep, intensely 243, 334, 527 (**dep(e** *adv.*)

depnes *n.* the depths (fig.) 417 (**depnes(se** *n.*)

dere *adj.* beloved, dear, precious 23, 621 etc. (**dere** *adj. 1.*)

dere *adv.* dearly 515 (**dere** *adv.*)

descendith, discendit *v. 3sg. pr.* descends 172sd; 1355sd; *imp. sg.* **descende** 137*A2* (**descenden** *v.*)

desesyd *p. p.* troubled, distressed 130*A2* (**disesen** *v.*)

desyre *n.* longing, desire 356 (**desir** *n.*)

desyre *v.* wish, desire 1021; *pl. pr.* **desyre** 1342 (**desiren** *v.*)

deté *n.* song 1010 (**dite** *n.*)

determyn *v.* decide upon 557 (**determinen** *v.*)

determynacyon *n.* investigation, definition, conclusion 496 (see note to ll.490–6) (**determinacioun** *n.*)

deth *n.* death 1204, 1212, 1218, *n. pl.* **dethis** 1206 (**deth** *n.*)

dette *n.* debt; **as is dette** as is due and necessary 373 (**dette** *n.*)

devyde *v. see* **dyvvyde**

devyl *n.* devil 469, 1083, 1101, 1157; *n. pl.* **develys** 1009 (**devel** *n.*)

devyr *n.* duty 109*A2* (**dever, -er** *n.*)

devyse *v.* manage (to provide) 64 (**devisen** *v.*)

devocyon *n.* devoutness, piety 494 (see note to ll.490–6), 527, 1435; *n. pl.* **devocyonys** prayers 1430 (**devocioun** *n.*)

devowtly *adv.* reverently, solemnly 97, 907 (**devoutli** *adv.*)

dewe, du *adj.* proper, appropriate 777; 41, 720 (**du(e** *adj.*)

dyffende *see* **defende**

diffynicyon *n.* limitation 1162 (**diffinicioun** *n.*)

dyffuse *adj.* complicated 696 (**diffuse** *adj.*)

dyght *p. p.* prepared 747, 786, 822 (**dighten** *v.*)

dygnyté *n.* authority, high office, excellence 38, 458 (**dignite** *n.*)

dylexcyon *n.* spiritual pleasure/love 494 (see note to ll.490–6) (**dileccioun** *n.*)

dysceyved *p. p.* deceived, tricked 1083 (**deceiven** *v.*)

dyscencyon *n.* disagreement, quarreling 1176 (**dissencioun** *n.*)

discendit *see* **descendith**

dyscerne *v.* make a judgement, come to a conclusion 689 (**discernen** *v.*)

dyscressyon *n.* sound judgement 494 (see note to ll.490–6) (**discrecioun** *n.*)

dyscus *v.* discuss, investigate 557 (**discussen** *v.*)

dysmayd(e) *p. p.* afraid, perturbed 902; 23*A2* (**dismaien** *v.*)

dyspeyre *v.* despair 1512 (?*n*) (**despeiren** *v.* or **despeir** *n.*)

dyspyce, dysspice, dys(s)pyse *v.* scorn, humiliate, reject 645; 61; 54*A2*; 38; *sg. pa.* **dyspysyd** 1131 (**despisen** *v.*)

displese *v. imp. pl.* be annoyed/offended 1031; *p. p.* **dysplesyd** 128*A2* (**displesen** *v.*)

dissese *n.* suffering, misfortune 1*A3* (**disese** *n.*)

dissponsacyon *n.* betrothal, marriage 585 (**desponsacion** *n.*)

dysspose *v. imp. sg.* settle, compose 1002 (**disposen** *v.*)

dyvers *adj.* various 560sd (**divers(e** *adj.*)

dyvvyde *v.* separate, divide 1190; *1sg. pr.* **devyde** 51 (**dividen** *v.*)

dyvvynacyon *n.* ?foresight 496 (see note to ll.490–6) (**divinacioun** *n.*)

dyvinyté *n.* the divine nature, God 1328 (**divinite** *n.*)

dyvvysyon *n.* disagreement, strife, estrangement 1181 (**divisioun** *n.*)

do *v.* do, act, perform, carry out (and as *aux.*) 37, 84, etc.; *1sg. pr.* **do** 783, 1025; *2sg. pr.* **dost** 151*A2*; *3sg. pr.* **doth** 60, 138 etc.; *2pl. pr.* **do** 133, 137 etc.; *3pl. pr.* **doth** 1007, 1295, 7*A1*; *sg. pr. subj.* **do** 96, 351, 565; *sg. pa.* **dyd** 268; *2sg. pa.* **dedyst** 58*A2*, 123*A2*; *pl. pa.* **dede** 645, 1374; *p. p.* **do** 122, 158, etc., **don** 428, 1351 etc., **done** 619; **frute was do** time of child-bearing was over 639; **lawe doth after** the law is in accord with 681; **all was don** everything was over 1585; **do way** stop! 74*A2* (**don** *v.*)

doloure *n.* grief 972 (**dolour** *n.*)

dom *n.* judgement 782; *n. pl.* **domys** decrees, judgements 49 (**dom** *n.*)

dominacyon, domynacyon *n.* authority, rule, majesty, lordship 1438; 1092 (**dominacioun** *n.*)

dompnesse *n.* dumbness 1446 (**dombenesse** *n.*)

dore *n.* door 1*A2*, 5*A2*, 8*A2* (**dor(e** *n.*)

dote *v.* become infatuated 854 (**doten** *v.*)

doughter *see* **dowtere**

doute, dowhte, dowte, dowth *n.* doubt, uncertainty 756, 52*A2*; 684; 712; 450 (**dout(e** *n.*)

dowm *adj.* dumb 1490, 1580 (**domb** *adj.*)

down(e) *adv.* down 66, 551 etc.; 1091, 1455 (**doun** *adv.*)

dowse *adj.* dear, sweet 613 (**douce** *adj.*)

dowte *v.* *1sg. pr.* doubt 1312 (**douten** *v.*)

dowteful *adj.* uncertain 712 (**douteful** *adj.*)

dowteles *adv.* without doubt 696 (**douteles** *adv.*)

dowtere, dowtyr, doughter *n.* daughter 275, 280 etc.; 333, 609 etc.; 18*A1* (**doughter** *n.*)

dowty *adj.* worthy, handsome 20*A1* (**doughti** *adj.*)

drawe *v.* bring 599; *p. p.* **drawyn** brought, admitted 277 (**drauen** *v.*)

dred(e) *n.* fear, apprehension 78, 553, 1299; 131, 653 etc. (**dred(e** *n.*)

drede *v.* *1sg. pr.* fear, dread 49, 58, 27*A2*; *3pl. pr.* **drede** 405, 1508 (**dreden** *v.*)

dredful *adj.* frightening 49, 689 (**dredeful** *adj.*)

dres *v.* prepare 683 (**dressen** *v.*)

dryve *v.* *imp. sg.* force, drive (fig.) 527 (**driven** *v.*)

du *see* **dewe**

durste *see* **dare**

dwell(e) *v.* remain, live, exist 670; 436, 923 etc.; *3sg. pr.* **dwellys** 376, **dwellyth** 388; *3pl. pr.* **dwelle** 1418 (**dwellen** *v.*)

dwere *n.* **withowtyn dwere** without doubt, truly 11*A2* (**dwere** *n.*)

ech *pron.* each 766 (**ech** *pron.*)

eche, iche *adj.* each 6, 541 etc.; 716 (**ech** *pron.*)

echon *pron.* each one 434, 518, 1224 (**ech on** *pron phrase*)

edyfied *p. p.* built, erected 400 (**edifien** *v.*)

ey(e) *n.* eye 363, 856; 1054, 170*A2*; (363, 856 ?*pl.*); *n. pl.* **eyn** 375, 424, 648, **eynes** 1084 (**eie** *n. 1.*)

eylsum *adj.* wholesome, sound 701 (**holsom** *adj.*)

eyte *num.* eight 1568 (**eighte** *card. num.*)

eyted *ord. num.* eighth 397 (**eightethe** *ord. num.*)

elde *n.* old 96 (**elde** *n.*)

elefnte *ord. num.* eleventh 415 (**elleventhe** *ord. num.*)

ellys *adv.* otherwise 456, 525, 1262 (**elles** *adv.*)

empres *n.* empress 1398 (**emperesse** *n.*)

enbrace *v.* afflict 7*A1* (**embracen** *v.*)

encrese *n.* growth 604 (**encres** *n.*)

ende *n.* end 1307; **withowtyn ende** 468, 548, 1127, 1174 (**ende** *n. 1.*)

ende *v. 1sg. pr.* end, conclude 1402 (**enden** *v.*)

endynge, hendyng *vbl. n.* ending, end 7; 915 (**ending(e** *ger.*)

endles *adj.* eternal, without end 1154, 1155, 1168 (**endeles** *adj.*)

endles *adv.* eternally 388 (**endeles** *adv.*)

endlesly *adv.* eternally 1063, 1145, 1290 (**endelesli** *adv.*)

endure *v.* continue, last, remain, suffer 7, 1134 (**enduren** *v.*)

enforme *v. imp. sg.* resolve, explain 712 (**enfourmen** *v.*)

enjoyd *see* **injouyid**

enjonyd *p. p.* united 1403 (**enjoinen** *v.*)

enmy *n.* enemy 470; *n. pl.* **enemyes** 382 (**enemi** *n.*)

ensens *see* **incense**

ensensyth *v. 3sg. pr.* censes 97sd (**ensensen** *n.*)

ensure *v. 1sg. pr.* assure 697; promise, assert 108*A2* (**ensuren** *v.*)

entent *n.* mind, purpose 1325; **to Goddys entent** as God wished 265 (**entente** *n.*)

entre *v. 3pl. pr.* enter 1355sd (**entren** *v.*)

equyté *n.* justice, impartiality 1194 (**equite** *n.*)

er, her, or *conj.* before 638; 337; 963, 1421 (**er** *conj. 1.*)

erste *adv.* before that 1073 (**erest** *adv.*)

erth(e), herthe *n.* earth 215, 235 etc.; 230, 346 etc.; 1548 (**erthe** *n.*)

erthely *adj.* earthly, of this earth 664, 1336 (**ertheli** *adj.*)

esyd *p. p.* comforted 131*A2* (**esen** *v.*)

eternal(l) *adj.* everlasting, eternal 45; 349 (**eternal** *adj.*)

euery, every *adj.* every 54, 603, 1541, 10*A1*; 8, 353 etc. (**everi** *pron.*)

everych *pron.* every one 742 (**everi** *pron.*)

evesong *n.* evensong, vespers 1541 (**eve(n-song** *n.*)

euyl, evyl *adj.* evil, slanderous, wicked 921; 194, 1045, 25*A2* (**ivel** *adj.*)

euyl, evyl *adv.* with difficulty 811; **evyl payd** annoyed, angry 197*A2* (**ivel(e** *adv.*)

evyn *adj.* **evyn crystyn** fellow Christian, fellow man 457, 468, 515 (**even** *adj.*)

evyn *adv.* impartially, truly 821; **evyn al at onys** all at the very same moment 1359 (**evyn** *adv.*)

euyr, evyr *adv.* perpetually, ever, always 1059, 222*A2*; 19, 76 etc. (**ever** *adv.*)

evyrmo(re) *adv.* at all times, always 1133; 48, 131 etc.; **and evyrmore** for all time 1432 (**evermo(r** *adv.*)

excede *v.* go beyond, transcend 556 (**exceden** *v.*)

excepcyon *n.* objection 1141 (**excepcioun** *n.*)

exercyse *v. 1pl. pr.* celebrate 35 (**exercisen** *v.*)

exilyd, exyled *p. p.* banished, driven away 126; 1205 (**exilen** *v.*)

exorte *v. 1.* call upon 83 (**exhorten** *v.*)

exorte *v.2* arise 1118 (see note) (**exorten** *v.*)

expownd *v.* interpret, explain 680 (**expounen** *v.*)

expres(se) *adv.* clearly, plainly, openly 682; 428 (**expres(se** *adv.*)

expresse *adj.* **masangere expresse** special messenger 1381 (**expres** *adj.*)

face *n.* face 66, 310 etc. (**face** *n.*)

fadere, fadyr *n.* father 503; 216, 285 etc.; *n. poss.* **faderys** 1371 (**fader** *n.*)

fay *n.* **in fay** in faith, truly 43*A2* (**feith** *n.*)

fayl *n.* **withowt fayl** certainly 6*A3* (**faile** *n.*)

faylen *v.* fail to obtain 1016 (**failen** *v.*)

fayn *adv.* gladly, willingly 574, 798, 1373 (**fain** *adv.*)

fayr(e) *adj.* in good condition, beautiful, lovely 136, 271 etc.; 633, 742 (**fair** *adj.*)

fayrest *adv.* most beautifully 872 (**fair(e** *adv.*)

fal *v.* fall, drop down 346; *1sg. pr.* **fall(e)** 512; 216, 759, 914, 951; *1pl. pr.* **falle** 1551; *imp. sg.* **falle** 707; *p. p.* **falle** 1089; **falle fast in age** really are getting old 1551 (**fallen** *v.*)

fame *n.* reputation, report 127, 194, 922 (**fame** *n.*)

famyt *p. p.* famished (fig.) 1071 (**famen** *v.*)

fare *v.* live, exist 268; *pl. pr.* **How fare ȝe?** How are you getting along? 134, **faryn** 575; *p.p.* **ferd(e)** got on 10*A2*, 21*A2* (**faren** *v.*)

far(e)wel, fareweyl *interj.* farewell, 969; 205, 939 etc.; 975, 976, 1376 (**faren** *v.*)

fast *adv.* quickly, really 108, 812 etc. (**fast(e** *adv.*)

fastyng *vbl. n.* fasting 41 (**fasting(e** *ger.* 2)

fawte *n.* fault, deficiency, imperfection 67, 520 (**faute** *n.*)

febylnesse *n.* weakness, infirmity 3*A1*, 7*A1* (**feblenesse** *n.*)

fede *v.* feed, eat 474, 538, 563, 1071; *imp. pl.* **fede** 534, 571 (**feden** *v.*)

feyth *n.* faith, belief 427, 503, 1170; **in feyth** certainly, indeed 208, 1454 (**feith** *n.*)

fel *adj.* violent, deadly 410 (**fel** *adj.*)

felachep(pe) *n.* company, companionship 630; 126, 485 (**felauship(e** *n.*)

felas *n. pl.* lads, friends 133 (**felau(e** *n.*)

fele *v.* *1sg. pr.* feel 485, 1356, 1369; *sg. pa.* **felt** experienced 540 (**felen** *v.*)

felle *v.* fell, strike down 218*A2*; *3sg. pr* **fellyth** 1520 (**fellen** *v.*)

fendys *n. poss.* devil's 218*A2* (**fend** *n.*)

fer *adj.* distant, far 1040, 10*A2* (**fer** *adj.* 1.)

fer *adv.* far 728, 1039 etc. (**fer** *adv.*)

fer(e) *n.* fellow 1296; companion 627 (**fere** *n.* 1.)

fer(e) *n.* fear 403; 521 (**fer** *n.* 1.)

fere *n.* fire 174 (**fir** *n.*)

fere *n.* **in fere** together 940, 1340 (**fere** *n.* 2)

fere *v.* *1sg. pr.* fear 61, 171; *3sg. pr.* **feryth** frightens 1013; *pr. p.* **feryng** 158 (**feren** *v.*)

ferforthe *adv.* **so ferforthe for þat** so much so that 1500 (**fer-forth** *adv.*)

fers *adj.* powerful 410 (**fers** *adj.*)

ferther *adv.* further 1569 (**ferther** *adv.*)

ferthermore *adv.* moreover 741, 1332, 216*A2* (**ferther-more** *adv.*)

fest *n.* feast, feast-day 33, 35, 44 (**feste** *n.*)

fewe *adj.* few 14 (**feue** *indef. pron.*)

fy *interj.* fie! 71*A2* (**fi** *int.*)

fyff, fyve *num.* five 191, 890; 477, 524, 545 (**five** *card. num.*)

fyfte *ord. num.* fifth 379, 518 (**fifte** *ord. num.*)

fyftene *num.* fifteen 350, 354, (as *ord. num.*) 439 (**fif-tene** *card. num.*)

fyfty *num.* fifty 1420 (**fifti** *card. num.*)

fylle *n.* **wepe my fylle** cry as much as I need 149*A2* (**fille** *n.*)

fynde *v.* find 808, 1223, 178*A2*; *1sg. pr.* **fynde** 539; *p. p.* **fownd(e)** 29; 1216, 1301 (**finden** *v.*)

fynialy, fynyaly *adv.* finally 1247; 1205 (**finialli** *adv.*)

fyrst *ord. num.* first; (as *adj.*) 274, 355, 1097; (as *n.*) 481, 926; (**first** *ord. num.*)

fyrst *adv.* first 319, 458 etc. (**first** *adv.*)

fle *v.* depart, turn aside 1195 (**flen** *v.*)

flesch(e) *n.* flesh 65*A2*; 1363 (see **bon** above) (**flesh** *n.*)

fleschly *adj.* carnal, physical 410 (**fleshli(ch** *adj.*)

flyth *n.* flight 1278 (**flight** *n.* 2)

floreschyth *v. 3sg. pr.* blossoms, bears leaves 872 (**florishen** *v.*)

flowre *n.* flower (fig.) 656, 974; *n. pl.* **flourys** 835 (**flour** *n.* 1.)

fo *n.* enemy 760, 1131 (**fo** *n.*)

fode *n.* food 538, 1071 (**fode** *n.* 1.)

foyson *n.* plenty, abundance 568 (**foisoun** *n.*)

folde *v.* give way, buckle 800 (**folden** *v.* 2)

foly *n.* sinfulness 29, 1061, 1203 (**folie** *n.*)

folk(e) *n.* people 575; 1071 (**folk** *n.*)

folwe *v.* come near 630; accompany, follow 933, 934; *imp. sg.* **folwe** 1034; *pr. p.* **folwyng** 12 (**folwen** *v.*)

foot *n.* foot 208*A2*; *n. pl.* **fete** 216, 294, 185*A2*, 186*A2* (**fot** *n.*)

foot-mayd *n.* maidservant 73 (**fot-maid(en** *n.*)

for *conj.* because, for, since 49, 51 etc. (**for** *conj.*)

for(e) *prep.* for, on account of, in exchange for 25, 53 etc.; 985, 1232; **For my barynes** as far as my infertility is concerned 168; **fore** (as *adv.*) on that account 1232 (**for** *prep.*)

forbede *v. sg. pr. subj.* forbid 841, 98*A2* (**forbeden** *v.*)

forfaderys *n. pl.* ancestors 1527 (**for(e-fader** *n.*)

forfete *n.* **dede . . . forfete** offended 40*A2* (**forfet** *n.*)

forgete *v.* forget 201 (**foryeten** *v.*)

forȝeve *v. imp. sg.* forgive 330 (**foryeven** *v.*)

forgyfnes *n.* forgiveness 169*A2* (**foryevenes(se** *n.*)

forlorn *p. p.* lost, damned 70*A2*, 158*A2* (**forlesen** *v.*)

forsake *v.* abandon, give up 898, 929, 112*A2*; *1sg. pr.* **forsake** 60*A2*, 184*A2*; *sg. pa.* **forsoke** 1156, **forsook** 1170 (**forsaken** *v.*)

forsothe *adv.* truly 67*A2* (**forsoth** *adv.*)

fortene, fourtene *num.* fourteen 268; 586, 600 etc.; (as *ord. num.*) fourteenth 433 (**four-tene** *num.*)

forth(e), furth *adv.* forward, out, on 259, 756 etc.; 1423, 150*A2*; 15*A1* (**forth** *adv.*)

forthy *adv.* **what forthy** notwithstanding 104*A2* (**for-thi** *pronominal adv.*)

forthryght *adv.* directly 451 (**forth-right** *adv.*)

foure, fowre *num.* four 1060, 1435; 1060, 1188, 1206, 1247 (**four** *num.*)

fourte *ord. num.* fourth 373, 517, 789 (**ferthe** *num.*)

fowle *adj.* shameful 127; sinful 1061 (**foul** *adj.*)

fowth *p. p.* fought, afflicted 411 (**fighten** *v.*)

fraternyté *n.* brotherhood 1330 (**fraternite** *n.*)

fre *adj.* fine 835, gracious 1036 etc. (**fre** *adj.*)

frelnes *n.* frailty, weakness 1172 (**frelnes(se** *n.*)

frendys *n. pl.* friends 14*A1*, 17*A3* (**frend** *n.*)

Frensche *adj.* French 56*A2* (**Frensh** *adj.*)

fro, from *prep.* from 2, 89 etc.; 7, 126 etc. (**from** *prep.*)

fruyssyon *n.* spiritual enjoyment 483 (see note to ll. 481–3) (**fruicioun** *n.*)

frute, frewte *n.* (fig.) child, offspring 60, 71 etc.; 194*A2* (**fruit** *n.*)

fruteful *adj.* fertile 102, 239; (as *n.*) those who have borne children 103, 309 (**fruitful** *adj.*)

ful *adj.* filled, full 171, 192 etc. (**ful** *adj.*)

ful(l) *adv.* very, fully, quite 79, 135 etc.; 646, 647, 747, 798 (**ful** *adv.*)

fulffyl(le) *v.* carry out, comply with, consummate 932; 628; *3sg. pr.* **fulfyl-lyth** fills 1519; *p. p.* **fulfylled** 1468, **fulfylt** 1273 filled (**ful-fillen** *v.*)

fully *adv.* completely, fully 1571 (**fulli** *adv.*)

furth *see* **forth(e)**

future *adj.* future, to come 2 (**futur(e** *adj.*)

gay *adv.* showily, splendidly 76*A2* (**gai** *adv.*)

game *n.* sport, business 75*A2*, 79*A2*; **game and gle** happiness 837; **neyther sport nere game** no fun, no joke 844 (**game** *n.*)

gan *see* **gyn**

gate, ȝate *n.* **Gyldyn/Goldyn Gate** 198, 221; gate 236 (**gate** *n.*)

generacyonys *n. pl.* people, generations 1500 (**generacioun** *n.*)

gentyllest *adj.* most noble 1393 (**gentil** *adj.*)

gete *v.* obtain, earn 11*A2* (**geten** *v. 1.*)

gyff, gyve, ȝeve *v.* give 1084; 499; 55, 695 etc.; *3sg. pr.* **gevyth** 462–4; *imp. sg.* **gyff** 1346; *sg. pa.* **ȝaff** 182, 1229; *p. p.* **ȝove** 308, **ȝovyn**, 453

gyldyn, goldyn *adj.* **Gyldyn/Goldyn Gate** the Golden Gate of Jerusalem 198 (see note), 221 (**golden** *adj.*)

gyn *v. pl. pr.* begin (or = *aux.* 'do') 800; *2sg. pr.* **gynnyst** 35*A2*; *3sg. pr.* **gynnyth** begins 1451, 30*A2*; *3sg. pa. aux.* **gan blys** blessed 1588, **gan tell** told 216*A2* (**ginnen** *v.*)

gynnynge *vbl. n.* beginning 7, 187 (**ginning(e** *ger.*)

gyse *n.* business, manner, fashion 31*A2*, 56*A2* (**gise** *n.*)

glad *adj.* happy, joyful 81, 175 etc. (**glad** *adj.*)

gladnes *n.* happiness, joy 222, 226, 367 (**gladnes(se** *n.*)

gle *n.* **game and gle** happiness 837 (**gle** *n.1*)

gloryous *adj.* magnificent, wonderful 1100 (**glorious** *adj.*)

go(n), goo, gone *v.* go, walk 44, 123 etc.; 298, 985 etc.; 8*A1*; 838, 118*A2*; *1sg. pr.* **go** 1277, 1433, 60*A2*; *3sg. pr.* **goth** 236sd; *pl. pr.* **go(n)** 242, 302 etc.; 250, 406; *imp. sg.* **go** 150*A2*, 153*A2*, 159*A2*; *imp. pl.* **gooth** 228, **go(th)** 142, 497, 14*A1*; 908, 994, 1424; *2sg. pr. subj.* **go** 108, 959; *pr. p.* **goynge** 560sd; *sg. pa.* **went** 29*A2*; *pl. pa.* **wenten** 1447; *p. p.* **go** 215, 1428 (**gon** *v.*)

God *n.* God; *n. poss.* **God(d)ys** God's (**God, god** *n. 1*)

god *n.* beneficial action 1227; *n. pl.* **godys** possessions 46, 51, **goodys** good things 1519 (**god** *n.*)

gode, good *adj.* good, favourable, beneficial 347, 1335, 62*A2*; 147, 206 etc. (**god** *adj.*)

Godhed(e), Godhyd *n.* the Deity, God 1260, 1355sd; 1395; 560 (**godhede** *n. 1*)

godly *adj.* divine, of God 440; **Fadyr godly** God the Father 1355sd (**godli** *adj.*)

godnesse, goodnes *n.* goodness 958; 20, 147, 1383 (**godnes(se** *n. 2*)

gold *adj.* gold 528sd (**gold** *adj.*)

Go(o)st *n.* **Holy Go(o)st** Holy Spirit 311, 461 etc.; 192 (**gost** *n.*)

gostly *adj.* spiritual 476 (**gostli** *adj.*)

gostly *adv.* spiritually, in spirit, in a spiritual way 355, 1013 (**gostli** *adv.*)

governe *v.* keep 20; *imp. pl.* **governe** look after 205 (**governen** *v.*)

gowne *n.* cloak 758 (**goune** *n.*)

grace, gras *n.* mercy, favour 68, 143 etc.; 593, 949; *n. pl.* **gracys** 526 (**grace** *n.*)

gracyous *adj.* merciful, benevolent, good, noble, beautiful 69, 239 etc. (**gracious** *adj.*)

gracyously *adv.* fortunately 1404 (**graciousli** *adv.*)

grame *n.* grief 125 (**gram(e** *n.*)

gramercy *interj.* thank you, many thanks 1352–5 etc. (**gramercy** *n. & interj.*)

graunt *v.* allow, permit, grant 650; *lsg. pr.* **graunt** 1144, **grawnt** 616; *sg. pr. subj.* 293; *p. p.* **grauntyd** 235, 135*A2* (**graunten** *v.*)

grecys, grees *n. pl.* steps 448; 350 (**gres** *n.*; **gre** *n.*1)

greff *n.* **thynkys no greff** do not be distressed 1*A3* (**gref** *n.*)

gret(e), grett *adj.* great 143, 1*A1* etc.; 1064, 1104; 62, 77 etc.; **grett age** old age 1271 (**gret** *adj.*)

gretynge *vbl. n.* greeting, salutation 1294, 1462 (**greting(e** *ger.*)

grettly *adv.* much, greatly 61, 136 etc. (**gretli** *adv.*)

grevyth *v.* *3sg. pr.* afflicts, saddens 1139; *p. p.* **grevyd** 1122 (**greven** *v.*)

gronyn *v.* groan, moan 759 (**gronen** *v.*)

grote *n.* groat, a silver fourpenny piece (used for coin of small value) 772 (**grot** *n.3*)

grounde, grond *n.* earth, ground 150; 6*A1* (**ground** *n.*)

grow *v. pl. pr.* grow 1461; *3sg. pr.* **growyht** appears 143; *sg. pa.* **grew** came 1408 (**grouen** *v.*)

ʒa *adv.* yes (and as an exclamation) 145, 246 etc.

ʒaff *see* **gyff**

ʒarde, ʒerd(e) *n.* rod, wand 778, 781 etc.; 822; 724, 742, 816; *n. pl.* **ʒardys** 721, 723, 734

ʒate *see* **gate**

ʒe, ye *pl. pron. subj.* you 50, 82 etc.; 6*A1*

ʒelde *v. pl. pr.* offer, yield 874

ʒer(e) *n.* year 1567; 35; *n. pl.* **ʒer(e), ʒerys** 1568; 181, 268 etc.; 275, 610, 1062, 1070; **of thre ʒer(e) age** three years old 262, 270sd, 447

ʒet(t), ʒit(t) *adv.* yet 753, 804, 987, 98*A2*; 102, 187 etc.; 340, 678, 47*A2*; 46*A2*, 111*A2*

ʒeve *see* **gyff**

ʒiff, ʒyff *see* **if(f)**

ʒyfte *n.* gift 1411

ʒyng(e), ʒonge *adj.* young 258, 977; 447, 768; 755, 852, 918, 51*A2*

ʒynge *n.* young (people): **bothe elde and ʒynge** everyone 96

ʒonge *see* **ʒyng(e)** *adj.*

ʒonger *adj.* younger 277

ʒou, ʒow, you *pl. pron. obj.* you 1589, 1590; 16, 17 etc.; 14*A1*, i5*A1*

ʒough *n.* youth 411

ʒour(e), ʒowre, your *pl. pron. poss.* your, yours 66, 78 etc.; 581, 599, 1*A2*; 48*A2*, 213*A2*; 14*A1*

ʒourself *pron.* yourself 471

ʒove, ʒovyn *see* **gyff**

ha *see* **a** *interj.*

habytacyon *n.* **in vs haue habytacyon** dwell in us 381 (**habitacioun** *n.*)

had, hadde, haddyst *see* **haue**

haddyd *see* **adde**

halle *n.* hall 713; **halle or boure** anywhere (lit. main public room or private apartment) 970 (**hal(le** *n.*)

halwyd *p. p.* holy, blessed 1022 (**halwen** *v.*)

han *see* **haue**

hand, hond(e) *n.* hand 723, 758 etc.; 786, 1539; 721 (?*pl.*), 208*A2*; *n. pl.* **handys** 294, 741, 828; þe **had in honde** had dealings with you 28*A2* (**hond(e** *n.*)

hand-mayden, -maydeʒe *n.* servant, hand-maiden 1350, 1362; 1499 (**hond(e** *n.*)

hap *n.* (good) fortune, chance 181*A2* (**hap** *n.*)

hard *adj.* terrible, difficult 693, 85*A2* (**hard** *adj.*)

haske *see* **aske**

hast *n.* eagerness, impatience 1263; **in hast** quickly 203, 636, 1428 (**hast(e** *n.*)

hast *v. pl. pr.* hasten, hurry 739; *imp. sg.* **haste** 1324 (**hasten** *v.*)

hast, hath *see* **haue**

hastyly *adv.* quickly 1414 (**hastili(e** *adv.*)

hate *v.* hate, shun 469; *2sg. pr.* **hatyst** 516; *3sg. pr.* **hatyth** hates 1149 (**haten** *v.*)

haue, hauyn, a *v.* have 122, 191 etc.; 884; 1159, 163*A2*, 165*A2*, 202*A2*; *1sg. pr.* **haue** 48, 122 etc.; *2sg. pr.* **hast** 153, 896 etc.; *3sg. pr.* **hath** 176, 220 etc.; *1pl. pr.* **haue** 70, 246 etc.; **han** 545, 794; *2pl. pr.* **haue** 206, 310 etc. **han** 254, 702 etc. **an** 900; *3pl. pr.* **haue** 31, 1115, **han** 400, 1094, **an** 150, 400; *sg. pr. subj.* **haue** 157, 381 etc.; *pr. p.* **havyng(e)** 1358; 1438; *imp. sg.* **haue** 199, 429 etc.; *imp. pl.* **hath** 588; *2sg. pa.* **haddyst** 80*A2*; *3sg. pa.* **had** 182, 183 etc.; *pl. pa.* **hadde** 642; *sg. pa. subj.* **had** 1201, 1202, 111*A2*, 201*A2*; *p. p.* **had** 209, 226 (**haven** *v.*)

he *pron.* he (**he** *pron. 1*)

hed *n.* head 132, 1089, 1552 (**hed** *n. 1*)

hed(e), heed, heyd *n.* **take hed(e)/heed/heyd** take note, pay attention, consider 18; 695, 824, 1325, 1332; 724; 595 (**hed** *n. 2*)

hedyr *adv.* hither, here 135, 502 etc. (**hider** *adv.*)

hef(f)ne, hevyn *n.* heaven 149, 216 etc.; 230; 21, 22 etc. (**heven** *n.*)

hey, hy(e), hyʒ(e) *adj.* great, important, lofty, sovereign 449, 1275, 1515; 1098; 1382; 458, 713 etc.; 26*A2*; **hye and lowe** everyone 594; **on hye** in heaven 174*A2* (**heigh** *adj.*)

heyd *see* **hed(e)**

heye, hy *adv.* up, high 828; loudly 905 (**heighe** *adv.*)

heyl *interj.* hail 1280 (**heil** *interj.*)

heyth, hyght *n.* height 1516; **in hyght** ?quickly 743; **Gramercy . . . on hyght** Great thanks! 1353 (**height(e** *n.*)

heyued *p. p.* raised 423 (**heven** *v.*)

helle *n.* hell 551, 991 etc. (**helle** *n.*)

helle-hownde *n.* hellhound, the devil 1149 (**helle** *n.*)

helmes *see* **almes**

help *v.* help 1008; *imp. sg.* **help** 131*A2*; *sg. pr. subj.* **help** 684, 798 (**helpen** *v.*)

helpe *n.* help 364 (**help** *n.*)

helpfful *adj.* kind, helpful 209 (**helpful** *adj.*)

helpyngys *vbl. n. pl.* acts of mercy, alms-deeds 1428 (**helpinge** *ger.*)

helth *n.* well-being, prosperity, salvation 1048, 1049, 1496 (**helth(e** *n.*)

hem *pl pron. obj.* them (**hem** *pron. pl.*)

hende *adj.* gracious, obedient 507, 598, 933 (**hend(e** *adj.*)

hendyng *see* **endynge**

hendyr *adj.* nearer at hand 568 (**hend(e** *adv.*)

hens *adv.* away, hence 344, 507 etc. (**hennes** *adv.*)

hent *v. 2pl. pr.* take 741 (**henten** *v.*)

her *see* **er**

her(e) *adv.* here 179, 285 etc.; 3, 9 etc. (**her** *adv.*)

her(e), hire, hyre *pron. obj./poss.* her 675; 10, 73 etc.; 260, 293, 294; 934, 1319, 159*A2* (**hir(e** *pron. 1* and *2*)

her(e) *pl. pron. poss.* their 97sd; 4, 27 etc. (**her(e** *pron. poss. pl.*)

herand *n.* errand, message 4*A2* (**erend(e** *n.*)

here *v.* hear 139, 212 etc.; *1sg. pr.* **here** 1045; *imp. sg.* **here** 418; *2pl. pr. subj.* **here** 127; *1/3sg. pa.* **herd(e)** 655, 1462; 611; *p. p.* **herd(e)** 176, 220, 292, 713; 358 (**heren** *v.*)

hereaftere *adv.* after this 555 (**her-after** *adv.*)

herebefore *adv.* before this 246 (**her-bifore(n** *adv.*)

herefore *adv.* for this 154, 1237 (**her-for** *adv.*)

hereto *adv.* to this 1191 (**her-to** *adv.*)

herynge *vbl. n.* speech, message 1292 (**hering(e** *ger.*)

herk(e) *v. imp. sg.* listen 731; 607; *imp. pl.* **herkyn** 598 (**herken** *v.*)

hert(e) *n.* heart 139, 153 etc.; 423, 711 etc.; *n. pl.* **hertys** 598, 647, 911, 1512 (**herte** *n.*)

herthe *see* **erth(e)**

herty *adj.* **with herty wylle** readily, willingly 153*A2* (**herti** *adj.*)

hert(y)ly *adj.* devout, heartfelt 1572; 662 (**hert(e)li(e** *adj.*)

hertyly, hertylyé *adv.* cheerfully, unrestrainedly 571; 4*A3* (**hert(e)li(e** *adv.*)

hes(e), his(e) *pron. poss.* his 1225; 23, 77 etc.; 24, 55 etc.; 1446 (**his** *pron. 1* and *2*)

hesely *adv.* comfortably 1033 (**esili** *adv.*)

hest *n.* command 620 (**hest(e** *n. 1*)

hestyd *v. sg. pa.* promised 661 (**hesten** *v.*)

hevy *adj.* sad, sorrowful 647 (**hevi** *adj.*)

hevy *v.* sadden 911 (**hevien** *v.*)

hevyly *adv.* miserable, sad 137 (**hevili** *adv.*)

hevyn *see* **hef(f)ne**

hevynes *n.* grief, dejection 123 (**hevines(se** *n.*)

hevynly *adj.* heavenly, of heaven 352, 1219 (**hevenli** *adj.*)

hy *see* **hey** or **heye**

hyde *v.* hide 132 (**hiden** *v.*)

hye *see* **hey**

hyest *n.* the supreme one, God 1305 (**heigh** *adj.*)

hyest *adj.* most worthy, most important, supreme 33, 151 etc. (**heigh** *adj.*)

hyght, hygth, hyth *p. p.* (be) called, (be) named 224, 214*A2*; 190; **hyth Elizabeth** is called Elizabeth 1441 (**hoten** *v. 1*)

hyʒ(e) *see* **hey**

hyʒe *v.* hurry 236; *imp. sg.* **hyʒe** 1261 (**hien** *v.*)

hyʒly *adv.* excellently, highly 1297 (**heighli** *adv.*)

hym *pron. obj.* him (**him** *pron.*)

hympne *n.* hymn 560sd (**imne** *n.*)

hymself *pron.* himself 140, 562 (**him-self** *pron.*)

hynde *adv.* near 146*A2* (**hende** *adv.*)

hyryd *p. p.* hired, rented 1032 (**hiren** *v.*)

his *see* **hes(e)** *and* **be(n)**

ho *interj.* stop! 1149 (**ho** *interj.*)

ho *pron. interr. and rel.* who 234, 339, 1337, 36*A2*

holde, holdyn *v.* consider, last out, retain, keep 1209; 884; *1sg. pr.* **hold** 5*A3*, **holde** 209; *sg. pr. subj.* **holde** 763 (**holden** *v.*)

holde *see* **old(e)**

holy *adj.* holy 27, 39 etc. (**holi** *adj.2*)

holyere *adj.* holier 186 (**holi** *adj.2*)

holyest *adj.* holiest 31, 871, 904 (**holi** *adj.2*)

holyly *adv.* devoutly 249 (**holili(che** *adv.1*)

hom *n.* home 138, 509 etc. (**hom** *n.*)

hom *adv.* home, homeward 123, 203, 6*A3* (**hom** *adv.*)

homward *adv.* homeward 118, 250, 10*A3* (**hóm-ward** *adv.*)

honour *v.* honour, worship 876; *1sg. pr.* **honoure** 790, **honowre** 1377 (**honouren** *v.*)

hool *adj.* whole 584 (**hol(e** *adj.2*)

hope *n.* hope 367, 391 (**hop** *n.1*)

hosbonde, hosbund, husbond(e) *n.* husband 234; 63*A2*; 67, 91 etc.; 507, 205*A2* (**hous-bond(e** *n.*)

hoso *pron.* whosoever 157, 760

hous(e), howse *n.* house 222, 242 etc.; 609; 1044; **Goddys hous** the temple 299, 370, 452 (**hous** *n.*)

housholde *n.* dwelling-place, members of the family 1041 (**hous-hold** *n.*)

how *interj.* (exclamation to draw attention) hoy! 1*A2* (**hou** *interj.1*)

how, whow *interr. adv.* how 133, 134, etc.; 103 (**how** *interrog. adv.*)

how, whow *conj. adv.* how 10, 69 etc.; 1326, 1333 (**how** *conjunctive adv.*)

howe, howyth *see* **owe** *v.*

hownde *n.* hound, dog 152 (**hound** *n.*)

howre *n.* hour, time 1442, 1488; *n. pl.* **howrys** 542 (**houre** *n.*)

humylyté *n.* humility 1354 (**humilite** *n.*)

hundryd, vndryd *num.* hundred 1568; 1060 (**hundred** *card. num.*)

I *pron.* I (**ich** *pron.*)

i-cast *v.* say (see note) 1430 (**icasten** *v.*)

iche *see* **eche**

ierarchie *n.* hierarchy (of angels) 1097 (**jerarchi(e** *n.*)

if(f), yf, ȝiff, ȝyff *conj.* if 71, 94 etc.; 650; 330, 399, 759, 1180; 1204; 64 (**if** *conj.*)

immortalyté *n.* immortality 391 (**immortalite** *n.*)

impossyble *adj.* impossible 1272, 1322 (**impossible** *adj.*)

in *prep.* in, on (**in** *prep.*)

inbassett *n.* message, mission 227, 1275 (**ambassade** *n.*)

incarnacyon *n.* incarnation (of Christ) 1343, 1387 (**incarnacioun** *n.*)

incense, ensens *n.* incensing, incense 1442; 26 (**encens** *n.*)

incensynge *n.* incensing, censing 1488 (**encensing** *ger.*)

incheson *n.* purpose 1395 (**enchesoun** *n.*)

incomparabyl *adj.* matchless, unequalled 201 (**incomparable** *adj.*)

inconuenyens *n.* harm, impropriety 1591 (**inconvenience** *n.*)

indede *adv.* truly, indeed 279, 403 etc. (**dede** *n.*)

indygnacyon *n.* displeasure, scorn 105 (**indignacioun** *n.*)

infynyte *adj.* (emendation) boundless, limitless 705 (**infinite** *adj.*)

influens *n.* power, influence 549 (**influence** *n.*)

informacyon *n.* instruction, explanation 480 (**informacioun** *n.*)

iniquité, iniquyté *n.* sin, wickedness 415, 1083; 1208 (**iniquite** *n.*)

injouyid *v. sg. pa.* rejoiced (in) (translating L. *exultauit*) 1496; *p. p.* **enjoyd** 1465 (**enjoien** *v.*)

innocent *adj.* without sin, innocent 549 (**innocent** *adj.*)

inquysissyon *n.* inquiry, investigation 361 (**inquisicioun** *n.*)

inspyracyon *n.* divine communication, inspiration 1385 (**inspiracioun** *n.*)

inspyred *p. p.* endowed, filled 192; *pr. p.* **inspyrynge** filling, enlightening 1464 (**enspiren** *v.*)

intelligence *n.* news, information 1444 (**intelligence** *n.*)

into *prep.* into (**in-to** *prep.*)

is, ys *see* **be(n)**

it, yt *pron.* it 6, 14 etc.; 13*A1* (**hit** *pron.*)

iwys, iwus *adv.* certainly, indeed 55, 67 etc.; 1579 (**iwis** *adv.*)

jape *v.* play, act foolishly 44*A2* (**japen** *v.*)

jentyl(l) *adj.* loving, dear, gracious (polite form of address) 607, 1043, 21*A2*, 182*A2*; 900 (**gentil** *adj.*)

joy(e) *n.* happiness, delight, joy 202, 240 etc.; 125, 232, 1495; *n. pl.* **joys** 191, 234 (**joie** *n.*)

joyful *adj.* happy, glad 231, 300 etc. (**joiful** *adj.*)

jugement *n.* punishment, sentence 456 (**jugement** *n.*)

jurny, jorney *n.* journey 763, 1425, 1431; 3*A1*, 12*A1* (**journei** *n.*)

kan, kannot *see* **can**

ken *v.* know, acknowledge, commend 1533; *1sg. pr.* **ken** 1467; *p. p.* **kende** called 1253 (**kennen** *v.*)

kende, kynde *n.* race, family 549; generation 1507; **of kende** by (his) nature, from (his) descent 1305 (**kind** *n.*)

kepe, kepyn *v.* keep, protect, look after 57, 92 etc.; 888; *sg. pr. subj.* **kepe** 940, 960; *imp. sg.* **kepe** 241, 865, 876, 1043; *pr. p.* **kepyng** 1288; *p. p.* **kept** 455, 1145, 1311 (**kepen** *v.*)

kepere *n.* guardian, protector 863 (**keper(e** *n.*)

kepyng *vbl. n.* protection 981 (**keping(e** *ger.*)

kyn *n.* family, race 789; *n. poss.* **in no kynnys wyse** under no circumstances 50*A2* (**kin** *n.*)

kyng(e) *n.* king 719, 736; 22, 184 etc. (**king** *n.*)

kynnysmen, kynsmen *n.* kindred, relations 757; 719, 732 (**kinnes-man** *n.*)

kynred(e) *n.* family, race 780; 83, 736 etc.; *n. pl.* **kynredys** 36 (**kinrede** *n.*)

kys *v.* kiss 329, 185*A2*, 187*A2*; *1sg. pr.* **kysse** 79, **cus** 559; *2sg. pr. subj.* **kys** 962; *sg. pa.* **kyssyd** 1588 (**kissen** *v.*)

knawe *see* **knowe**

kne *n.* knee 707, 710, 1052; *n. pl.* **knes** 238, 512, 951, 1466, **kneys** 551 (**kne** *n.*)

knele *v.* *1sg. pr.* kneel 487; *imp. pl.* **knelyth** 499; *pr. p.* **knelende** 146, **knelynge** 710 (**knelen** *v.*)

knowe, knawe *v.* know, acknowledge 596, 132*A2*; 517, 1207; *1sg. pr.* **knowe** 1419; *2sg. pr.* **knowist** 128*A2*; *3sg. pr.* **knowyth** 140, 575; *pl. pr.* **know(e)** 1152, 1161; 943, 982, 1386; *imp. pl.* **knowyth** 16*A1*; *pr. p.* **knowyng(e)** 1310, 1413; 362, 767; *sg. pa.* **knew** 101*A2*; *pl. pa.* **knew** 1337; *sg. pa. subj.* **knew** 493 (**knouen** *v.*)

knowlage *v. 1sg. pr.* acknowledge, admit 203*A2* (**knowlechen** *v.*)
knowlech(e) *n.* knowledge, information 699; 706 (**knoulech(e** *n.*)
krepe *see* **crepe**
kusse *n.* kiss 241 (**cos** *n.*)

labore, labour *n.* work, occupation 1029, 1*A1*; 475 (**labour** *n.*)
laboryn *v.* work, labour 1040; *p. p.* **laboryd** 400, 12*A2* (**labouren** *v.*)
lady *n.* lady (mainly as a form of address, or for the Virgin Mary); **Oure
    Ladyes** of the Virgin Mary 578, 1567 (**ladi(e** *n.*)
lame *adj.* crippled 801, 811 (**lame** *adj.*)
lamentacyon *n.* lamenting, mourning 1112 (**lamentacioun** *n.*)
langage *n.* words, rumour 921, 1045 (**langage** *n.*)
lanterne *n.* lantern 1355 (**lantern(e** *n.*)
lappyd *v. sg. pa.* enveloped, sealed 1446 (**lappen** *v.*)
last *adj.* **at þe last** at last, at length 640 (**last(e** *adj. sup.*)
late *adv.* late 203 (**lat(e** *adv.*)
late *see* **let(e)**
laue *n.* loaf 848 (**lof** *n.2*)
lawe *n.* law, teaching 514, 535 etc.; *n. pl.* **lawys** 492 (**laue** *n.*)
lede, ledyn *v.* lead, guide, direct 284, 651 etc.; 897; *1sg. pr.* **lede** 1*A1*; *sg. pr.
    subj.* **lede** 971; *p. p.* **ledde** brought 614 (**leden** *v.*)
lefful *adj.* lawful, permissible 686 (**lefful** *adj.2*)
left(e) *see* **leve** *v.1*
leggys *n. pl.* legs 800 (**leg** *n.*)
ley *v.* place, stake 294; *1sg. pr.* **ley** 772 (**leien** *v.*)
lely *n.* lily 816 (**lilie** *n.*)
lenger(e) *adv.* longer 564; 1150 (**lenger(e** *adv. com.*)
lerne *v.* learn, teach 284, 492, 535; *2sg. pr.* **lernyst** 1020; *3sg. pr.* **lernyth**
    1012; *imp. pl.* **lerne** 1173; *p. p.* **lernyd** 1562 (**lernen** *v.*)
lernyd *p. p.* (as *n.*) learned, educated (people) 15 (**lernen** *v.*)
lese *v. 2pl. pr.* destroy 849; *p. p.* **lore** 1120, **lorn** 1580 lost (**lesen** *v.*)
leste *v.* last, continue, endure 922, 1127; *1sg. pr.* **leste** 170; *3sg. pr.* **lestyght**
    885 (**lasten** *v.1*)
leste *v. imp. sg.* listen 626 (**listen** *v.2*)
let(e), lett, late *v. imp. sg./pl.* let, allow 285, 12*A1*, 74*A2*; 74, 276 etc.; 298,
    853, 186*A2*; 88, 280, 1163; **let(t) be(ne)** 74*A2*; 853; 186*A2* give up, stop
    (**leten** *v.*)
lett *v. imp. sg.* stop, hinder 150*A2* (**letten** *v.*)
letterys *n. pl.* letters, characters 545 (**lettre** *n.*)
leve *n.* leave 9*A3*; **take ... leve** say goodbye 319, 979, 1586 (**leve** *n.*)
leve *v.1* leave 316; *p. p.* **leve** 572, **left(e)** 90; 558 (**leven** *v.1*)
leve, levyn *v.2* live 293, 1248; 248, 631 etc.; *1sg. pr.* **leve** 170; *3sg. pr.* **levyth**
    151; *pr. p.* **levynge** 544; *sg. pa.* **levyd** 265; *p. p.* **levyd** 246 (**liven** *v.1*)
levers *n.pl.* living people 1335 (**liver(e** *n.2*)
levynge *vbl. n.* livelihood, living 11*A2* (**living** *ger.*)
levyr *adj.* **haue/had levyr** prefer, would rather 111*A2*, 133*A2* (**lef** *adj. &
    adv.*)
lewd *n.* the uneducated, laymen 15 (**leued** *adj.*)
ly *v.* lie, remain 1063; *3sg. pr.* **lyce** 678, **lyse** 1230, **lyth** 2*A1*; *pl pr.* **ly** 1079,
    lye 6*A1*; *3sg. pr. subj.* **ly** 1164; *p. p.* **loyn** 1062 (**lien** *v.*)
lyberary *n.* a body of learning/knowledge 535 (**librari(e** *n.*)
lyberté *n.* **at hese lyberté** freely 1210 (**liberte** *n.*)

lycens *n.* permission 9*A3* (**licence** *n.*)
lyff, lyve *n.* life 121, 284 etc.; 479, 522 (**lif** *n.*)
lyfte *v.* lift, raise 828; *3sg. pr.* **lyftyth** 141; *p. p.* **lyfte** 363 (**liften** *v.*)
lyght *n.* light 464, 1355 (**light** *n.*)
lyght *adj.* easy, kindly, insignificant 535, 820 (**light** *adj.2*)
lyist *v.* *2sg. pr.* are lying 43*A2* (**lien** *v.*)
lyke *adj.* similar, like 189, 528sd; likely 1421 (**lik** *adj.*)
lyketh *v.* *3sg. pr.* gives pleasure, appeals 479 (**liken** *v.1*)
lyknes *n.* appearance, shape, image 460, 1296 (**liknes(se** *n.*)
lippis *n. pl.* lips 1446 (**lip(pe** *n.*)
lyst *v. pl. pr.* please 142; *sg./pl. pr. subj.* **lyst** 168, 1173 (**listen** *v.1*)
lystenyth, listenyth *v. imp. sg./pl.* listen 1038 (*sg.*), 1561; 594 (**listenen** *v.*)
lytel, lytyl *adj.* little, brief 133; 1032, 1323sd, 1479 (**litel** *adj.*)
lytenyth *v.* *3sg. pr.* lightens 1009 (**lighten** *v.1*)
lyth *adj.* light, bright 174 (**light** *adj.1*)
lythly *adv.* hastily, casually 582 (**lightli** *adv.*)
lytyl *adv.* little 1372 (**litel** *adv.*)
lo *interj.* lo, look! 318, 577 etc. (**lo** *interj.*)
lofte *n.* **on lofte** up high 423 (**loft** *n.*)
loyn *see* **ly**
loke *v.* look, see 149; *pl. pr.* **loke** 137, **look** 1020; *imp. sg./pl.* **loke** 498, 599 etc.; *pr. p.* **lokynge** 424 (**loken** *v.2*)
londe *n.* land; **on londe or on watyr** everywhere 959; **out of londe** away 22*A2* (**lond** *n.*)
long(e) *adj.* long 753, 1031; 655, 1086, 121*A2* (**long** *adj.1*)
longe *adv.* long 795, 885 etc. (**longe** *adv.*)
longyng *adj.* yearning 404 (**longen** *v.*)
lord(e) *n.* lord (mainly used in addressing God); *n. poss.* **Lorde-is** 392, **Lordys** 228, 442 etc. (**lord** *n.*)
lordyngys *n. pl.* sirs 594 (**lording(e** *n.*)
lore *n.* teaching 1173 (**lor(e** *n.2*)
lorn *see* **lese**
lost *p. p.* lost 1202 (**losen** *v.*)
lot *n.* (emendation) turn, appointed time 1436 (**lot** *n.1*)
loth *adj.* disinclined, unwilling 1554 (**loth** *adj.*)
lothe *n.* hate 178 (**lothen** *v.*)
lothfolest *adj.* most hateful, most despicable 151 (**lothful** *adj.*)
loue, love, lovyn *v.* love 886; 284, 457; 470, 515; *2sg. pr.* **lovyst** 155; *3sg. pr.* **lovyth** 1153, 4*A3*; *imp. sg./pl.* **love** 459, 461 etc.; *sg. pa.* **lovyd** 459; *p. p.* **lovyd** 1133 (**loven** *v.1*)
loveday *n.* day of reconciliation 1247 (**love-dai** *n.*)
lover *n.* friend, lover 1245 (**lover(e** *n. 2*)
lovyd *p. p.* praised 332 (**loven** *v.1*)
lovyngest *adj.* most loving 164 (**loven** *v.1*)
lowde *adv.* loud 1468 (**loude** *adv.*)
lowe *adj.* humble 966; **bothe hye and lowe** all people 594 (**loue** *adj.*)
lowly *n.* the humble, the meek 1516 (**louli** *adj.*)
lownes *n.* humility 1499 (**lounes(se** *n.*)
lusty *adj.* full of life, in good shape 136 (**lusti** *adj.*)

magesté *n.* sovereignty, majesty 72, 1067, 1098 (**mageste** *n.*)
magnyficens *n.* greatness, munificence 163 (**magnificence** *n.*)

may *n.* maiden 771 (**mai** *n.*)

may *v.* *1/3sg. pr.* **may** 6, 90 etc.; *2sg. pr.* **mayst** 837, 845; *pl. pr.* **may** 21, 84 etc., **mow** 1126, 1548, 23*A3*; *sg. pa.* **myght** 1166, 1182, 1477, **myth** 234; *pl. pa.* **myth** 278; *pa. subj.* **myght** 1118, **myth** 574, 1267, 1415 (**mouen** *v.3*)

mayd(e) *n.* maiden, virgin 805, 838 etc.: 306, 354 etc. (**maid(e** *n. & adj.*)

mayd-childe *n.* girl-baby 71 (**maide-child** *n.*)

mayden, maydyn, maydon *n.* maiden, virgin 869, 1463; 286; 529, 752 etc.; *n. pl.* **maydenes** 484, 682, **maydenys** 477, 497 etc., **maydonys** 1036 (**maiden** *n.*)

maydenhed *n.* maidenhead, virginity 1058 (**maidenhede** *n.*)

mayn *n.* strength 818 (**main** *n.*)

maynteyn *v.* preserve, support 1041 (**maintenen** *v.*)

mayster *n.* master 135, 137 etc. (**maister** *n.*)

mak(e) *v.* make, compose, create 686; 45, 59 etc.; *1sg. pr.* **make** 92*A2*; *2sg. pr.* **makyst** 173, 1021; *3sg. pr.* **makyht** 1007, **makyth** 132, 179, 1015, 1323sd; *pl. pr.* **make** 66, 97sd; *sg. pr. subj.* **make** 5, 81, 399; *sg./pl. pa.* **mad(e)** 305, 1231, 1582; 273, 330 etc.; *p. p.* **mad(e)** 9, 288 etc.; 1094 (**maken** *v.*)

make *n.* companion, spouse 671, 725, 894, 182*A2* (**make** *n.1*)

makere *n.* creator (God) 543, 1156 (**maker(e** *n.*)

males *n.* hatred, malicious behaviour 1104 (**malice** *n.*)

man *n.* man; *n. poss.* **mannys** 233, 422 etc.; *n. pl.* **men** (**man** *n.*)

maner(e) *n.* kind, kinds, way, manner 29, 539, 666; 788, 941, 954, 1309; (**maner(e** *n.*)

many *adj.* many 132, 674 etc. (**mani** *adj. & n.*)

mankende, mankynd *n.* mankind 197, 398, 1172, 172*A2*; 158*A2*; *n. poss.* **mankende** 1345 (**man-kind(e** *n.*)

manna *n.* manna 528sd (see note) (**manna** *n.*)

mary(n) *v.* marry 19*A1*; 871; *p. p.* **maryde** 768; **maryde** 12, 751, 754, 805 (**marien** *v.*)

masangere *n.* messenger 731, 1381 (**messager** *n.*)

massage *n.* message 1384 (**message** *n.*)

matere *n.* matter, business, subject, story 5, 9 etc.; *n. pl.* **materys** 582 (**mater(e** *n.*)

matremony *n.* marriage 904 (**matrimoin(e** *n.*)

me *pron. obj.* me, myself (**me** *pron.2*)

mech(e *adj.* much, great 163, 1087; 1130 (**much(e** *adj.*)

mede *n.* reward 476, 1429; **God do . . . mede** may God reward . . . 96, 565; **qwyte my mede** reward me 826 (**mede** *n. 2*)

meditacyon *n.* meditation 481 (see note to ll.481–3) (**meditacioun** *n.*)

meke *n.* the humble, the lowly 141 (**mek** *adj.*)

meke *adj.* humble, gentle 361, 373 etc. (**mek** *adj.*)

meke *v.* bring down, make submissive 1067 (**meken** *v.*)

mekely *adv.* humbly, submissively 80, 95 etc. (**mekli** *adv.*)

mekenes *n.* humility 63, 421, 1348 (**meknesse** *n.*)

mekest *adj.* humblest 529, 546 etc. (**mek** *adj.*)

mell *v.* mix, join 669 (**medlen** *v.*)

membyr *n.* part of the body 1360 (**membre** *n.*)

memorye *n.* memory 354 (**memori(e** *n.*)

men *v.* mean 749; *3sg. pr.* **menyth** 634, 34*A2*; *p. p.* **ment** intended 543 (**menen** *v.1*)

mende *n.* mind 199, 367 etc.; **haue mende on/of** remember 163, 429, 1066; **haue good mende** remember well how 307 (**mind(e** *n. 1*)

mene *adj.* intervening 1390 (see note) (**mene** *adj. 2*)

meracle *n.* miracle, extraordinary feat 351, 449, 839 (**miracle** *n.*)

mercy(e) *n.* mercy 9, 64 etc.; 1064 (**merci** *n.*)

mercyabyl *adj.* merciful 1146, 1169 (**merciable** *adj.*)

mercyfful, mercyful(l) *adj.* merciful 121; 86*A2*; 546 (**merciful** *adj.*)

mery *adj.* cheerful, happy, glad 211, 338, 394, 1417 (**miri(e** *adj.*)

meryer *adj.* happier 77 (**miri(e** *adj.*)

merveyl *n.* wonder, marvel 834 (**merveille** *n.*)

merveylyth *v. 3sg. pr. impers.* **me merveylyth** I am puzzled/amazed 1151, 1406; *imp. sg.* **merveyle** wonder 529 (**merveillen** *v.*)

mervelyous *adj.* wonderful, extraordinary 188, 445, 1292 (**merveillous** *adj.*)

mesemyth *v. impers. 3sg. pr.* it seems to me 1141, 1183

mete *n.* food, eating 531, 539, 564 (**mete** *n. 1*)

mete *v.* meet 199, 221, 868; *pl. pr. subj.* **mete** 76; *pr. p.* **metyng** 13 (**meten** *v. 4*)

methynkyht *v. impers. 3sg. pr.* it seems to me 809

metyng(e) *vbl. n.* meeting 81, 240, 1450; 255 (**meting(e** *ger. 4*)

mevyd *see* **movyth**

my, myn *pron. poss.* my (**min** *pron.*)

myght, myth *n.* strength, power 449, 462 etc.; 180; *n. pl.* **myghtys** 313 (**might** *n.*)

myght *see* **may** *v.*

myghty(e) *adj.* great, valiant 409; 1068 (**mighti** *adj.*)

myghtyest *adj.* most ?powerful 1503 (**mighti** *adj.*)

mylde *adj.* gentle, humble 73, 221 etc. (**milde** *adj.*)

myle *n.* mile 212; *n. pl.* **myles** 1420 (**mile** *n.*)

minister *n.* attendant priest 560sd; *n. pl.* **ministerys** 97sd (**ministre** *n.*)

mynyster, mynystryn *v.* perform services, look after, serve 73; 491; *pl. pr.* **mynistere** 28 (**ministren** *v.*)

mynistracyon, mynystracyon *n.* administering of religious services, service 1437, 1442; 31, 529 (**ministracioun** *n.*)

mys *v.* be lacking 987 (**missen** *v. 1*)

myschevyd *p. p.* injured, ruined 1138 (**mischeven** *v.*)

myschevys *n. pl.* misfortunes, sufferings 1087 (**mischef** *n.*)

myself(f) *pron.* myself 515; 886 (**mi-self** *pron.*)

mysse *n.* evil, misfortune, sin 960 (**mis** *n.*)

mysthought *p. p.* thought wickedly/wrongly, misjudged 169*A2* (**misthinken** *v.*)

mystrost *n.* doubt 1490 (**mistrust** *n.*)

myswrought *p. p.* sinned 152*A2*, 167*A2* (**miswerken** *v.*)

mo, moo *adj.* more 106; 1411; **withowtyn mo** alone, at once 14*A3* (**mo** *adj.*)

mod, mood *n.* mind, attitude, heart 63*A2*; 1052 (**mod** *n.*)

modyr *n.* mother; *n. pl.* **moderys** 187, 1574 (**moder** *n.*)

mon(e) *n.* regret, uneasiness 41*A2*; 836, 86*A2* (**mon** *n. 1*)

monyth *n.* month 1320; *n. pl.* **mon(e)this, mon(e)thys** 1042; 1543; 1571; 1484 (**month** *n.*)

more *adj.* more, greater 202, 234 etc. (**mor(e** *adj. comp.*)

more *adv.* more, again 74, 76 etc. (**mor(e** *adv.*)
morny *adj.* mournful, sad 1052 (**morni** *adj.*)
most *adj.* greatest, most 313, 1387, 12*A3* (**most** *adj. sup. & n.*)
most *adv.* most 73, 172 etc. (**most** *adv. sup.*)
mote *n.* speck, particle 856 (**mot.** *n.1*)
mot(e) *v. sg. pr. (subj.)* may 503; 4, 24 etc.; *sg. pa.* **must(e)** 614, 628 etc.; 611, **mut** 1478; *pl. pa.* **must(e)** 36, 44 etc.; 457, **mut** 230; *sg. pa. subj.* **mut** 77; *impers.* **vs must sofron** 129; *combined with pron.* 'Γ **moty** 1418 (**moten** *v. 2.*)
movyth *v. 3sg. pr.* prompts, guides 1151; *3sg. pa.* **mevyd** tempted, prompted 1102 (**meven** *v.*)
mownteynes *n. pl.* mountains (fig.) 363 (**mountain(e** *n.*)
mowthe *n.* mouth 1017, 187*A2* (**mouth** *n.*)
multyply *v. 3pl. pr.* increase in numbers, breed 136; *p. p.* **multyplyed** 398 (**multiplien** *v.*)
murne *v. 1sg. pr.* mourn, grieve 1054 (**mornen** *v.*)
must(e), mut *see* **mot(e)** *v.*

nay *interj.* no 210, 331 etc. (**nai** *interj.*)
name *n.* name (frequently used in asseverations, 'In God's name!', etc.) 46, 68 etc.; *n. pl.* **names** 905, **namys** 480, 493 (**name** *n.*)
namely *adv.* especially, in particular 1384, 1427 (**nam(e)li** *adv.*)
nat *see* **not(t)**
natural *adj.* physical 532 (**natural** *adj.*)
nature *n.* human kind, the character and being of man 178; sexual contact 196 (**natur(e** *n.*)
ne *conj.* nor 8*A1* (**ne** *conj.1*)
necessary *adj.* necessary 982 (**necessari(e** *adj.*)
nede *n.* necessity, need 145, 567 etc. (**ned(e** *n.*)
nede *adv.* of necessity 129 (**ned(e** *adv.*)
nedful *adj.* necessary 688, 938 (**ned(e)ful** *adj.*)
nedy *n.* those in need (of salvation), the poor 1111, 1519 (**nedi** *n.*)
nedyth *v. 3sg. pr.* needs 157, 1225, 1288; *pl. pr.* **nede** 1285 (**neden** *v.*)
neyborys *n. pl.* neighbours 124, 757 (**neighebor** *n.*)
neyther *pron.* neither 102 (**neither** *pron.*)
neyther, nother, nothyr *conj.* neither 844; 8*A1*; 642 (**neither** *conj.*)
ner(e) *adv.* near, nearly 811, 1458; 728, 178*A2* (**ner** *adv.2*)
ner(e) *conj.* nor 540; 642, 844 (**ner** *conj.*)
nest *adv.* next 1355sd (**next(e** *adv.*)
never, nevyr *adv.* never 101*A2*, 204*A2*; 102, 185 etc. (**never** *adv.*)
nevyrmore *adv.* never again 191*A2* (**never-mor(e** *adv.*)
nevyrþeles(se) *adv.* nevertheless, however 104*A2*; 756 (**never-the-les** *adv.*)
nevyrþemore *adv.* not at all, never 1170 (**never-the-mor(e** *adv.*)
new(e) *adj.* new, another 1402; 35 (see note) (**neue** *adj.*)
newly *adv.* recently, again 56*A2* (**neuli** *adv.*)
ny, nyh *adv.* **ny almost** very nearly 801; near 46*A2* (**neigh** *adv.*)
nyght, nyth *n.* night 337, 533, 1085; 1049 (all in phrases 'day and night/night and day') (**night** *n.*)
nyn *num.* nine 1042 (**nin** *num.*)
nyn *conj.* nor 15, 424, 1477 (**ne** *conj. 1*)
nynte *ord. num.* ninth 403 (**ninthe** *num.*)

nynty *num.* ninety 181 (**ninti** *num.*)

no *adj. and adv.* no (**no** *adj. and adv.*)

noyis *n. pl.* harms, sufferings, pains 416 (**noi** *n.*)

noyous *adj.* dangerous, painful 416 (**noious** *adj.*)

nome *p. p.* taken 778 (**nimen** *v.*)

non *adj.* no 5, 194 etc. (**non** *adj.*)

non *pron.* none 540, 677 etc. (**non** *pron.*)

nor *conj.* nor 186, 331, etc. (**nor** *conj.*)

norchyth *v. 3sg. pr.* nourishes, sustains 434 (**norishen** *v.*)

not *v. 1sg. pr.* do not know (= **ne wot**) 231

not(t), nat *adv.* not 69, 123 etc.; 149, 1360; 14, 571, 3A1 (**not** *adv.*)

nother, nothyr *see* **neyther** *conj.*

nothyng(e) *adv.* not at all 967; 825, 211A2 (**no-thing** *adv.*)

nothynge *pron.* nothing 469, 1272, 1322 (**no-thing** *pron.*)

nought, nowth, not *pron.* nothing 380, 1473; 504; 161 (**nought** *pron.*)

nouht, nowght, nowth, notht *adv.* not at all 665; 150A2; 1042, 1199, 1278, 23A2; 2A2 (**nought** *adv.*)

now(e) *adv.* now 16, 22 etc.; 598 (**nou** *adv.*)

o, oo *num.* one 1217, 1360; 1412 (**o** *num.*)

O *interj.* O (for invocation) 527, 1018 etc (**o** *interj.*)

obedyence *n.* obedience 373 (**obedience** *n.*)

obey *v.* carry out, obey 518 (**obeien** *v.*)

oblocucyon *n.* error, awkwardness 5 (see note) (**oblocucioun** *n.*)

obscure *adj.* difficult to understand 5, 696 (**obscure** *adj.*)

observe *v.* keep, conform to 688 (**observen** *v.*)

obstynacye *n.* obstinacy, hardness of heart 1103 (**obstinaci(e** *n.*)

occapyed *p. p.* employed, occupied 579 (**occupien** *v.*)

oc(c)upacyon, ocupasyon *n.* employment, work, activity 580, 1389; 497; 2A1 (**occupacioun** *n.*)

of *adv.* **come of** come along, do not delay 1324 (**of** *adv.*)

of(f) *prep.* of, from, out of, for 4, 9 etc.; 780, 1355 (**of** *prep.*)

offendyd *v. sg./pl. pa.* displeased, sinned against 331, 1154; *p. p.* **offendyd** 171 (**offenden** *v.*)

offens *n.* sin, wrong 158, 1061, 1122 (**offens(e** *n.*)

offeryng, offryng(e) *vbl. n.* religious offering 105; 97sd, 720, 738, 791; 777, 790, 793, 820 (**offring(e** *ger.*)

offyr, offre *v.* present, offer to God 733, 777, 11A1; 65, 305, 783; *1sg. pr.* **offyr** 816, **offre** 787; *pl. pr.* **offre** 26, 313, **offere** 722; *imp. pl.* **offyr** 813, **offeryth** 98, 107; *p. p.* **offeryd** 1142, **offred** 11, **offryd** 193, 259, 658 (**offren** *v.*)

offyse *n.* duty, function 1095 (**office** *n.*)

ofte *adv.* often 411, 1390 (**oft(e** *adv.*)

oftyntyme(s) *adv.* frequently 120A2; 857 (**often-times** *adv.*)

oy *interj.* hear ye! 735 (**oyes** *interj.*)

old(e), holde *adj.* old 755, 762 etc.; 296, 610 etc.; (as *n.*) 691 (**old(e** *adj.*)

omnypotent *adj.* all-powerful 19 (**omnipotent(e** *adj.*)

on(e) *pron.* one 209, 584 etc.; **a merveyl one** a real wonder 834 (**on** *pron.*)

on *prep.* on, of, in (**on** *prep.*)

on *num.* one, single 52, 276 etc.; **in on** together, in unity 436 (**on** *num.* and **in-on** *adv. & adj.*)

ondo *see* **vndo**

onest *adj.* honourable, suitable 1176 (**honest(e** *adj.*)
ony *n.* honey 1019 (**honi** *n.*)
ony *see* **any** *adj., pron.*
onys *adv.* once 127, 522 etc. (**ones** *adv.*)
only *adv.* ?alone 1512 (**onli** *adv.*)
onto, vnto *prep.* unto, to 595, 606 etc.; 27, 197 (**unto** *prep.*)
opynd *p. p.* revealed 136*A2* (**openen** *v.*)
opynly *adv.* openly, in public 110*A2* (**openli** *adv.*)
or *see* **er** *conj.*
or(e) *conj.* or 456, 959, 970, 1190; 1591 (**or** *conj.*)
ordeyn *v.* arrange, make ready 985, 1237; *sg. pa.* **ordeyned** established 1435 (**ordeinen** *v.*)
ordenaryes *n. pl.* authorities, rules 518 (see note) (**ordinari(e** *n.*)
ore *n.* mercy; **þin ore** in thy mercy 247 (**or(e** *n. 2*)
oth *n.* oath; **withowte oth** assuredly 1551 (**oth** *n.*)
other, tothere *adj.* other 671, 694, 28*A2*, 39*A2*; 489 (**other** *adj.*)
othere *pron.* the other, others 1190, 1341 (**other** *pron.*)
ought *see* **owght**
our(e) *pron. poss.* our 95, 125 etc.; 18, 33 etc.; **oure** ours 794 (**our(e** *pron.*)
out(e), owte, owth *adv.* out 856; openly, clearly 680; 148*A2*; 663, 1039 (**out(e** *adv.*)
out/owth(of) *prep.* out of 108, 22*A2*; 508 (**out(e** *prep.* and **out(e of** *prep.*)
overthrowyht *v. 3sg. pr.* throws down 141 (**overthrouen** *v.*)
ovyr *adv.* over 257 (**over** *adv.*)
ovyrcomyth *v. 3sg. pr.* surpasses 1177 (**overcomen** *v.*)
ow *interj.* oh! 34*A2* (**ou** *interj.*)
owe, owyn *adj.* own 984; 460, 620 etc. (**ouen** *adj.*)
owe *v. pl. pr.* own; **for what þat ȝe owe** at all costs (lit. for all that you own) 600; *3sg. pr.* **howyth** ought 805; *2pl. pr.* **howe** ought 876; ?*3pl. pr.* **owyght** 882 (**ouen** *v.*)
owght, owgth, ought *pron.* anything 572; at all 736; 4*A2* (**ought** *pron.*)
owught *adv.* at all 1415 (**ought** *adv.*)

pace *see* **pas(se)**
pacyens *n.* pacience 581, 588, 1589 (**pacience** *n.*)
pay *n.* liking, pleasure 827 (**pai(e** *n.*)
payd *p. p.* pleased 297; **evyl payd** displeased 197*A2* (**paien** *v.*)
palsye *n.* palsy 1552 (**palesi(e** *n.*)
parde *interj.* indeed, in truth 163*A2* (**parde** *interj.*)
pardon *n.* indulgence, remission of part of the punishment for sin 1568 (**pardoun** *n.*)
parfyte *adj.* perfect 1357, 1361 etc. (**parfit** *adj.*)
parlement *n.* conference, council 590 (**parlement(e** *n.*)
parochonerys *n. pl.* parishioners 56 (**parishoner** *n.*)
part *n.* part, portion 55, 56, 57; *n. pl.* **partys** 51 (**part** *n.*)
parte *v.* depart 18*A3*; *3sg. pr. subj.* **parte** 963 (**parten** *v.*)
pas *n.* step, way 348 (**pas(e** *n.*)
pas(se) *v.* pass, go, exceed 1210; 945; *3sg. pr.* **passyth** 610; *pl. pr.* **pace** 582, **passe** 257, **passyn** 600; *3sg. pr. subj.* **pace** 121*A2* (**passen** *v.*)
passage *n.* pregnancy 1320; **be mene passage** in the intervening time 1390 (see note) (**passage** *n.*)
passyon *n.* (Christ's) Passion 1593 (**passioun** *n.*)

past *p. p.* past 2, 26*A3* (**passen** *v.*)

pasture *v.* graze, put out to pasture 135 (**pasturen** *v.*)

patryarchys *n. pl.* fathers of the Old Testament 1094 (**patriark(e** *n.*)

pawsacyon *n.* **to make pawsacyon** to pause, linger 587 (**pausacion** *n.*)

peyn(e) *n.* suffering, grief, torment 183, 456; 1232, 1363, 1424; *n. pl.* **peynes** 1062, 1086, 1134 (**pein(e** *n.*)

peyneth *v. 3sg. pr.* grieves, torments 1231; *p. p.* **peynyd** 1429 (**peinen** *v.*)

pepyl *n.* people 106, 263, 519, 1426 (**peple** *n.*)

peraventure *adv.* perchance, perhaps 382 (**paraventur(e** *adv.*)

perellys *n. pl.* dangers 2 (**peril** *n.*)

perfyght *adv.* perfectly 132*A2* (**parfit(e** *adv.*)

performe *v.* carry out 881 (**performen** *v.*)

perysch(e) *v.* pass away, come to an end, die 1204; 1064, 1189; *p. p.* **peryschyd** 1201 (**perishen** *v.*)

perpetual *adj.* endless, everlasting 456 (**perpetuel(le** *adj.*)

persevere *n.* recipient, receiver 1344 (**perceiver(e** *n.*)

person(e) *n.* being, person (of the Trinity) 162; 6, 1329; *n. pl.* **personys** 3, 276, 312, 465 (**persoun(e** *n.*)

perteyneth *v. 3sg. pr.* is necessary/appropriate for 40 (**pertenen** *v.*)

pes *n.* peace, quiet 17, 1177 etc.; *n. poss.* **Pesys** 1228 (**pes** *n.*)

peté, pety, pyté *n.* pity, mercy 1055; 172, 576, 125*A2*; 1065, 1093 (**pite** *n.*)

petycyons *n. pl.* requests 513 (**peticioun** *n.*)

pygth *n.* pith, essence 1006 (**pith** *n.*)

pyke *v.* pick 856 (**piken** *v.*)

pylgrimys *n. pl.* pilgrims 53 (**pilgrim** *n.*)

pylgrymagys *n. pl.* pilgrimages 1428 (**pilgrimage** *n.*)

pyté *see* **peté**

place, plas *n.* place, house, position 251, 270 etc.; 348, 947 (**place** *n.*)

plage *n.* affliction 1446 (**plage** *n.*)

planetys *n. pl.* planets 374 (**planet(e** *n.*)

pleand *v. pr. p.* playing, performing 3 (**pleien** *v.1*)

pleyn *adv.* fully 457 (**plein** *adv.*)

pleynge-fere *n.* play-fellow, companion 1378 (**pleiinge** *ger.*)

pleynyn *v.* complain 110*A2* (**pleinen** *v.*)

plenté *n.* prosperity, fruitfulness 604 (**plente** *n.*)

plesauns *n.* **to þi plesauns** pleasing to you, to please you 517 (**plesaunce** *n.*)

plese *v.* please 6, 343, 705; *3sg. pr.* **plesyth** 827, 1092 etc.; *3sg. pr. subj.* **and/if it plese** 169, 303 etc.; *pr. p.* **plesynge** 287; *sg. pa.* **plesyd** 1131; *p. p.* **plesyd** 176, 1198 (**plesen** *v.*)

plesynge *vbl. n.* pleasure 94, 988 (**plesing(e** *ger.*)

pleson *n.* satisfaction 1179 (**pleson** *n.*)

plight *n.* state, situation 129*A2* (**plight** *n.*)

pore *n.* power 1511 (**pouer(e** *n.*)

pore *n.* poor people 1519; *n. poss.* **porys** of the wretched 1112 (**povre** *adj.*)

pore *adj.* poor 53, 573, 575, 168*A2* (**povre** *adj.*)

povert(é) *n.* poverty, need 56; 992 (**poverte** *n.*)

powsté *n.* power, domination 218*A2* (**pouste** *n.*)

pray, prey *v.* pray 144, 145, 335, 954; 146, 1192; *1sg. pr.* **pray** 17, 172 etc., **prey** 1078, 14*A1*; *1pl. pr.* **pray** 704, **prey** 698; *3pl. pr.* **pray** 814; *pr. p.* **prayng** 817, **praynge** 1479; *3pl. pa.* **preyd** 648 (**preien** *v.1*)

prayere, prayour, prayr, prayȝer, preyour *n.* prayer 176; 161, 655 etc.;

803; 473; 220; *n. pl.* **prayers** 526, 1115, 1142, **prayerys** 1095, **prayorys** 162 (**preier(e** *n.*)

praty *adj.* neat, handsome 1032 (**prati(e** *adj.*)

pratyly *adv.* carefully, cleverly 348 (see note) (**pratili** *adv.*)

precyous *adj.* precious, of great worth 1593 (**precious(e** *adj.*)

preyse *v.* praise 1005; *imp. pl.* **prayse** 207 (**preisen** *v.*)

preysenge, preysyng(e) *vbl. n.* praise, praising 1017; 874, 1531; 1478 (**preising(e** *ger.*)

prerogatyff *n.* special privilege 1367 (**prerogatif** *n.*)

presence, presens *n.* presence 1391; 28, 161 etc. (**presence** *n.*)

present *n.* present, gift 560sd; *n. pl.* **presentys** 560sd (**present(e** *n. 2.*)

present *adj.* present 2, 6 etc. (**present(e** *adj.*)

present(e) *v.* present, dedicate, offer 276; 1095; *3pl. pr.* **presente** 270sd (**presenten** *v.*)

presentacyon *n.* presentation to the service of God 578 (**presentacioun** *n.*)

preserve *v. sg. pr. subj.* protect 16 (**preserven** *v.*)

prest *n.* priest 61, 318, 1439; *n. pl.* **prestes** 303, 561, **prestys** 26, 30 etc. (**prest** *n. 3.*)

prest *adj.* ready 622 (**prest** *adj.*)

presume *v.* act presumptuously 103; *sg. pa.* **presumyd** 1171 (**presumen** *v.*)

presumpcyon *n.* presumption, arrogance 1160 (**presumpcioun** *n.*)

pretende *v. imp. sg.* direct, set forward 348 (**pretenden** *v.*)

preuylage *n.* special right 1386 (**privilege** *n.*)

preuyly *adv.* secretly, unobtrusively 773 (**priveli(e** *adv.*)

prevyde *v. imp. pl.* search 1211 (**previden** *v.*)

prevydens *n.* preparation 583 (**previdence** *n.*)

pryde *n.* ostentation, show 133 (**pride** *n. 2.*)

prince, prynce *n.* **prince of prestes** high priest 303, 749; 30, 94, 561, 1438 (cf. **bus(s)chop** *n.*) (**prince** *n.*)

pryncypal *adj.* most important, excellent 1395 (**principal** *adj.*)

priuité *n.* secrecy 134*A2* (**privete** *n.*)

procede *v.* come, go, continue, move on 60, 281 etc.; *pl. pr.* **proced** 259 (**proceden** *v.*)

proces(se) *n.* story, order of events 1451; 16; **be proces** in due course 223 (**proces** *n.*)

profecyes *see* **prophesye**

profite, profyte *v.* benefit, avail, grow 6; 161, 1475 (**profiten** *v.*)

pronunciacyon *n.* speaking, setting forth 3 (see note) (**pronunciacioun** *n.*)

prophesye *n.* prophecy 1538, 173*A2*; *n. pl.* **profecyes** 70 (**propheci(e** *n.*)

prophesyed *v. pl. pa.* prophesied, spoke by inspiration 1581 (**prophecien** *v.*)

prophetys *n. pl.* prophets (of the Old Testament) 1094, 1115 (**prophet(e** *n.*)

propyr *adj.* genuine, true 379 (**propre** *adj.*)

prosperité *n.* good fortune 154 (**prosperite** *n.*)

prostrat *adj.* prostrate 162, 526 (**prostrat(e** *adj.*)

proude, prowde *n.* the proud 141; 1512 (**proud** *n.*)

proverbe *n.* proverb, saying 81*A2* (**proverb(e** *n.*)

prow *n.* advantage, good 89*A2*, 27*A3* (**prou** *n.*)

prowde *adj.* proud, eminent 1515 (**proud** *adj.*)

psalme *n.* psalm, canticle 1027, 1492, 1538; *n. pl.* **psalmes** 1003, **psalmys** 354, 1018, 1022, **psalmus** 1010 (**psalm(e** *n.*)

punchement *n.* punishment 1155 (**punishement** *n.*)

punchyth *v. imp. ?sg.* punish, chastise 159 (**punishen** *v.*)
pure *adj.* chaste, pure 286 (**pur(e** *adj.*)
purest *adj.* most pure 1264 (**pur(e** *adj.*)
purveyd *v. sg. pa.* provided, prepared 224*A2* (**purveien** *v.*)
puttyn *v.* put, place 73*A2*; *3sg. pr.* **puttyth away** gets rid of 1009; *imp. pl.*
   putt 1185; *3sg. pa.* **put** 1515; *p. p.* **put away** rejected 1011 (**putten** *v.*)

quod *v. sg. pa.* said 1084 (**quethen** *v.*)
qwake *v. 1sg. pr.* tremble, shake 78, 553, 180*A2* (**quaken** *v.*)
qwan *see* **whan**
qwedyr *v. 1sg. pr.* shake 180*A2* (**quaveren** *v.*)
qwelle *v.* kill 97*A2*|(**quellen** *v. 1.*)
qweme *v.* please, satisfy 1184 (**quemen** *v.*)
qwen *n.* queen (see also note to l. 282) 282, 1398 (**quen(e** *n. 2.*)
qwens *conj.* whence, where 364
qwere *conj.* where 1211
qwhat *see* **what** *pron.*
qwhyl *see* **whil** *conj.*
qwy *see* **why** *adv.*
qwyk(e) *adj.* living 1023; **qwyk with childe** pregnant 1271 (**quik** *adj.*)
qwyle *n.* **abyde a qwyle** wait a moment 100 (**While** *sb.*)
qwyte *v. imp. sg.* **qwyte my mede** reward me 826 (**quiten** *v.*)

rage *v.* be sexually active 870 (**ragen** *v.*)
rather *adv.* rather 110*A2* (**rather(e** *adv. comp.*)
rave *v.* act passionately 850 (see note) (**raven** *v. 1.*)
rebate *v.* diminish 200 (**rebaten** *v.*)
receyve *v.* accept, receive, take in 488, 532, 740, 746 (**receiven** *v.*)
recomende *v. 1sg. pr.* give respects, commend, commit 1401; *imp. sg.* 565,
   1371; *pr. p.* **recomendynge** 560 (**recommenden** *v.*)
reconsyliacyon *n.* reconciliation 1114 (**reconsiliacioun** *n.*)
reconsylid *p. p.* reconciled, restored to participation (in the services of the
   temple) 309 (**reconcilen** *v.*)
record *v.* bear witness to, celebrate 906 (**recorden** *v.*)
recure *v. 1pl. pr.* obtain 699 (**recuren** *v.*)
rede *v.* read, find 492, 997, 1025; *1sg. pr* **rede** advise 250, 15*A1*; *1pl. pr.* **rede**
   1571, **redyn** 919; *sg. pr. subj.* **rede** guide 975 (**reden** *v.1*)
redempcyon *n.* redemption, deliverance 1073, 1212 (**redempcioun** *n.*)
redy *adj.* ready, prepared 47, 82 etc. (**redi** *adj. 3.*)
redolent *adj.* fragrant 540 (**redolent** *adj.*)
refreschynge *vbl. n.* spiritual refreshment 11*A3* (**refreshing(e** *ger.*)
refuse *v. 1sg. pr.* reject 105; *pr. p.* **refusynge** 993 (**refusen** *v.*)
regina *n.* queen 548 (**regina** *n.*)
regyon *n.* the earth 548, kingdom 1219 (**regioun(e** *n.*)
regne *n.* reign, rule 1307 (**regne** *n 1.*)
reynyth *v. 3sg. pr.* reigns 1394; *pr. p.* **reyneng** 548, **reynyng** 1307 (**regnen**
   v.)
relacyon *n.* advice, instruction 698 (**relacioun** *n.*)
relevys *n. pl.* the remains, what is left over 573 (**relef(e** *n.*)
remedy *v.* cure, put right 1557 (**remedien** *v.*)
remembyr *v.* remember 272 (**remembren** *v.*)
ren *v.* run 761 *p. p.* **ronne** run 1219 (**rennen** *v.l*)

renew *v.* restore, bring back 1400 (**reneuen** *v.1*)

repelle *v. imp. sg.* overcome 1104 (**repellen** *v.*)

repentyd *v. sg. pa.* repented, was contrite 1103 (**repenten** *v.*)

report *v. pl. pr.* report, describe 85 (**reporten** *v.*)

repreff *n.* shame, disgrace 177, 115*A2* (**repreve** *n.*)

repreff, reprove *v.* shame, censure 3*A3*; reject, find fault with 666; *p. p.* **reprevyd** scorned 643 (**repreven** *v.*)

reputacyon *n.* estimation, repute 1341 (**reputacioun** *n.*)

rescu *n.* rescue, deliverance 1339 (**rescoue** *n.*)

reson, resoun *n.* reason 15; 1165 (see note); **sey grett reson** speak very reasonably, bring forward good arguments 1178 (**resoun** *n.2*)

resonable *adj.* reasonable, moderate 474 (**resonable** *adj.2*)

resorte *v.* go, return, resort 88, 1137 (**resorten** *v.*)

respyt *n.* delay 133*A2* (see note) (**respit(e** *n.*)

rest *v.* rest 1455 (**resten** *v.1*)

restynge *vbl. n.* pause 1323sd (**resting(e** *ger.1*)

res(s)tore *v.* make amends for, set right, renew 1107, 1168 etc; 1125 (**restoren** *v.*)

returne *v. imp. pl.* go back, return 118, 222 (**returnen** *v.*)

reuerens *n.* due respect, reverence 72 (**reverence** *n.*)

reverently *adv.* with veneration, devoutly 1466 (**reverentli** *adv.*)

revyled *v. sg. pa.* scorned, abused 307; *p. p.* **revylyd** 128, 644 (**revilen** *v.*)

rewarde *v.* reward 1594 (**rewarden** *v.*)

rewlyd *p. p.* **be rewlyd** behave, conduct oneself, act 452, 716 (**reulen** *v.*)

rewthe *n.* a matter of regret, pity 1121 (**reuth(e** *n.*)

ryche *n.* the wealthy, the rich 1520; *n. pl.* **ryches** wealth 993 (**riche** *adj.*; **riches(se** *n.*)

ryche *adj.* rich, great, powerful 986, 991 (**riche** *adj.*)

ryff *adv.* readily 893 (**rif(e** *adv.*)

ryght *n.* right 198*A2*; **of ryght** truly 465; **Ryght** the character *Justicia* 1178 1203 (**right** *n.*)

ryght *adj.* true, right 1088, 1511 (**right** *adj.*)

ryght, ryth, ryht *adv.* right, very, just, altogether 217, 301 etc; 251, 613 etc; 784.833 (**right(e** *adv.*)

ryghtffulnes *n.* righteousness, justice 1153 (**rightfulnes(se** *n.*)

ryghtful *adj.* just, righteous 50, 1153 (**rightful** *adj.*)

ryghtwysnes *n.* justice 1162; **Ryghtwysnes** the character *Justicia* 1152, 1167, 1193, 1201 (**rightwisnes(se** *n.*)

ryng(e) *n.* ring 891; 893 (**ring** *n.*)

ryse *v.* rise, 1113, swell 30*A2*; *imp. pl.* **ryse** 21*A3* (**risen** *v.*)

rodde *n.* rod, staff, wand 770, 804 etc.; *n. pl.* **roddys** 769 (**rod(de** *n.*)

ronne *see* **ren**

rownde *adv.* around, through 1219 (**round(e** *adv.*)

rowse *v.1* proclaim 611 (**rosen** *v.*)

rowse *v.2* ?stir 1045 (but perhaps part of the previous verb) (**rosen** *v.*)

ruyne *n.* fall 1266 (**ruin(e** *n.*)

sa *see* **so** *adv.*

sacrefice, sacrefyce, sacrefyse, sacrifice, sacryfice, sacryfyse *n.* sacrifice. offering 95; 45; 39; 84; 59, 75, 99, 641; 37 (**sacrifice** *n.*)

sad *adj.* solemn, serious, sorrowful 4, 79, 208, 967 (**sad** *adj.*)

sage *n.* wise person 1449; **redyn in old sage** find in the wisdom of the old 919 (**sage** *n.*)

sage *adj.* wise 1317 (**sage** *adj.*)

say, sey(n) *v.* say 18, 47 etc.; 68, 200 etc.; 708sd, 1232, 1323; *1sg. pr.* **say** 732, 745, 760, 159*A2*; **saye** 858, **sey** 1286; *2sg. pr.* **seyst** 156, 633, 1145, 1147; *3sg. pr.* **seyth** 97sd, 528sd etc.; *2pl. pr.* **sey** 279; *3pl. pr. ?subj.* **sey** 1178; *imp. sg.* **say** 1259, **sey** 452, 860 etc; *imp. pl.* **say** 1430, **sey** 692; *pr. p.* **seyng(e)** 270sd; 1489; *1/3pl. pa.* **seyd** 219, 1480 etc; *2pl. pa.* **seydest** 1123; *p. p.* **sayd** 260, **seyd** 4, 186 etc., **seyn** 1540 (**seien** *v.*)

sake *n.* **for mannys sake** our of consideration for man 69*A2*; **a Godys sake** (an exclamation of surprise) for God's sake 1416 (**sake** *n.*)

salutacyon *n.* greeting, the Annunciation 12, 555, 592 (**salutacioun** *n.*)

salvacyon, savacyon *n.* salvation, deliverance 1238; 1345 (**savacioun** *n.*)

same *pron.* same 200; − **at same** that place 1421; −**e same** the same praise 1532 (**sam(e** *pron.*)

same *adj.* same 183, 306, 733 (**sam(e** *adj.*)

sank *p. p.* penetrated 243 (**sinken** *v.*)

sapyens *n.* Wisdom (God the Son) 1237 (**sapience** *n.*)

sat *see* **sytt**

saue, save *v.* save 158*A2*, 172*A2*; 1121; *3sg. pr. subj.* **saue** 852, 961 etc.; *p. p.* **savyd** 368, 1158, 1269 (**saven** *v.*)

savyour *n.* saviour, deliverer 197, 225 (**saveour** *n.*)

savowrys *n. pl.* smells 539 (**savour** *n.*)

sawe *n.* speech, decree, words 595, 601; *n. pl.* **sawys** words 536 (**sau(e** *n.2*)

sawtere *n.* psalter 1004, 1026; **Oure Laydes sawtere** 1567 (see note); **sawtere-book** the psalter 997 (**sauter** *n.*)

schadu *v.* over-shadow, enfold 1315 (**shadwe** *n.*)

schame *see* **shame**

schamfast *adj.* shy 1426 (**shamefast(e** *adj.*)

schappe *n.* shape, form 1358 (**shap(e** *n.*)

sche *see* **she**

scheeld, shylde *v. 3sg. pr. subj.* protect, shield 89; 1050 (**sheld** *n.*)

schent, shent *p. p.* disgraced 33*A2*; 278, 53*A2* (**shenden** *v.*)

schryve *v.* hear confession, administer absolution 491 (**shriven** *v.*)

sclepyr *adj.* **sclepyr of tonge** ready to gossip/spread scandal 920 (**sliper** *adj.*)

scripture, scrypture *n.* the Bible 687; 492, 694 (**scripture(e** *n.*)

se *n. 1* sea 1088 (**se** *n.1*)

se *n. 2* seat, throne, inheritance 1306 (**se** *n.2*)

se(n) *v.* see 21, 50 etc; 285; *1sg. pr.* **se** 93, 237, 219*A2*; *2sg. pr.* **seest** 181, **seyst** 1042; *3sg. pr.* **seyth** 177; *pl. pr.* **se** 446, 829, 831, 873; *imp. sg.* **se** 489, 1350; *imp. pl.* **se** 142, 1211; *pr. p.* **seinge** 1445, **seynge** 412; *p. p.* **sen** 254, 170*A2*, **sene** 857, 91*A2*, **seyn** 577, 775, **seyne** 1426 (**sen** *v.1*)

secunde *ord. num.* second 361, 515, 927, 1329 (**second** *num.*)

sed(e) seed *n.* offspring, progeny 1528; 649; 656 (**sed** *n.*)

sees ses *v.* cease, stop 93, 1155; 1196, 1200, 1453 (**cesen** *v.*)

sefne, seven *num.* seven 151, 374, 490, 513; 819 (**seven** *num.*)

sefnte, sefte *ord. num.* seventh 521; 391 (**seventh(e** *num.*)

seyst, seyth, seynge, seyn *see* **say sey(n)** *v.* and **se(n)** *v.*

seke *n.* the sick 86 (**sik** *adj.*)

seke *v.* look for, search, seek 214; *imp. pl.* **seke** 1213; *pr. p.* **sekynge** 1449; *p. p.* **sowte** searched 1215 (**sechen** *v.*)

sekyr *adv.* truly indeed 23*A2* (**siker** *adv.*)

seme *v. impers.* seem, appear 1187; *3sg. pr.* **semyth** 25*A2*; **semyth me** it seems to me 277, 440 (**semen** *v.2*)

sen *conj.* since 129 (**sin** *conj.*)

send(e), sendyn *v.* send, grant 728; 566, 649, 706; *pl. pr.* **send** 166; *3sg. pr. subj.* **send** 71, 147, **sende** 23, 505, 941, 1049; *sg. pa.* **sent** 656, 162*A2*; *p. p.* **sende** 1251, **sent** 153, 253 etc. (**senden** *v.2*)

sentens *n.* words, (dramatic) parts, speech, judgement, opinions 4, 260, 695, 1185 (**sentence** *n.*)

sequens *n.* liturgical piece sung at Mass after Alleluia and before Gospel 97sd (**sequence** *n.*)

sere *n.* sir 82, 100 etc.; *n. pl.* **serys** 98, 499, 764, 88*A2* (**sir(e** *n.*)

serteynly *adv.* truly 111*A2* (**certainli** *adv.*)

sertys *adv.* certainly, indeed 637, 780 (**certes** *adv.*)

seruaunt, servaunt *n.* servant (of God) 289; 274, 314; *n. pl.* **servauntys** 442, 568, 1224 (**servaunt** *n.*)

serve, servyn *v.* serve (God) 472, 511 etc; 120; *pr. p.* **servyng** 52 (**serven** *v.1*)

service, ervise, servyce, servyse *n.* service 305; 676; food, part of a meal 562, 570; 670, 52*A2* fare; liturgical service of the temple 97 (**servis(e** *n.*)

ses *see* **sees** *v.*

sesyd *p. p.* in possession 127*A2* (see note) (**seisen** *v.*)

sete *n.* seat 1516; *n. pl.* **setys** 151 (see note), places 1515 (**sete** *n.2*)

sethe *see* **syth** *and* **sythe**

sette *p. p.* fixed, set 375 (**setten** *v.*)

sew *v.* appeal 1399 (**seuen** *v.1*)

sex *num.* six 1060, 1484 (**six** *num.*)

sexte *ord. num.* sixth 385, 519, 1320 (**sixt(e** *num.*)

shake *v. 2pl. pr.* shake 1552 (**shaken** *v.*)

shalle *see* **xal**

shame, schame *n.* shame, disgrace, reproach 89, 92 etc; 71*A2*; diffidence, shyness, bashfulness 536 (**shame** *n.*)

shamfastnes *n.* shyness 1299 (**shamefastnes(se** *n.*)

she, sche *pron.* she 138, 184 etc.; 73, 140 etc.(**she** *pron.*)

shenschepe *n.* disgrace 1050 (**shendship(e** *n.*)

shent *see* **schent**

shepherdys *n. pl.* shepherds 205 (**shepherd(e** *n.*)

sherherdys *n. pl.* (probably an error for 'shepherds') 130 (see note)

shewe *v.* show 180, 1024; *3sg. pr.* **shewyth** 166; *2pl. pr.* **shewe** 1546; *3pl. pr.* **shewyth** 536; *p. p.* **shewyd** 254 (**sheuen** *v.1*)

shylde *see* **scheeld**

short *adj.* brief, short 589 (**short** *adj.*)

shortely *adv.* **shortely to say** to speak briefly 454 (**shortli** *adv.*)

shoue *v.* push, drive 664 (**shouven** *v.*)

shryle *adv.* (emendation) loudly, shrilly 147*A2* (**shril(le** *adv.*)

shuld(e *see* **xuld(e)**

syde *n.* side 489, 694, 1072 (**side** *n.*)

syghys *n. pl.* sighs 79 (**sigh(e** *n.*)

syght, syth *n.* **in/within syght** openly 446, 787; **to se ʒow in syth** to see you 1405; **to þi syght** before you, in your presence 1090; *n. pl.* **fleschly syghts** the sight of physical things 410 (**sight(e** *n.*)

sygne, syne *n.* sign, indication 802; 440; *n. pl.* **sygnes** 536 (**signe** *n.*)

syknes *n.* sickness, misery 1079 (**siknes(se** *n.*)

sympelest *adj.* most insignificant, humblest 291, 544 (**simple** *adj.*)

sympyl *adj.* humble, poor 418, 820 (**simple** *adj.*)

sympyl *adv.* **sympyl as we kan** simply, in the way we know 144 (**simpli** *adv.*)

syn *v.* *2pl. pr.* sin 72*A*2; *sg. pa.* **synnyd** 1164; *p. p.* **synnyd** 1123 (**sinnen** *v.*)

syn *prep.* since 1484 (**sin** *prep.*)

synfolest *adj.* most sinful 166 (**sinful** *adj.*)

synful(l) *adj.* sinful 150, 825; 31*A*2 (**sinful** *adj.*)

synful(l) *n.* sinful people 1399; 86 (**sinful** *adj.*)

syng(e) *v.* sing 905; 97sd, 212, 560sd; *pl. pr.* **synge** 1596; *pr. p.* **syngyng(e)** 172sd; 528sd; *p. p.* **songe** 1540 (**singen** *v.*)

syngulere *adj.* individual, special 1386 (**singuler(e** *adj.*)

syngulyrly *adv.* specially 192 (**singulerli** *adv.*)

synne *n.* sin 178, 469 etc. (**sinne** *n.*)

systere, systyr, sustyr *n.* sister 1152; 1167; 1378; *n. pl.* **systerys** 487, 510 etc. (**suster** *n.*)

syt *see* **sytt**

syth *see* **syght**

syth(e), sethe *conj.* since 1241; 29*A*2; since when 1490 (**sitthe** *conj.*)

sythe, sethe *adv.* afterwards 11, 1360; 474 (**sitthe** *adv.*)

sytt *v.* sit 1455; *1sg. pr.* **sytt** 1056; *3sg. pr.* **sytt** 138, 252, 980. **syttyht** 873, **syttyth** 160, **syttys** 174*A*2; *pr. p.* **syttynge** 770; *sg. pa.* **sat** 1479; **it syt** it is fitting 1175; **syttynge** fitting, appropriate 1187 (**sitten** *v.*)

skyes *n. pl.* skies 376 (**ski(e** *n.*)

skyl *n.* right 880; **good skyl** quite right 934 (**skil** *n.*)

skore *v.* scour, clean 1544 (**scouren** *v.*2)

slawndyr *n.* disgrace, shame 62 (**sclaundre** *n.*)

sle *v.* kill 128; *3sg. pr.* **sleyth** 139 (**slen** *v.*)

slepe *v.* sleep 1148; *2pl. pr.* **slepe** 337; *3sg. pr. subj.* **slepe** 528 (**slepen** *v.*)

slyde *v.* *3pl. pr.* slip down, fall 56 (**sliden** *v.*)

smytyht *v.* *3sg. pr.* strikes 334 (**smiten** *v.*)

so, sa *adv.* so 7, 169 etc; 1528 (**so** *adv.*)

so *conj.* so 48, 54 etc. (**so** *adv.*)

sobbe *v. pl. pr.* sob, weep 1079 (**sobben** *v.*)

sobyr *adj.* serious, temperate 967 (**sobre** *adj.*)

socour(e) *n.* assistance protection 1399; 792 (**socour** *n.*)

socowre *v.* assist, relieve 649 (**socouren** *v.*)

soferauns *n.* endurance 409 (**sufferaunce** *n.*)

sofreynes, sovereynes, sovereynys *n. pl.* friends (a term of polite address to the audience) 577; 254, 1434; 1561 (**soverain** *n.*)

sofron *v.* allow, endure, bear 129; *3sg. pr.* **soferyth** 129 (**sufferen** *v.*)

softe *adj.* gentle 421 (**soft(e** *adj.*)

solacyth *v.* *3sg. pr.* cheers, comforts 1405 (**solasen** *v.*)

solas *n.* comfort 505 (**solas** *n.*)

solemply *adv.* formally 193 (**solempneli** *adv.*)

solempn *adj.* solemn, important 906 (**solempne** *adj.*)

solennyzacyon *n.* rite, religious celebration 33 (**solempnisacioun** *n.*)

som *see* **sum**

son(e) *n.* son 182, 184 etc; 210, 311 etc; *n. poss.* **sonys** 1387 (**sone** *n.*)

sond(e) *n.* messenger 9*A*1; 24*A*2; **sownde** message 1274 (**sond(e** *n.*)

sone *adv.* soon 148, 566 etc. (**sone** *adv.*)

song *n.* song 1010 (**song** *n.*)

songe *see* **syng(e)**

sonne *n.* sun 1407 (**sonne** *n.*)

sore *adv.* greatly, grievously, deeply 49, 58 etc. (**sore** *adv.*)

sory *n.* those in distress 86 (**sori** *adj.*)

sorwe *n.* sorrow, grief 81, 92 etc; *n. pl.* **sorwys** 200 (**sorwe** *n.*)

sorwyth *v. 3sg. pr.* grieves, sorrows 160 (**sorwen** *v.*)

sote *see* **swete**

sothe *n.* truth 1337; **in soth(e)** indeed, truly 812, 984, 1449; 1216 (**soth** *n.*)

sothly *adv.* truly 288, 1405 (**sothli** *adv.*)

sovereyn, soveryen *adj.* sovereign, supreme 458; 537 (**soverain** *adj.*)

sovereynes, sovereynys *see* **sofreynes**

sovereynly *adv.* above all 457 (**soverainli** *adv.*)

sowyht *v. 3sg. pr.* sews 138 (**seuen** *v. 2*)

sowle *n.* soul 240, 422 etc; *n. pl.* **sowles, sowlys** 1007; 208, 1078 (**soul(e** *n.*)

sownd *adj.* **saue þe/ȝow sownd** keep you safe 961, 972 (**sound(e** *adj.*)

sownde see **sond(e)**

sowte *see* **seke** *v.*

space, spas *n.* **þis space** at this time 1332, 162*A2*; time 589 (**space** *n.*)

spak *see* **speke**

spare *v.* spare, cease, hold back, save 269, 571, 1175; *3sg. pr.* **sparyth** 179; *imp. sg.* **spare** 159, 563 (**sparen** *v.*)

spech(e) *n.* words, talking, speech 1580, 221*A2*; 269, 297; *n. pl.* **speches** 1175 (**spech(e** *n.*)

specyal *adv.* in particular 43 (**special(e** *adv.*)

specialy, specyal(l)y, specyalye *adv.* especially, in particular 1558; 32, 336 etc; 1142; 1380 (**specialli** *adv.*)

specyfy *v.* specifically arrange 1374 (**specifien** *v.*)

sped(e) *n.* help, fortune 261; 147; **in sped** quickly 358, 418 (**sped(e** *n.*)

spede *v.* prosper, help, succeed 949, 995, 1431, 3*A1*; *3sg. pr. subj.* **spede** 842, 969 etc. (**speden** *v.*)

spedful *adj.* prosperous, fortunate 691 (**spedeful** *adj.*)

speke *v.* speak 139, 1555; *3sg. pr.* **spekyth** 7*A2*; *pl. pr.* **speke** 1553, 2*A2*; *3sg. pa.* **spak** 1527, 1579; *p. p.* **spoke** 173*A2* (**speken** *v.*)

spelle *n.* words, speech 221*A2* (**spel** *n.*)

spyryt(e) *n.* (Holy) Spirit 135*A2*; spirit 1496; *n. pl.* **spyrytys of vertu** the angels 1333 (see note) (**spirit** *n.*)

sport *n.* amusement; **neyther sport nere game** no fun at all 844 (**sport(e** *n.*)

spowsage *n.* marriage 606 (**spousage** *n.*)

spowse *n.* spouse (husband or wife) 607, 612 etc. (**spous(e** *n.*)

spowsyng *vbl. n.* marriage 683 (**spousing(e** *ger.*)

sprede *v. 3sg. pr. subj.* extend (over) 973 (**spreden** *v.*)

sprynge *v.* arise 194 (**springen** *v.*)

staff *n.* staff, stick 760, 763 (**staf** *n.*)

stage *n.* **in stage** ?for a period of time, ?in your house 923 (**stage** *n.*)

stande, standyst *see* **stonde** *v.*

starkly *adv.* stoutly, boldly 1433 (**starkli** *adv.*)

staunche *v.* satisfy 1072 (**staunchen** *v.*)

steppys *n. pl.* footsteps 150 (**step** *n.*)

ster(e)d *p. p.* moved, roused, encouraged, incited 388, 1008; 1410 (**stiren** *v.*)

sterrys *n. pl.* planets 819 (**sterre** *n.*)

stewyn *n.* **of gracyous stewyn** ?for a kindly response, ?of kindly judgement 817 (**steven(e** *n. 1*)

stylle *adv.* still, yet, always 988, 1164, 1570, 1577 (**stille** *adv.*)

stody *n.* studying 361 (**studi(e** *n.*)

stok *n.* stump, stick 835 (**stok** *n. 1*)

stond(e) *v.* stand 8*A1*; 26*A2*; *2sg. pr.* **standyst** 1344; *pl. pr.* **stande** 806; **it doth now stonde with me** I am placed 944 (**stonden** *v. 1*)

stonys *n. pl.* stones 97*A2* (**ston** *n.*)

stray *v.* stray 142 (**straien** *v.*)

straunge *adj.* odd, unnatural 755 (**straunge** *adj.*)

strem *n.* stream (fig.) 386 (**strem** *n.*)

strenght *n.* strength 385; *n. pl.* **strenghthis** 467 (**strength(e** *n.*)

stryff *n.* discord, quarrelling, dispute 895, 191*A2* (**strif(e** *n.*)

stryve *v.* debate, struggle 525 (see note) 845 (**striven** *v.*)

strongere *adj.* stronger 185 (**strong** *adj.*)

substancyall *adj.* **in godys substancyall** wealthy, prosperous 46 (**substancial** *adj.*)

such, swiche, swych *pron.* such people 679; 691; 188 (**swich** *pron.*)

such(e), suech, swych(e) *adj., adv.* such 665, 682, 139*A2*; 339, 191*A2*; 411; 52*A2*; 478, 1211 (**swich** *adj.*; **swiche** *adv.*)

suete *see* **swete**

suffyce *v.* suffice, be enough 584; *3sg. pr.* **sufficyth** 537, 587 (**suffisen** *v.*)

sufficyent *adj.* adequate 1223 (**sufficient** *adj.*)

suffre *v.* suffer, undergo 1221, 1232; *imp. sg.* **suffyr** 1148 (**sufferen** *v.*)

sum, som *adj.* some 158, 754 etc.; 20*A1* (**som** *adj.*)

sum *pron.* some, a part 1026, 1491 (**som** *pron.*)

supplicacyon, supplycacyon *n.* petition, humble request 1115; 1094 (**supplicacioun** *n.*)

supportacyon *n.* support, help 1590 (**supportacioun** *n.*)

sure *adj.* deliberate, careful 4 (see note) (**seur** *adj.*)

sure *adv.* surely, certainly 1223 (**seur** *adv.*)

surely *adv.* truly, certainly 1406 (**seurli** *adv.*)

sustenauns *n.* livelihood, food 987 (**sustenaunce** *n.*)

sustentacyon *n.* sustenance, nourishment 531 (**sustentacioun** *n.*)

swage *v.* allay, appease, lessen 921 (**swagen** *v.2*)

swelle *v.* swallow 382 (**swolwen** *v.*)

swem(e) *n.* grief 78; shame, pity 1189 (**swem** *n.*)

swemful *adj.* distressing, mournful 66 (**swemful** *adj.*)

swemynge *vbl. n.* grieving, mourning 334 (**sweming(e** *ger.*)

swepe *v.* sweep 1544 (**swepen** *v.*)

swete, sote, suete *adj.* sweet, dear, pleasant 67, 292 etc; 26; 869 (**swet(e** *adj.*)

swetter *adj.* sweeter 1019 (**swet(e** *adj.*)

swettnes *n.* gentleness, mildness (translating L. *mansuetudo*) 430 (**swetenes(se** *n.*)

swiche, swych *see* **such** *pron.*

swych(e) *see* **such(e)** *adj., adv.*

tabernakyl *n.* dwelling, shrine 1549 (**tabernacle** *n.*)

take *v.* take, give, offer 38, 280 etc.; *1sg. pr.* **take** 75, 169 etc.; *imp. sg.* **take** 717, 723 etc.; *imp. pl.* **take** 18, **take** 1300, 186*A2*, **takyth** 595, 735; *pr. p.* **takynge** 1360; *3sg. pa.* **toke** 1586; *p. p.* **take** 896 (**taken** *v.*)

talkyd *p. p.* spoken 14 (**talken** *v.*)

talkyn *vbl. n.* talking, words 18 (**talking(e** *ger.*)

tary *v. imp. sg./pl.* delay, remain 744, 1082; *2sg. pr.* **taryst** 795; *1sg. pa.* **taryed** 124*A2* (**tarien** *v.1*)

teche *v.* teach 491 (**techen** *v.*)

tedyous *adj.* tedious, wearisome 14 (**tedious** *adj.*)

tell(e) *v.* tell, reckon, declare 216*A2*; 232, 715 etc.; *1sg. pr.* **tell** 668, 1038, **telle** 1060, 156*A2*; *imp. sg.* **telle** 636, 1268, 32*A2*, 211*A2*; *imp. pl.* **telle** 285, 4*A2*; *1sg. pa.* **told** 88*A2*; *3sg. pa.* **tolde** 282, 1448; *p. p.* **told** 18*A1*, **tolde** 608, 1491 (**tellen** *v.*)

temple, tempyl(l) *n.* temple 11, 37 etc.; 520, 612, 614, 640; 11*A1* (**temple** *n. 1*)

temptacyon *n.* temptation 409, 1236 (**temptacioun** *n.*)

ten *num.* ten 453, 1568 (**ten** *num.*)

tende *v.* attend, look after 495; *2pl. pr.* **tende** 498 (**tenden** *v. 1*)

tende *ord. num.* tenth 409 (**tenth(e** *num.*)

tenderest *adj.* most loving 889 (**tender** *adj.*)

tendyr *adj.* tender; **tendyr age and zyng** extreme youth 258 (**tender** *adj.*)

tendyrly *adv.* gently, carefully 498, 595 (**tenderli** *adv.*)

tene *n.* harm, injury 1053 (**tene** *n.2*)

tene *v. 3sg. pr. subj.* disparage, censure 677 (**tenen** *v.*)

tent *n.* attention; **take tent** pay attention, take heed 717, 735, 49*A2* (**tent(e** *n.2*)

teryeng *vbl. n.* delaying 278 (**tariing(e** *ger. 1*)

terys *n. pl.* tears 66, 177 (**ter(e** *n.*)

terme-tyme *n.* **both terme-tyme and tyde** at all times (limited and unlimited time) 903 (**terme** *n.*)

than, þan *adv.* than 1019, 110*A2*, 116*A2*; 152, 154 etc. (**than** *conj.*)

than(ne), then, þan *adv.* then 12, 62 etc.; 157, 475 etc.; 1537; 206, 468 etc. (**thanne** *adv.*)

thank *v.* thank 252, 537, 1556, 24*A3*; *1sg. pr.* **thank** 154, 726 etc.; *pl. pr.* **thank** 1589; *3sg. pr. subj.* **thank** 327; *imp. pl.* **thank** 2*A3*; *pr. p.* **thankynge** 1572 (**thanken** *v.*)

þare *see* ther(e), þer

that, þat *pron.* that 25*A2*; 257 (**that** *pron.*)

that, þat *rel. pron.* that, which, who 197, 736, 1226, 1336; 17, 19 etc. (**that** *rel. pron.*)

that, þat *conj.* that, so that 368, 573, 705, 6*A1*; 3, 5 etc (**that** *conj.*)

that, þat *adj.* that 267, 1227; 19, 204 etc. (**that** *def.art. & adj.*)

the, þe *pron. obj.* thee 155, 417 etc.; 108, 139 etc. (**the** *pron.2*)

the, þe *def. art.* the 26, 57 etc.; 3, 7 etc. (**the** *def.art.*)

the(n) *v.* prosper, thrive 1418; 751 (**then** *v.*)

thedyr *adv.* thither, there 88 (**thider** *adv.*)

thedyrward *adv.* to that place, thither 300 (**thiderward** *adv.*)

thei, they, þei *pron.* they 343, 639, 674, 1447, 19*A1*; 27, 136 etc.; 84, 567 etc. (**thei** *pron.*)

them *pron. obj.* them 645, 1582 (**theim** *pron.*)

thens *adv.* thence, from there, forward 810, 1166 (**thennes** *adv.*)

þer *pron. poss.* their 81, 721 (**their(e** *pron.*)

ther(e), þer, þare, thore, þore *adv.* there, then, in that case 161, 490 etc.; 481, 722 etc.; 52, 74 etc.; 104, 345, 1235 etc.; 1123; where 1142 (**ther** *adv.*)

þerby *adv.* by that 1011, 1202 (**ther-bi** *adv.*)

therefore, þerffor, therffore, þerffore, therfor(e), þerfor(e) *adv.* therefore 107, 1183; 1556; 1163; 17; 12*A1*; 867, 947 etc.; 1237; 27, 276 etc. (**ther-for(e** *adv.*)

þerin *adv*. in that, there 476, 1033, 1063 (**ther-in(ne** *adv*.)

therkeness *n*. darkness 1009 (**therknes(se** *n*.)

þerof *adv*. of it, of them 571, 573, 1006, 1427 (**ther-of** *adv*.)

therto, þerto *adv*. of that, to that, thereto 315; 878, 881, 1554 (**ther-to** *adv*.)

þerwith *adv*. with that, therewith 13, 427 etc. (**ther-with** *adv*.)

these, þese *adj*. these 369, 484 etc.; 70, 448 etc. (**thes(e** *adj*.)

þese *pron*. these 1230 (**thes(e** *pron*.)

thi, þi(n), thy(n) *pron. poss.* thy, thine 727, 4*A1*; 101, 151 etc.; 105, 176 etc.; 713, 1081, 1127; 1071, 1121 etc.; (used absolutely) **þin** 794 (**the** *pron. 2*)

thynge, þinge *n*. thing 445, 504 etc.; 34*A2*; *n. pl.* **thyngs** 579, 1021, 1503 (**thing** *n*.)

thynk(e) *v*. think 1477, 1524; 1274; *1sg. pr.* **thynk** 1294, **thynke** 1199, *3sg. pr.* **thynk** 353; *3pl. pr.* **thynkth** 1323; *imp. pl.* **thynk** 333, **thynkys** 1*A3*; *3sg. pa.* **thought** 661 (**thinken** *v. 2*)

this, þis, thys *pron*. this 33, 34 etc.; 16, 63 etc.; 129, 1370, 206*A2* (**this** *pron*.)

this, þis *adj*. this 9, 685 etc.; 1, 5 etc. (**this** *adj*.)

thyself, þiself, þiselph *pron*. thyself 33*A2*; 168, 468, 1331; 917 (**thi-self** *pron*.)

tho, þo *pron*. those 38; 39, 81 etc. (**tho** *pron. 2*)

thore, þore *see* **ther(e), þer**

thorwe, þorwe, thour *prep*. through 1269, 1328; 219*A2*; 1400 (**thurgh** *prep*.)

thou *see* **thu, þu**

thought *n*. thought, intention, mind 511, 1474 etc.; **with a thought** immediately, in a trice 1276; *n. pl.* **thoughtys** 1199 (**thought** *n*.)

thought *v. 3sg. pa. impers.* **hym thought** it seemed to him 1489 (**thinken** *v. 1*)

thow, þow *conj*. though 528, 1284, 109*A2*; 1170, 1171 etc. (**though** *conj*.)

thowsand *num*. thousand 1060, 1568 (**thousand** *num*.)

thre *num*. three 51, 275 etc. (**thre** *num*.)

threttene *num*. (as *ord. num.*) thirteenth 427 (**thritene** *num*.)

threttye *num*. thirty 1070 (**thriti** *num*.)

thryd(de) *ord. num.* third 57; 367, 516, 928 (**thrid** *num*.)

thryes *adv*. three times 79 (**thrice** *adv*.)

thryff *v*. prosper, have good fortune 851, 877 (**thriven** *v*.)

thrysté *n*. thirsty 1072 (**thirsti** *adj*.)

thu, þu, thou *pron*. thou 181, 469, 1147, 1281; 100, 101 etc.; 831 (**thou** *pron*.)

thus, þus *adv*. thus, in this way, so 128, 167 etc.; 253, 465 etc. (**thus** *adv*.)

tyde *n*. time; **both terme-tyme and tyde** at all times 903 (**tid(e** *n*.)

tydnge *n*. news 218; *n. pl.* **tydyngys** 206, 369 (**tiding(e** *n*.)

tyl *conj*. until 93, 345 etc. (**til** *conj*.)

tyl(le) *prep*. till, to 268; 364 (**til** *prep*.)

tyme *n*. time 41, 59 etc. (**time** *n. 2*)

to *see* **two** *num*.

to *adv*. too 1130, 1167, 26*A2*, 124*A2* (**to** *adv. 2*)

to *prep*. to (**to** *prep*.)

togedyr *adv*. together 618, 704, 1126

to–hym–ward *adv*. towards him 238

toke *see* **take**

tokyn *n*. sign, token 104, 155, 102*A2*; **in tokyn** as a sign 198, 1270
tomorwe *n*. tomorrow 1082
tomorwe *adv*. tomorrow 168
tonge, tounge *n*. speech, words, speaking 920, 1453; 232
to-say *v*. *pl. pr.* say 72*A2*
tothere *see* **other** *adj*.
toure, towre *n*. dwelling, tower 796; 24
towchyd *v*. *3sg. pa.* was connected/associated with 103*A2*
towne *n*. town 756
tray *n*. pain, grief 1053 (**Tray** *sb¹*.)
transgressyon *n*. sin 1139
trast *v*. trust, believe 638
travayl, traveyll *v*. journey, travel 10*A3*; 13*A1*
traveyl *v*. labour 1382
trekyl *v*. trickle, run 66
Trenyté *see* **Trinité**
tresowre *n*. treasure (fig.), dear one 976
trespace, trespas *n*. wrong, sin 165*A2*; 87*A2*
trew(e) *adj*. faithful 1335; 902 (**True** *a*.)
trewly *adv*. certainly, indeed 701, 804
trewth(e), trowth(e) *n*. truth, the character *Veritas* 1119, 1143 etc.; 1127,
    1133; 809; 1215; **with trewth** honestly, truly 1041; **take ... trewth** to
    pledge one's faith 886; **in trowth(e)** truly 809, 1191
tribulacyon, trybulacyon *n*. distress, affliction 156; 1136
tribus *n*. *pl.* tribes (of the children of Israel) 32, 62
tryne *adj*. threefold 560 (**Trine** *a. & sb.*)
Trinité, Trinyté, Trynité, Trynyté, Trenyté *n*. the Trinity, God 1233,
    1549; 120, 1396; 1459, 68*A2*; 1303, 1375; 874
trobyl *n*. trouble, distress 357
trobyl *v*. *3pl. pr.* disturb, distress, worry 674; *3sg. pr.* **trobelyth** 685; *p. p.*
    trobelyd 1293
tron(e) *n*. throne (also fig.) 252, 1366; 560, 832 etc.
trost *v*. *1sg. pr.* trust, have faith in 792; *3pl. pr.* **trust** 387
trow *v*. believe, think, trust 81*A2*; *1sg. pr.* **trowe** 567, 1420, 1553
turnyd *v*. *3sg. pa.* turned, reversed into, went 125, 1282, 1466
turtyl *n*. turtle-dove (also fig.) 1376; *n. pl.* **turtelys** 75
twey(n) *num*. two 1126; 75, 454 etc.; *poss*. **here tweyners** of the two of
    them 1450
tweyners *see* **twey(n)**
twelfte *ord. num.* twelfth 421
twenty *num*. twenty 296, 1435
two, to *num*. two 1420; 1146, 1574

veyn *adj*. unprofitable, worthless 579; **in veyn** uselessly 400
veynglory *n*. worthless pride, vainglory 397
velany *n*. wickedness, sin 103*A2*, 114*A2*
vengeabyl *adj*. vengeful, cruel 1167, 99*A2*
vengere *n*. avenger, punisher 178
venymyd *p. p.* (emendation) envenomed, poisoned 150 (**Venom** *v*.)
venjauns *n*. vengeance 26*A3*
verament *adv*. truly 1329
very *adv*. true, real 1194

veryfye *v.* prove true, confirm the truth of 171*A2*
veryly(e) *adv.* truly 134, 139 etc.; 1441
vertu *n.* power, virtue 1315, 1333, 1410; *n. pl.* **vertuys** 517, 1006, 1176
vertuysful *adj.* virtuous, full of virtue 1012
vertuous *adj.* virtuous, good 201*A2*
vesytacyon *n.* visitation, affliction 1555
vesyte *v.* visit, come to 1074, 1390
vesselys *n. pl.* dishes 566
vexacyon *n.* trouble, distress 411
virgyn(e) *n.* virgin, maiden 871; 1264, 1471
virginyté *n.* virginity 1311
vndyr *prep.* under 294
vndyrstande, vndyrstonde *v.* understand 748, 764; 209*A2*; *1sg. pr.*
  vndyrstande 1385; *imp. sg.* **vndyrstond** 717; *imp. pl.* **vndyrstondyth**
  1434
vndyrtake *v.* *1sg. pr.* promise, pledge myself 729
vndo, ondo *v.* *imp. pl.* open 1*A2*, 5*A2*; 8*A2*
vndowteful *adj.* confident, sure 391
vndryd *see* **hundryd**
vnyté *n.* unity (of God) 1197, 1246, 1269
vnkende, vnkynde *adj.* unnatural, ungrateful 1129; 1121
vnknowlage *n.* ignorance 130*A2*
vnprofytable *adj.* worthless 1224
vnto *see* **onto**
vnwurthy *adj.* unworthy, undeserving 1298
vnwurthynes *n.* unworthiness, lack of merit 1445
voydnes *n.* emptiness, oblivion, futility 1520
voys *n.* voice 418
vow *v.* *1sg. pr.* vow 72
up, vp *adv., prep.* up 65, 98 etc.; 448, 769
upon, vpon *prep.* upon 495; 1516
vpryght *adj.* or *adv.* erect; directly, straight 448
vptoke *v.* *3sg. pa.* took up, raised, supported 1523
us, vs *pron. obj.* us 23, 64 etc.; 24, 29 etc.
vsage *n.* practice, habitual use 1322, 1388
vsyth *v.* *3sg. pr.* practises, performs 1014

way *adv.* (shortened form of 'away') **do way** 74*A2* (*see* **do** *v.*)
way, wey *n.* way 352, 731, 1047; 212, 215; *n. pl.* **weys** 406, 971
wake *v.* wake, watch, keep vigil 41, 528
walk *v.* *1sg. pr.* walk 168*A2*; *pr. p.* **walkyng** 762
wand(e), whande, wond *n.* rod, stick, wand 758; 766; 750; 11*A1*
wardeyn *n.* guardian 863
ware, was *see* **be(n), bene**
wasche *v.* wash 1544
watyr *n.* water (*see* **londe**) 959
we *pron.* we
wedde *v.* marry 612, 838, 841, 177*A2*; *1sg. pr.* **wedde** 893; *imp. sg.* **wedde**
  891; *imp. pl.* **weddyth** 50*A2*; *p. p.* **weddyd** 679, 1254, 222*A2*
weddyng *vbl. n.* wedding, marriage 599, 635
wede *n.* clothing (fig.) 1240
wedyr *see* **whedyr** *adv.*

wey *see* **way**
wel(e), well, weyl *adv.* well 91, 246 etc.; 493, 722 etc.; 1038, 8*A1*; 619
welaway *interj.* (an exclamation of sorrow) alas! 57*A2*, 78*A2*
welcom(e), wellcome *interj.* welcome 135, 188*A2*; 624, 1559; 9*A2*
weldygh *v.* ?*3sg. pr.* accepts, receives 821
wellys *n. pl.* wells (fig.) 1084
welth *n.* prosperity, happiness 961; *n. pl.* **welthis** worldly goods 993
wen *v.* think 754; *1sg. pa.* **wend** 1372 (**Ween** *v.*)
wench *n.* girl, woman 51*A2*
wende *v. 1* go 931, 144*A2*; *imp. sg.* **wend þi way** 731
wende *v. 2 pl. pr.* think (confusion over the past tense of **ween** seems more
   likely than that the form is past here; cf. **Wend** *v².*) 568
went, wenten *see* **go(n)**
wepe *v.* weep, cry 90, 335, 1085, 149*A2*; *1sg. pr.* **wepe** 162, 240, 526, 1054;
   2sg. pr. **wepyst** 147*A2*; *pl. pa.* **wepte** 646
wepynge *vbl. n.* weeping, crying 93, 220, 151*A2*
werd(e) *n.* world 174, 225, 506, 904, 1528, 1537; 54
werdly *adj.* of the world 986
were *see* **be(n)**
were *v.* wear 1240
wery *adj.* weary, exhausted 1421, 1454
weryn *see* **be(n)**
werk(e) *n.* work, doing 223*A2*; 1328; *n. pl.* **werkys** 229, 833, 1169, 1537
werke, werkyn *v.* do, perform, carry out, create, make 729, 1268; 727; *p. p.*
   wrought 506, 1046, 1471, 8*A2*
wern *see* **be(n)**
wers(e) *adj.* worse 1473; 152
wete *v.* know, imagine 134, 1222; *1pl. pr.* **wete** 69; *2pl. pr. subj.* **wete** 867
   (**Wit** *v¹.*)
wete *v. 3sg. pr. subj.* ?acknowledge, ?grant 14*A3* (?**Wit** *v¹.*; *v².*)
whan, qwan *conj.* when 198, 393 etc.; 1407
whande *see* **wand(e)**
what, qwhat *pron. interr. and rel.* what 18, 121 etc.; 173
what *adj.* what, whatsoever 232, 609 etc.
what(h) *interj.* what! 841; 806
whatso *pron.* whoever 603
whatsoevyr *pron.* whatever 214
wheche *see* **which** *adj.*
whedyr, wedyr *adv.* whither, where 100, 118*A2*, 119*A2*; 145*A2*
when *see* **whan**
where-as *adv.* where 909
whereffore, wherfor(e) *conj.* for which reason, therefore 105; 613; 41*A2*
wherevyr *conj.* wherever 959
wherso *conj.* wherever 970, 20*A3*
why, qwy *adv.* why, for what reason 50, 167 etc.; 100*A2*
which(e) *pron.* which, who 35, 153 etc.; 224, 440 etc.
which, wheche *adj.* which 215, 1307; 1004
whyght, wythe *n.* person, being 1473; 201*A2* (**Wight** *sb.*)
whyght *see* **white**
whil, whyl, qwhyl *conj.* while 289; 22*A2*; 170
white, whyte, whyght *adj.* white 734, 742, 778, 781; 270sd; 721, etc.; 785
whith *see* **with**

who(o) *pron. interr. and rel.* who 680, 1014 etc.; 1166

whom *pron. obj.* whom 182, 805, 1255, 1467

whonde *v. imp. sg.* hesitate, hold back 211*A2*

whos(e), whoos *pron. poss.* whose 179, 506, 1101; 724; 47*A2*

whow *see* **how** *interr.* and *conj. adv.*

wyde *adj.* wide 54

wyde *adv.* widely 135

wyff, wyve *n.* wife 58, 76 etc.; 847

wykkyd *n.* wicked people 643

wykkydnes *n.* evil, wickedness 1199

wyl(l), wylle *n.* will, desire, intention 729, 826 etc.; 884, 930, 213*A2*; 362, 632, 1572, 153*A2*

wyl(l), wole *v. 1sg. pr.* will, wish 130, 629 etc.; 669, 1040, 288; 95*A2*; *2sg. pr.* **wylt** 635, 1024, 1120, **wytte** 100; *3sg. pr.* **wyl** 69, 846 etc., **wol** 860, **wole** 61, 64 etc., **woll** 16*A1*; *1pl. pr.* **wyl** 97, **wole** 267, 905, 906, 1033, **wul** 146; *2pl. pr.* **wyl** 1323, 4*A2*, **wole** 50, 478 etc.; *3pl. pr.* **wole** 1399, **woll** 19*A1*; would, should *1sg. pa.* **wold** 346, 1373, **wolde** 87, 134, 574, 798; *2sg. pa.* **woldyst** 1068, 176*A2*; *3sg. pa.* **wold** 754, 911, 165*A2*, 202*A2*, **wolde** 584, 649 etc.; *3pl. pa.* **wolde** 1203, 1428, 115*A2*; (expressing fervent desire) **wolde God** 774, 1068 (for detailed discussion of forms see **Will** *v¹*.)

wylde *adj.* unruly, wanton, self-willed 967

wyllde *n.* cruel people 643

wys *adv.* truly, indeed 302, 1554 (**Wis** *adv.*)

wysdam *n.* wisdom 463, 506 etc.

wys(s)e *adj.* wise 672, 1159, 1328; 40; (as *n.*) 691

wyse *n.* way, manner 189, 666 etc.

wysest *adj.* wisest 709

wysly *adv.* sensibly 205

wysse *v. 3sg. pr. subj.* guide 958

wyst *v. 1sg. pa. subj.* knew 100*A2*; *p. p.* **wyst** 163*A2*

wyte *v.* accuse, blame 200*A2*

with, whith *prep.* with 8, 13 etc.; 297; as *adv.* 411 (all forms except 297 are expansions of abbreviations)

withall *adv.* with 217

withdrawe *v.* draw back from 516

wythe *see* **whyght**

withinne *adv.* **withinne and withowt(e)** throughout, everywhere 422, 1215

within(ne) *prep.* in 787; 1331

without(yn), withowte, withowth, withowtyn *prep.* without 196, 7*A3*; 836, 895; 1117, 1217 etc.; 380; 468, 548 etc.

withowt(e) *adv. see* **withinne** *adv.*

wytt *n.* intelligence, mind, reason 675, 818, 1177; *n. pl.* **wyttys fyve/fyff** the five senses (sometimes mental faculties in general) 524, 890

wo *n.* grief, affliction 759, 762 etc.

wo *adj.* sorrowful, woeful 213

woman *n.* woman 70, 1364, 1440; *n. pl.* **women** 1281, 1291, 1469

wombe *n.* womb 179, 1302 etc.

wonyng *n.* dwelling-place 909 (**Wonning, woning** *vbl. sb.*)

wonte *adj.* accustomed 1248 (**Wont** *pa.pple.*)

woo *interj.* woe! 1076

worchep, wurchep(pe) *v.* worship 989; 472, 653, 776, 210*A2*; 1548
worchepful *adj.* honoured, worshipful 82
word(e), wourde, wurde *n.* word, message, speech, command 102*A2*;
    1351; **Goddys holy wourde** the blessing of God 109; 727, þe **wurde of**
    God Christ 1475; *n. pl.* **wordys** 672, 1293, 1312, **wourdys** 78, **wurdys**
    14, 66
wore, worn *see* **be(n)**
wo(u)rthy, wurthy *adj.* worthy, deserving 99, 1367; 207; 149, 290 etc.
wost *see* **wot(e)**
wot(e), wott *v. 1sg. pr.* know 119*A2*; 215; 946; *2sg. pr.* **wost** 463 (**Wot** *v.*)
wounde *n.* wound 1221
wounde *v.* wound (fig.) 153
wrake *n.* **withowtyn wrake** without dispute 727
wrecche, wretche *n.* miserable/useless person 152, 1473; 1129; *n. pl.*
    wrecchis 1076, 1473, 1547
wretchydnes *n.* misery 1111
wretyn *p. p.* written 1539
wrytynge *vbl. n.* **be wrytynge** according to the Bible 185
wronge *n.* wrong 123*A2*, 199*A2*
wroth(e) *adj.* angry 1553; 330
wrought *see* **werke, werkyn**
wundyrful *adj.* marvellous, excellent 833
wurchep(pe) *see* **worchep** *v.*
wurchep *n.* honour, worship 85, 815, 821, 822
wurde *see* **word(e)**
wurthyest *adj.* most worthy/honourable 1471

xal(le), shalle *v. 1sg. pr.* shall, will 48, 170 etc.; 238, 759; 109; *2sg. pr.* **xalt**
    199, 223 etc., **xalte** 221; *3sg. pr.* **xal** 73, 190 etc.; *pl. pr.* **xal** 18, 65 etc., **xall**
    316, 368, 510, **xalle** 119, **xul** 533, 720 etc.; *2sg. pr. ?subj.* **xalle** 715;
    should, would *1sg. pa.* **xuld** 841, 850 etc., **xulde** 1489; *3sg. pa.* **xuld** 29,
    194 etc., **xulde** 14, 54 etc.; *pl. pa.* **xuld** 665, **xulde** 282, 342 etc., **shulde**
    382; **shuld I haue here** if I were to have her 849

ye *see* **ʒe**
yf *see* **if(f)**
yis *adv.* yes 15*A1*
ylle *adv.* badly, sinfully 151*A2* (**ille** *adv.*)
you *see* **ʒou, ʒow**
your *see* **ʒour(e)**
ys *see* **be(n)**
yt *see* **it**

List of proper names
and *dramatis personae*

References are given here to proper names that appear in the text or stage directions (sd), and to speakers' names (sn). All line references are given for names occurring in the text and stage directions unless they are very numerous, when a single reference followed by 'etc.' is given. One line reference only is normally given for speakers' names, followed by 'etc.' if the name occurs more than once.

Initial 'Y' has been treated as 'I' in the alphabetical sequence.

For 'God', 'Lord', 'Trinity', which are not listed here, see the Glossary.

Abysakar 593sd; high priest/bishop in the temple at Mary's betrothal (*see also* **Episcopus**, and note to 593sd)
Abraham 1340, 1526, 1528
Adam 547, 1123, 1201, 1340; **Adamys** 1088
Angelus 175sn etc., **Aungell** 555sn
An 333, **Anna** 66sn etc., 508sd, 550, **Anne** 10 etc., 90sn, 270sd; wife to Joachim, mother of Mary

Babylony 352; (fig.) Babylon, the physical world, opposed to Jerusalem, the spiritual one

Chorus 111sn etc.; the choir in the temple
Clennes 482; with **Compassyon, Contryssyon, Fruyssyon, Meditacyon,** one of the five allegorical maidens, Mary's companions in the temple (*see also* **virgines**, and note to 11.481–3)
Compassyon 482, *see* **Clennes**
Contemplacio 1sn etc.; the linking narrator, expositor and occasionally actor
Contryssyon 482, *see* **Clennes**
Cryst 1, 8, 70; **Crystys** 1593

Dauid 431, 736, **Dauyd** 719, **Dauyth** 1003, **Davyd** 1256, 1306, 1340, 1434, **Davyth** 429; **Dauidis** 789, **Dauyd** 732, 10*A1*, **Dauythis** 780; King David
Declaracyon 496; with **Deliberacyon, Determynacyon, Devocyon, Dylexcyon, Dyscressyon** and **Dyvynacyon,** one of the seven allegorical priests, Mary's teachers in the temple (see note to 11.490–6)
Deliberacyon 494; **Determynacyon** 496, *see* **Declaracyon**
Deus 137*A2*sn; **Deum** 294sd, 310sd; God
Devocyon 494; **Dylexcyon** 494; **Dyscressyon** 494; **Dyvynacyon** 496, *see* **Declaracyon**

Egypt 184
Elizabet 20*A3*sd, **Elizabeth** 1441 etc., 1462sn etc., 20*A3*sd, **Elyzabeth** 13
  etc.; wife of Zacharias, mother of John the Baptist
Episcopus 114sn etc., *see* **Abysakar** *and* **Isakar**
Eva 1282; Eve

Fadyr godly 1355sd, *see* **Pater**
Filius 115, 1199sn; **Filij** 323, 325, 500, 916; **Filio** 1529; God the Son (*see also*
  Sone)
Fruyssyon 483, *see* **Clennes**

Gabriel 1275sn, 1392sn, **Gabryel** 1300sn etc., 1251 etc., **Gabryell**
  214*A2*
Galylé 42, 1252; the land of Galilee
Gyldyn/Goldyn Gate 198, 221; one of the gates of Jerusalem (see note to
  1.198)

Hierusalem 390, *see* **Jerusalem**
Holy Goost 192, **Holy Gost** 311 etc., 1355sd, **Holy Spyryt** 135*A2*, *see*
  Spiritus Sanctus

Ysaac 182; Isaac, son of Abraham and Sarah
Ysaie 1066; the prophet Isaiah
Isakar 307sn, **Isakare** 569, **Isaker** 97sd, **Ysakar** 26sn etc., 30 etc., 97sd,
  Ysakare 561; high priest/bishop in the temple (*see also* **Episcopus**)
Israel 383, 412, 414, 1521, 1523; another name for the patriarch Jacob, and
  from that the name of the chosen people of God

Jacob 1307; the patriarch Jacob
Jeremye 1084; the prophet Jeremiah
Jerusalem 36, 44 **Jherusalem** 198, 352, 388; the city of Jerusalem and its
  spiritual counterpart
Jesses 549; of Jesse
Jhesu 560sd, 1304, 1397, **Jhesus** 16 etc.
Joachim 105sd, 271sn, 508sd, **Joachym** 10 etc., 42sn etc., 270sd, 310sd;
  husband of Anne, father of Mary
John 1575, 1578, 1588; John the Baptist
Joseph 12 etc., 748sn etc., 883sd; husband of Mary
Juda 1419; ?the land of Judah. (It is not quite clear whether the playwright is
  thinking of Montana as a city of Judah, or Juda as a city 'in montana', in
  the hills, or in Montana.)
Justicia 1151sn etc., 1250, *see* **Ryght**

Locyfere 1107; Lucifer, the fallen angel

Maria 287sn etc., 545, 552, 1403sd, 1566, **Mary** 190 etc., 1323sd, 1355sd,
  1403sd, 186*A2*sn, 223*A2*sn, 20*A3*sd; **Mariam** 886sd; the Virgin Mary
Meditacyon 481, *see* **Clennes**
Mercy 1151 etc.; one of the four daughters of God (*see also* **Misericordia**)
Minister 112sn etc., 560sd; **ministerys** 97sd; **ministris** 500sd; **Ministro**
  110sd; assistant priests
Misericordia 1135sn etc., 1249, *see* **Mercy**
Montana 1418, *see* **Juda**

Mownt Syon 387, (**mons**) **Syon** 389, 395; an area of Jerusalem, often used for the whole city, especially in a spiritual sense

Nazareth 43, 1035, 1253
Nuncius 735sn; the bishop's messenger

Our Lady 256, 258, 1355sd, **Oure Lady** 270sd, 1448, 1577, 1585, 1596; **Oure Ladyes** 578, 1567, *see* **Maria**

Pater 115, 1108sn etc.; **Patris** 323, 325, 500, 916; **Patri** 1529; God the Father (*see also* **Fadyr godly**)
Pax 1175sn, 1250, *see* **Pes**
Pes 1182, 1198, 1205; **Pesys** 1228; Peace, one of the four daughters of God (*see also* **Pax**)
Primus generacionis Dauid 776sn etc.; **Secundus g. D.** 780sn etc.; **Tercius g. D.** 785sn etc.; **Quartus g. D.** 789sn etc.; representatives of the family of David
Primus Pastor 135sn etc.; **Secundus Pastor** 143sn etc.; **Tertius Pastor** 145sn etc.; Joachim's shepherds

Quartus . . ., *see* **Primus** . . .

Rachel 183; wife of Jacob, mother of Joseph and Benjamin
Rebecca 927, 932sn; one of Mary's maidens
Ryght 1178, 1203; **Ryghtwysnes** 1167, 1193, 1201; Justice, one of the four daughters of God (*see also* **Justicia**)

Sampson 185; Samson
Samuel 186; the prophet Samuel
Sapyens 1237; a name for Christ (*see also* **Wysdam**)
Sara 181; wife of Abraham, mother of Isaac
Secundus . . ., *see* **Primus** . . .
Senior (Tribus) 82sn, 94sn; one of the elders of the family of David
Sephor 934sn, 67*A*2sn, **Sephore** 928; one of Mary's maidens
Sone of þe Godhed 1355sd, *see* **Filius**
Spiritus Sanctus 115, 1243sn etc.; **Spiritus Sancti** 323, 325, 500, 916; **Spiritui Sancto** 1530; the Holy Spirit (*see also* **Holy Goost** etc.)
Susanna 3*A*2sn, **Susanne** 926, 930sn; one of Mary's maidens

Tercius/Tertius . . ., *see* **Primus** . . .
Trewth 1119, 1143, 1178, 1202, 1203, **Trowthe** 1215; one of the four daughters of God (*see also* **Veritas**)

Veritas 1119sn etc., 1249, *see* **Trewth**
virgines 500sd, 510sd, *see* **Clennes**

Virtutes 1092sn; representatives of the third hierarchy of angels (see note to 1092sn)
Vox 804sn; the oracular voice in the temple

Wysdam 1196; a name for Christ (*see also* **Sapyens**)

Zacharye 1550, **Zakarie** 1587, 20*A*3sd, **Zakary** 1456, **Zakarye** 1417, 1439, 1576, 1579; Zacharias, husband of Elizabeth, father of John the Baptist, a priest in the temple

List of Latin words, phrases, etc. in text and stage directions

Ad dominum cum tribularer clamaui; et exaudiuit me. 359–60 (Gradual psalm 1)
Adiutorium nostrum in nomine domini,
    Qui fecit celum et terram.
    Sit nomen domini benedictum:
    Ex hoc nunc et usque in seculum. 110–13
Ad te leuaui oculos meos; qui habitas in celis. 377–8 (Gradual psalm 4)
Ad virgines 510sd
Alma chorus domini nunc pangat nomina summi. 907
Aue 1562, 1595 (twice), 215*A2*; *Ave* 1402, 1480
Ave gracia plena dominus tecum 1279, 1563; *Aue Maria gracia plena dominus tecum uirgo serena* 1403sd
Ave regina celorum 1596
Beati omnes qui timent dominum: qui ambulant in vijs eius. 407–8 (Gradual psalm 9)
Benedicat vos diuina maiestas et vna deitas
    + Pater + et Filius + et Spiritus Sanctus. 114–15
Benedicite 748, 160*A2*
Benedicta sit beata Trinitas. 97sd
Benedictus 1582, 1583
Benedixisti domine terram tuam 1028
De profundis clamaui ad te domine: domine exaudi uocem meam. 419–20 (Gradual psalm 11)
Domine non est exaltatum cor meum; neque elati sunt oculi mei. 425–6 (Gradual psalm 12)
Ecce nunc benedicite dominum: omnes serui dominj. 443–4 (Gradual psalm 15)
Ecce quam bonum et quam jocundum; habitare fratres in vnum. 437–8 (Gradual psalm 14)
et benedictus Fructus uentris tui 1565–6
Et clamant omnes 831sd
Et explexendo osculabit patrem et matrem 330sd
Et genuflectet ad Deum 294sd
Et hic cantent: Benedicta sit beata Trinitas 874sd
Et hic osculabunt pariter omnes 1250sd
et idem Joseph 883sd
Et recedet cum ministris suis. Omnes virgines dicent: Amen. 500sd
Et redit flendo 108sd
Et refudit sacrificium Joachim 105sd
et sic deinceps usque ad finem quindecim psalmorum 355sd
Et sic transient circa placeam 1433sd
Exultet celum laudibus resultet terra gaudijs archangelorum gloria sacra canunt solennia. 172sd

Festum Encenniorum 34

Hic Joachim et Anna recedent domum 508sd

In conuertendo dominus captiuitatem Syon; facti sumus sicut consolati. 395–6
(Gradual psalm 7)

In nomine Patris et Filij et Spiritus Sancti 323, 325, 500, 916

Jhesu corona virginum 560sd

Jhesus 1566

Joachym flectendo ad Deum sic dicens 310sd

Letatus sum in hijs que dicta sunt mihi; in domum domini ibimus. 371–2 (Gradual
psalm 3)

Leuaui oculos meos in montes; vnde ueniat auxilium mihi. 365–6 (Gradual psalm
2)

Magnificat 1583

Magnificat (the complete text with *Gloria Patri*) between 1493 and 1535

Maria 1566

Memento domine Dauid; et omnis mansuetudinis eius. 431–2 (Gradual psalm 13)

Ministro cantando 110sn/sd

Misericordia et Veritas obviauerunt sibi,
Justicia et Pax osculate sunt. 1249–50

Nisi dominus edificauerit domum; in uanum laborauerunt qui edificant eam. 401–2
(Gradual psalm 8)

Nisi quia dominus erat in nobis dicat nunc Israel; nisi quia dominus erat in nobis.
383–4 (Gradual psalm 5)

nunc ad Mariam, sic dicens 886sd

Propter miseriam inopum Et gemitum pauperum Nunc exurgam. 1108–10

Qui confidunt in domino sicut mons Syon: non commouebitur in eternum qui habitat
in Hierusalem. 389–90 (Gradual psalm 6)

regal sacerdocium 40

Sepe expugnauerunt me a iuuentute mea; dicat nunc Israel. 413–14 (Gradual
psalm 10)

Signando manu cum cruce solenniter et recedant tribus extra templum 116sd

summi sacerdotes 1437

Tunc venit Abysakar episcopus 593sd

Veni creator spiritus 708, *Veni creator* 708sd (twice)

Veritas mea et misericordia mea cum ipso 1147

Vovete et reddite 687